BORDER FETISHISMS:
Material Objects in
Unstable Spaces

Zones of Religion
Edited by Peter van der Veer

Also published in the series:

Appropriating Gender: Women's Activism and Politicized Religion in South Asia
Amrita Basu & Patricia Jeffrey

Conversion to Modernities
Peter van der Veer

BORDER FETISHISMS:
Material Objects in
Unstable Spaces

Edited by Patricia Spyer

ROUTLEDGE
New York and London

Published in 1998 by
Routledge
29 West 35th Street
New York, NY 10001

Published in Great Britain by
Routledge 11 New Fetter Lane
London EC4P 4EE

Library of Congress Cataloging-in-Publication Data
Border fetishisms : material objects in unstable spaces / by Patricia Spyer.
        p.   cm. — (Zones of religion)
    "This book is the result of a conference on the topic 'Border fetishisms' that was held in December 1995 at the Research Centre Religion & Society at the University of Amsterdam"—
Acknowledgements.
    Includes bibliographical references and index.
    ISBN 0–415–91856–1 (hardcover). — ISBN 0–415–91857–X (pbk.)
    1. Fetishism—Congresses.   2. Acculturation—Congresses.
3. Colonies—Congresses.   I. Spyer, Patricia, 1957–   .
II. Series.
GN472.B65   1998
306.4—DC21   97–21461
                                                            CIP

Contents

Illustrations

Acknowledgments

This book is the result of a conference with the title "Border Fetishisms" that was held in December 1995 at the Research Centre Religion and Society at the University of Amsterdam. In addition to the authors whose essays are collected here, Leora Auslander, Inge Boer, Johannes Fabian, Peter Geschiere, Thomas Holt, Prahbu Mohapatra, Shoma Munshi, Danilyn Rutherford, Marc Shell, and Bonno Thoden van Velzen also took part in the "Border Fetishisms" conference. Their contributions, comments, and ideas enriched the conference and this book, and I would like to express my gratitude to them here. The conference received financial support from the University of Amsterdam, The Royal Dutch Academy of Sciences, The Netherlands Foundation for Scientific Research, and Crea Studium Generale, for which I am very grateful. Special thanks are due to Peter van der Veer for encouraging me to pursue this project and for seeing it through its present stage as both a colleague and as editor of the Zones of Religion series. I also express my appreciation to my other colleagues at the Research Centre Religion and Society—Gerd Baumann, Birgit Meyer, Peter Pels, and Peter van Rooden—for their help, humor, intellectual stimulation, and vital support at different stages along the way. Inge Boer, Webb Keane, Prahbu Mohapatra, Annelies Moors, and Adela Pinch all proved invaluable when it came to the practical and intellectual tasks involved in organizing this book. Rafael Sánchez's sound advice and enthusiasm never flagged from the first moment the idea for a "Border Fetishisms" conference popped into my head through the final details of putting together the present collection, and I thank him much for this. I also thank Ingrid van den Broek for her truly good spirits and detailed attention during the conference and its organizational prelude, and for her dedicated work on the manuscript thereafter. Finally, at Routledge I am grateful to Maureen MacGrogan, her assistant, Laska Jimsen, and Bill Germano for their work on this project.

The following institutions and persons kindly gave their permission to reproduce the photographs and illustrations included in this book: photographs of "Two Surinamese *Obeahs*" and a "Regent in Official Costume," Tropenmuseum, Amsterdam, the Netherlands; "Design of PNG two kina note," "Designs of PNG five, ten, and twenty kina notes," and "Cover of the textbook *Money*," the Department of Education of Papua New Guinea and The Bank of Papua New Guinea; "Housewife—1960" and "Housewife—1970" and "Highlanders Shopping in a Service Supermart," Maslyn Williams, *In One Lifetime* (1970).

Unless otherwise noted, all translations are by the authors of the essays in which they appear.

Patricia Spyer
Amsterdam, February 1997

Introduction

Patricia Spyer

Border Fetishisms, the title of this collection, is deliberately oxymoronic. Neither here nor there, past or future, fully absent or unambiguously present, the notion of a border fetish is meant precisely to foreground the unresolvable oscillations, the restless toing-and-froing, and the cultural, commercial, and political crossings that distinguish fetish formations. In the wake of Pietz's illuminating genealogy of the fetish as an idea-problem in which the historic trajectory of the word itself and the fetish's specificity to situations of encounter emerge as crucial, the present volume focuses on a variety of border fetishisms in which different economies of the object and distinct valuations of things, persons, and their relations are at play (Pietz 1985; 1987; 1988; cf. Apter & Pietz 1993). In this view the concept of the fetish is intimately linked to the history of European expansion, to the discourses and power relations developed within novel cross-cultural landscapes, as well as to the Enlightenment elaboration of fetishism to typify precisely that which was held to be irrational, misguided, founded on fancy or "caprice." Since first described outside of Europe by Portuguese and then Dutch merchant-adventurers as the pidgin *fetisso* on the Gold and Slave coasts of West Africa in the sixteenth and seventeenth centuries, the fetish has been a composite, border phenomenon.

Fetish's characteristic hybridity applies to its most literal manifestation or apparent haphazard piecing together out of heterogeneous elements as, for instance, the fetish brooms of Susan Legêne's essay here—"freakish" palm branches encrusted with lumps of resin, chalk, cowrie shells, nails, beads of diverse colors, and hung with small brass chains, dotted with paint, and wrapped with cotton thread. Or, somewhat differently, the iconography of the coins and paper currency of postcolonial Papua New Guinea discussed by Robert Foster, which draws together traditional "monies" from disparate regions falling within the boundaries of state territory—things like pearl-shells, clay pots, and pigs—would be another example in which, moreover, the new money constructs the new nation as itself a fetish in the sense of a composite fabrication. Hybridity also infuses the fetish's initial role as the material sign of a cross-cultural agreement—trade treaties and other commercial contracts between Europeans and Africans were often sworn on fetissos in an attempt by the former to ensure the latter's compliance with the terms of the agreement. In this capacity, the fetisso figured not only as the physical reminder of a border crossing but increasingly came to stand in the eyes of the Europeans—as evidenced by mercantilist denunciations of the time—for a confusion of the religious and the economic or, in other words, for a denial of the proper boundaries between things and the distinctions these are held to delineate.

One unifying aim of the contributions collected here is to gain a better sense of the fissured, performative spaces where the fetish moves (as it were!) by exploring the forms of difference that fetishism both marks and negotiates in the process of producing or alluding to novel, creative hybridities. If the articles that follow suggest some different ways of thinking of the fetish, and if interdisciplinary in orientation, they all pay close attention to the specificities of time and place distinguishing the contact zones (Pratt 1992), boundary markers, and border incidents that the fetish in its migrations variously territorializes, unsettles, displaces, and reaffirms. It should not surprise that the bulk of the historic situations that contributors focus on here are well positioned within the history of European expansion, its colonizing projects, and postcolonial aftermaths, and relate, more generally, to the opening of new markets and territories. They range in focus from early talk about rarity, wonder, and the shuffle of things (Pels); to Christian missionization in Sumba, Eastern Indonesia in the first decades of this century and today (Keane); and the nineteenth-century conversion of recently emancipated Surinamese slaves with the concomitant baptism of their objects as "fetishes" by Dutch colonizers (Legêne); from government fears, fantasies, and programs aimed at "cargo cult" activity in one of the last colonial frontiers, present day Papua New Guinea (Foster); the great turn-of-the-century feather hunt in the far islands of the Dutch East Indies (Spyer); the European luxury market in lace in late Georgian England (Pinch); the rag trade at home (Stallybrass) and abroad (Spyer); to the social and political mobility of persons and property in (post)colonial contemporary Palestine (Moors). In the fissured colonial and postcolonial spaces that are the historical terrain for most of these articles, the fetish continually oscillates between a Eurocentric and an Other dimension, between recognition and disavowal, absence and (negative) presence. Gesturing as it does toward a beyond that guarantees its own futurity as well as toward a posited past moment of origin, the fetish more generally is never positioned in a stable here-and-now and thereby confounds essentializing strategies that aim for neat resolutions and clear-cut boundaries among things and between persons and objects.

Perhaps this is why the remaining essay in this collection that explores the notion of border fetish foregrounds the represention of representation itself as a crucial problem. For Michael Taussig, the ultimate, overlooked fetish and public secret in its own right is that "mother of all borderlands" and unfathomable territory that is the face. Both screen and window to the soul, the face holds out a promise of insight that it never can fulfill and, like Subcomandante Marcos of Zapatista fame, continually displaces itself along a chain of unmaskings and remaskings that describes the shifting game of political peekaboo played by this trickster folk hero with that most masked of entities, the state.

It is more than anything else in its capacity to fix and unsettle borders and the essentialisms that these hold in place that fetishism, following Pietz, demarcates a "space of cultural revolution" (1985: 11), or one that invites comparison between distinct social orders, possibilities, and schemes and that, in so doing, also opens up the possibility for cultural criticism. It is with this possibility in mind that contributors here are especially attuned to the "sinister pedigree" (Pietz 1985: 5) of the fetish concept as a derogatory term for the illusions of Others and thus the repetition of an all too familiar hegemonic move that inevitably sets in every time the concept is invoked negatively. At the same time, they also hone in on the border zones that fetishisms trace out by considering the effects of the crossings through which relations between subjects and objects may be reassessed, redrawn, and at times overturned, and how thereby distinctions such as those of gender, class, race, ethnicity, and nationality might be negotiated, transgressed, and perhaps most of all, exposed. Along these same lines, several articles focus on the ways in which various fetishisms generate social hierarchies and differences while at the same time opening up novel spaces for the construction of agency.

Robert Foster argues forcefully that once people pay attention to the material matter of money, thereby recovering money's characteristic erasure and dematerialization, the possibility also emerges for them to question the connection between themselves and money's source, the state.

Gold, another globalized fetish object, is a prize possession that is acquired by Palestinian women upon their marriage and subsequently worn and transacted by them in a wide range of settings. In her contribution, Annelies Moors draws attention to the marked disregard of Euro-American observers to these women's gold as opposed to the veil, which they repeatedly seize upon as the material expression of Muslim women's oppression by their men as well as a sign of the erasure of individuality that such subordination would further entail. Her detailed discussion of the wide range of variety in kind, carat, and liquidity value of the gold worn by women of different class and regional backgrounds shows how they variously construct and display the visible signs of their autonomy on their bodies, thereby complicating the more familiar picture of Muslim and Middle Eastern patriarchy held in place, as it were, by the veil. Objections voiced by Palestinian women to their alleged objectification by the old dower payments—"am I a donkey that he has to pay for me?"— or the objectification of their person that some associate with the new urban token dowers—"is she a cow that he needs to see her?"— suggest that what it is to be "modern," married, and a woman describes a contested and much debated field in present-day Palestine.

Like the articles by Moors, Spyer, and Stallybrass, Adela Pinch's elegant and nuanced piece also deals with clothing and its accoutrements. Lace, a border in itself and a classic fetish-object, evokes the national boundaries between England and France and the regulations pertaining to international traffic in luxury goods. If lace and other articles of clothing were the objects of the (primarily) female genteel shoplifting of late Georgian England, a bit of lace in Pinch's account does much more than disclose the burdens placed especially on women in an emerging consumer culture. Nor is Pinch satisfied with merely exposing the true meaning of shopping, as such would be revealed by its transgression in shoplifting, with the latter's underscoring of the compulsive power accorded to things by the commodity fetishism of a capitalist society. Lace, in her reading, is also the site of a vicious class warfare that pits genteel women shoplifters against the "shopocracy" that stands between them and the coveted goods. If then, at certain moments, these genteel female shoplifters might be construed as critically engaging prevailing

Georgian notions of gender, their practice also spoke vehemently in a rhetoric of class contempt of a desire to buttress the eroding visible boundaries of social position and privilege. In my own contribution, European colonizers writing about a Moluccan island's human inhabitants and birds at the height of Dutch imperialism construct an authoritative, utopian *imaginaire* for themselves that covers over their own sense of off-centeredness vis-à-vis the metropole. In their writings, these late nineteenth-century visitors to Aru insist repeatedly on a separation between "savage" bodies and "civilized" clothes, thereby underscoring the impossibility that the island's natives would ever approximate the European civilization that the colonizers in giving out their clothes also aimed to introduce. At the same time, in descriptions as detailed as those of Aruese in European and Eurasian dress, the colonizers invest the archipelago's famed birds of paradise with the signs of a fully fledged, fetishized, "tropical Gothic" vision of monarchical and uncompromised rule.

The material relations between bodies and things and the fetish object's "irreducible materiality" (Pietz 1985: 7) raise a number of issues that are explored by different contributors—the relationship between materiality and immateriality and the hierarchical ranking of spirit and matter that is still with us today as an Enlightenment legacy; and, relatedly, the powers that things have to entrance, raise hopes, generate fears, evoke losses, and delight as well as the social attitudes towards the wide range of sentiments produced in the face of such *objets chargés*. To be sensuous is, indeed, to *suffer*, in the sense of being acted upon (Marx in Pietz 1993: 144), and it is especially this aspect of fetishism that also has the potential to move our discussions beyond the idea of social constructionism. While the latter represents a great insight that has borne considerable fruit in work produced both interdisciplinarily and across a range of disciplines, theoretically this perspective begs the question of how and why certain things exercise the immense powers they do over persons and collectivities. The disadvantage, in other words, of a social constructionist perspective is that it tends to flatten out the passions, energies, and motivations with which, in the case of fetishism, things are so fiercely invested (cf. Taussig 1993: xiii–xix). Social constructionism explains away the extraordinary power that with fetishism is precisely the problem.

If at the conclusion of her article, Pinch calls somewhat cautiously for a phenomenological or psychoanalytic understanding of the force of things within a historical approach to the emotions these elicit, Peter Pels's characterization of the fetish as an agressive "matter that strikes back" is probably the most phenomenologically informed statement of the present collection. Opposed to animism as a "spirit *in* matter" resulting from human interventions, in relation to which its aliveness always remains derivative, fetishism for Pels is a "spirit *of* matter," by which difference he would foreground the possibility "that the materiality of things can stand in the way of, and deflect, the course of human traffic." With this in mind Pels cites Freud's famous assertion that "when the fetish comes to life . . . some process has been suddenly interrupted" (Freud in Pels). Yet if for Freud this interruption remains a human-derived one—call it repression or simply "forgetfulness" that allows the fetish to assume a life of its own—for Pels acknowledging the spirit *of* matter as an independant force offers the fetish "a chance to unfold its otherness." This, in turn, means recognizing the physicality of things and their capacity to carry over certain forms of signification from one context of human behavior to another, as well as to strain or transcend the human designs and constructions to which they are subject.

Here, however, we are somewhat beyond the "striking" distance of the fetish and more within the realm of resistance posed by the material itself or what Norman Bryson refers to as the "*authentically self-determining* level of material life" (Bryson 1990: 12–15; cf. Pinch, this volume). For Bryson, the "low-plane reality" of things like the tankards, jugs, and plates familiar from European still-life painting describes the slow, creeping rhythm of alternations in their basic shape and differs dramatically from the abrupt, dictatorial swings of fashion—indeed, often and tellingly spoken of thus, fetishistically—where the evidence of "the tooth of time" is almost immediately apparent and can have important social effects (Spyer). In Foster's account, the matter of money—its physical, coin and paper phenomenal reality—was something that repeatedly threatened to undermine the programs launched by the Australian colonial government in Papua and New Guinea that were aimed at dematerializing the matter of money with an eye toward discouraging the cargoism they feared it might otherwise elicit. Thus, fostering a practice of saving among the colony's population and familiarizing New Guineans with the new system of banks meant highlighting money's material fragility as well as the fetishistic pleasure a person might derive from showing off his bankbook to friends.

If the return of its materiality to money potentially elicits fetishistic desires or may become the avenue for social criticism of the powers-that-be, it can also have important shock value. Such I would argue is, for instance, the effect of a photo in a *Granta* collection titled *Money* that depicts "banknotes abandoned in the courtyard of the National Bank of Cambodia after Pol Pot suppressed all money" (*Granta* 49, winter 1994: 89). The eery vision of these "dead fetish hulls" (Legêne) strewn across the former bank's deserted lot relies for its effect on the overlooked spectral character that the immaterial, supra-sensitive exchange value money normally has and not on any knowledge of the larger killing fields that historically surrounded this scene of wreckage (though that of course doesn't help). Vis-à-vis money, the shock effect of this photo can go either way—by exposing its normalized fetish status under capitalist conditions or, inversely, by reinforcing it.

For Dutch Calvinist missionaries on the island of Sumba in the early decades of this century, who with the islanders themselves are the focus of Webb Keane's fine contribution, the ubiquity of sacrificial meat in all aspects of Sumbanese social life and its difficult-to-deny practical implications stood in the way of their attempts to segregate pagan and Christian religious practice, as well as, more theologically, spirit and matter. Many of the missionaries saw in the converts' consumption of meat that had been ritually dedicated to pagan spirits a transgression of "the injunction in 1 Corinthians 8 and 10 in which Paul warns against eating sacrifices as tantamount to 'fellowship with devils.' " Not unlike the double-bind in which Foster argues Australian colonizers were caught in their programs regarding money, antiprohibitionists in this heated debate argued that by emphasizing the materiality of meat over its symbolic purpose, the mission ran the risk of enforcing rather than diminishing the power ascribed to material things—if meat is only symbolic, these antiprohibitionists claimed, it should have no effects on the souls that consume it.

In his paper on "Marx's Coat," Peter Stallybrass wonders how it is that material things have come in for such contempt. For Marx himself, as Stallybrass so wonderfully shows, material things, at least theoretically speaking, were never the problem—something which is, indeed, often misunderstood. Rather, for Marx the erasure under capitalism of the material particularity of, let's say, a coat and its inscription with the immateriality of the phantomlike commodity form is the issue and one with which he was, indeed, all too familiar. Stallybrass's narrative takes us back and forth between the writing by Marx of *Capital* and the material circumstances of his own life, which time after time drove Marx to the pawnshop with the prized possessions of his household, where these were emptied of the memories, possibilities, and respectability that they in all their particularity subsumed for his family. Fetishizing commodities, Stallybrass insists, entails a reversal of the whole history of fetishism with the impassioned response to the material, tangible, sensuous character of things in the latter substituted under capitalism by an intense focus on the invisible, spooky quality that commodities as exchange values have. Thus, much as in the daily life of the Marx household in London in the 1850s and 1860s (where, among many other things, Marx's great coat migrated back and forth to the pawnshop), a coat puts in an early appearance in the first pages of *Capital* only to disappear—once it assumes commodity status—immediately thereafter. If *Capital*, following Stallybrass, can be glossed as Marx's attempt to give the coat back to its owner, the stories Marx told to his children disclose a utopia in which the marvelous toys sold by a magician toyshop owner to the devil to redeem his never-ending debts return of their own accord back to their owner. Denying the alienation that corresponds to the moment of sale, these magical toys insist somewhat giftlike on the powerful play that exists between persons and things, and in returning draw a charmed circle around the magician toyshop owner, his enchanted toys, and the Marx children who listened to their father invent these happy tales.

The fear of the power that things might have together with what Pinch calls "the thematics of things coming too close" surfaces dramatically in several contributions. Most of these also intimate how the excessive worry about things goes hand in hand with a concern for the autonomy of persons, pointing thereby, as Stallybrass argues, to an intimate connection between the historically situated contempt for material things and the "impossible project of the transcendental subject." One aspect of this may also be the fear that, according to Keane, dogs fetish discourse, namely, that the observer who accuses Others of the mistake of fetishism might herself be seduced into error, and in so doing collapse the important "double consciousness" on which the fetish discourse turns—on the one hand, "absorbed credulity" and, on the other, "degraded or distanced incredulity" (Pietz 1985: 14).

Efforts to stabilize the boundaries between persons and things thus also often entail an assertion of the distinctions between differently valued persons. Legène's contribution clearly shows, for instance, how the baptism of recently emancipated Surinamese slaves as Christians coincides with the naming of their former *obeah* brooms as "fetishes," and the redefinition of these objects as pertaining to the Maroon escaped slave populations. By way of a displacement of the "fetishes" onto the Maroons, this double baptismal event reinstates the "fetish" as the frontier marker of Christian colonial civilization.

In other colonial situations, talk about the fetish and attempts to establish the proper boundaries between persons and things covered over anxieties about racial miscegenation. Foster speaks, for instance, of the elision of cargo cult and miscegenation "inasmuch as both are taken to be cognate forms of confusion, of radical heterogeneity and unacceptable coupling." Similarly, Spyer argues that for the Europeans frequenting Aru at the high point of colonial racism in the Dutch East Indies, the physical fact of being confronted with native bodies in one's own colonizer clothes and the sheer materiality of this form of "contact" may have had profound, unsettling effects.

In both Keane's and Pinch's contributions, the disturbing effects of things coming too close provoke embodied responses that, once again, underscore the project of creating an autonomous subject, albeit quite differently. If in Keane's example this project is inspired by the Protestant suspicion of outward, materialized representations, in Pinch's discussion of the schizophrenic Lola Voss, her fear of being overwhelmed by the world translates into a pathological dread of shopping and a phobia of clothes. Notwithstanding the great difference between these two examples, the bodily reactions provoked in each are uncannily the same. Protestant converts in Sumba close their eyes when they pray to avoid the temptations of the fetishized word, and by thus marking off the boundary between exterior and interior allow their speech to "come from the heart." Being the next best thing to bodies, and therefore the most threateningly intimate, clothing was what Lola Voss was especially terrified of; when induced to shop she could only do so with her eyes shut. And it might not be pushing it too far to suggest that European colonizers confronted by the off-centered "look" that was reflected, I argue, back to them by Aruese "savages" made over in quasi-metropolitan clothes, might have at times, been tempted to close their eyes as well.

With these insights we have arrived at that "bottom line of being a social being," at the face that is the focus of Michael Taussig's contribution. One of the reasons that the face fascinates Taussig is that, much like the fetish holding out a promise of fulfillment and ultimate arrival, the face seems to initiate access to a beyond. But like the fetish the face, as it were, never arrives. A blush in this perspective is therefore a sign that the looked-for, longed-for innerness, the kind of haven that those shutting in their eyes aim to mark off, is an impossibility. In Tierra del Fuego in the 1920s, the most important lesson that a young person could learn in the initiation rituals that Taussig draws upon, was not about the illusions of masking but instead the realities of demasking. The successive demaskings in the ritual and the fact that what was revealed to the initiates was mask after mask after mask or, in other words, masks all the way down, rendered, following Taussig, the reality of the spirit world represented by the chain of masks all the more powerful and real.

Whether explicitly or implicitly, the articles in this collection seem to concur that the point is neither to demagicalize the fetish (as Karl Marx in the stories he told to his children also seemed to imply), nor is it to normalize the commodity (though, admittedly, Marx's efforts to undermine the latter are more famous). Treated as an other to the commodity, the fetish valorizes and normalizes the social relations of capitalism (in whichever of its historical moments), in the same way that shoplifting from a certain perspective normalizes shopping. Yet for Marx the commodity and the fetish were in fact one and the same. It was by bringing the two together as a curious hieroglyphic hybrid that he aimed to show the "mist-envelopped regions" and thereby the absolute strangeness of the normal capitalist everyday. For Marx, moreover, the law of equivalence governing the workings of the capitalist marketplace itself covered over a critical excess—that of surplus value. (I am indebted to Prahbu Mohapatra for this argument.) Another way of getting—more concretely—at much the same thing, or of resisting either demagicalizing the fetish or normalizing the commodity, is to take seriously the protestations of the (anti)heroine in the first section of Pinch's piece, the genteel shoplifter who insists in court that "lace is not necessary to my happiness," admitting thereby the possibility that it very much might or could be. Rather than divesting the *objets chargés* of diverse historical moments and circumstances of their powers, this volume argues for the inclusion of material things—whether as fetishes or, more loosely, fetishes after a fashion, within the wider calculus of human sufferings and joys.

REFERENCES

Apter, Emily and William Pietz (eds) (1993) *Fetishism as Cultural Discourse,* Ithaca: Cornell University Press.

Bryson, Norman (1990) *Looking At The Overlooked: Four Essays on Still Life Painting,* Cambridge: Harvard University Press.

Granta 49 (winter 1994) Issue "Money," Bill Buford (ed).

Pietz, William (1993) "Fetishism and Materialism: The Limits of Theory in Marx," in Emily Apter and William Pietz (eds) *Fetishism as Cultural Discourse,* Ithaca: Cornell University Press.

————. (1988) "The Problem of the Fetish, IIIa," *Res* 16, 105–123.

————. (1987) "The Problem of the Fetish, II," *Res* 13, 23–45.

————. (1985) "The Problem of the Fetish, I," *Res* 9, 5–17.

Pratt, Mary Louise (1992) *Imperial Eyes: Travel Writing and Transculturation*, London: Routledge.

Taussig, Michael (1993) *Mimesis and Alterity: A Particular History of the Senses*, New York: Routledge.

1

Calvin in the Tropics: Objects and Subjects at the Religious Frontier

Webb Keane

It is common to treat the various ideas grouped under the word "fetishism" as fundamentally concerned with material objects. Thus William Pietz begins his history of the concept by distinguishing the fetish in its "irreducible materiality" from the idol, which is the iconic image of some immaterial original (1985: 7). But the allure that the supposed fetish holds for some and the anxiety it provokes in others have less to do with objects than with the problems that objects pose for subjects. For example, Marx's (1967) commodity fetish is not simply a way of misunderstanding goods but a way humans misunderstand themselves. In the process of attributing life to things, they lose some of their own humanity and come to treat themselves as objects in turn.

The imputation of fetishism carries a strong charge; more than mere error is at stake. Indeed, something of the original religious character of the concept of fetishism seems to remain amidst its subsequent, more secular, exfoliations. In its secular uses, talk about fetishism may hint at dangers; in the religious context, the danger becomes apparent. Consider the Dutch missionary D.K. Wielenga's account of the ancestral ritualists on the eastern Indonesian island of Sumba: "The primitives confound that which is a fruit of the imagination with the reality, the objective with the subjective, the outer phenomena with their own spirit life" (1909: 332).[1] As a missionary, Wielenga has the task not simply of education and correction but, above all, salvation. This mission makes evident that the confounding of the objective and subjective has dire, even eternal, consequences.

But talk about fetishism often seems to harbor a sense of thrill and anxiety as well, as if the danger threatens not only the fetishist but also the outsider who, it would seem, should not taken in by the error. For some of the approaches that have been developed since Freud, this may be because the fetish remains a temptation even to those whose knowledge would deny the existence of that which they desire (see Apter and Pietz 1993; Ivy 1995). In the case of some traditions of Protestantism, it may have to do with the way in which other people's illusions threaten the very autonomy of the subject, for the autonomy of the human subject is not unproblematic even for the Protestants themselves. In this essay I explore these ramifications of the idea of fetishism by looking at the encounter between Dutch Calvinists and the practitioners of ancestral ritual on Sumba. I suggest that the difficulties posed for Calvinists by Sumbanese understandings of the relations among subjects and objects go well beyond the theological niceties beloved of colonial missionaries. They may reveal certain problems endemic to efforts to stabilize the boundaries between persons and things, or to determine the status of language in human activities. To see this means listening to how Calvinists articulate some of the core concerns of the West's self-understood modernity.

THE FETISH AS HISTORICAL ENCOUNTER

Despite its isolated, even pastoral, surroundings, the twentieth-century colonial mission on Sumba was inseparable from the larger background of Dutch industry and commerce.[2] Since Weber (1958), of course, the relationship between Protestantism and capitalism has been common disputational coin. Leaving aside the Weberian question of historical causality, it is apparent that when Protestants on Sumba draw on the discourse of fetishism, several aspects of their relationship to their context come to the fore. One is the missionaries' own ambivalence, torn as they are between economic rationality and spiritual commitment. As I have discussed elsewhere (Keane 1996), the Dutch saw Sumbanese ancestor ritualists as both excessively materialistic and as believing in too many spirits, as too calculating and as irrationally blinded to economics by their moral commitments.

The island of Sumba came under Dutch rule during the final period of the expansion and consolidation of the East Indies early in this century.[3] Having little to offer those with more worldly ambitions, the island was left almost entirely in the hands of a small band of missionaries. Official policy sought to prevent competition between rival missions by distributing them among discrete territories; most of Sumba was placed under the tutelage of a conservative sect of the Reformed (or Orthodox Calvinist) Church (Gereformeerde Kerken). In 1947, not long before Sumba entered the independent Republic of Indonesia, the tiny indigenous congregation formed the autonomous Sumbanese Christian Church (Gereja Kristen Sumba), which continues to have close ties to the Dutch church to this day. Despite the efforts of several generations of missionaries and indigenous evangelists, and increasing pressure from the Indonesian state, however, at the time of my first visit to the district of Anakalang in 1985, the unconverted *marapu* (ancestral spirit) followers formed the majority of the population of West Sumba and remained a strong presence in East Sumba.[4] Although it was becoming increasingly apparent that Christians would soon be dominant, resistance by *marapu* followers could be quite vociferous.

Despite the important changes that have transpired over this century's colonial and post-colonial periods, the encounter between Christians and *marapu* followers has produced recurrent discourses about their differences. The themes to which these discourses return again and again can be made apparent in two quotations. One is from the early years of the Dutch mission, the other from a conversation I had with a Sumbanese gospel teacher in 1993.

The first quotation comes from D.K. Wielenga. He was the first missionary to spend a long period on Sumba, persevering despite having been wounded in a spear attack and twice seeing his house destroyed by arson. In 1909, not long after his arrival, he described the religion of the Sumbanese in this way:

> The two constituents of the nature religion . . . [are] the dogma that everything has a soul, that is, *fetishism*, the worship of sensual perceptible objects, as having souls . . . [and] the dogma that the soul is free in its movement and not bound to a fixed body, *spiritualism*, the worshipping of the souls of the dead and of the invisible spirits in the air (1909: 332; emphases in the original).

He wrote this passage while still fairly new to Sumba, and thus relied more heavily on the comparative religion of the day than in his later, more ethnographically precise, writing. But this passage is useful precisely in its generality, for it shows in broad outlines what was at stake for the Protestant. The errors of paganism do not lie, for example, in immorality, cruelty, or absence of faith. Rather, the fundamental problem is the pagan's confusion about what kinds of beings inhabit the world, and how animated material things really are. Their confusion is twofold: first, taking what is really inanimate (matter) to be animate, and second, mistaking the attributes of the visible (that is, material) and invisible. Fetishistic error revolves around questions of animacy or agency, and visibility or materiality.

The second quotation comes from Bapak U.S. Kadiwangu. His father had been a powerful *ratu* (ritual specialist), and his brother had succeeded to the office. He himself had been among the small number of children of the nobility to be selected by the Dutch for a formal education, and was eventually ordained as a minister. When I knew him, he was an elderly man with the bittersweetness of someone who had spent a lifetime with little evangelical success, only now, in retirement, to witness the emergence of a Protestant majority. With quiet pride he told me in 1993 how he preached in the 1940s and 1950s:

> I'd ask them, why are they afraid of the *marapu*? "Because they created us, and if we don't respect them, we'll get sick." I'd tell them, "Yes, that's true, we must be afraid. We're afraid because we can't *see* Him. So the ancestors used gold, gongs, spears, those humans [i.e. the spirits of earlier, now deceased, ancestors]—they became signs that Lord God is there—like a king or a *ratu*—people fear them because of their power. So now we don't need to pray. God doesn't want us to bring chickens anymore. God sent me so you can return to God—not that wood, not that rock [i.e. traditional altars]. What saves us isn't wood, rock, cattle, but Lord Jesus."

Like Wielenga, Pak Kadiwangu stresses the error of using objects in ritual, attacking their use in *marapu* ritual, as well as the fallacy of ascribing divinity to ancestors who were mere humans. He sees this in terms of substitution, the material taking the place of the spiritual.

Both men mention the difference between the visible and invisible, which raises the fundamental religious problem of presence. *Marapu* follower and Christian alike must in some way contend with the fact that the deity is invisible and (usually) silent. *Marapu* followers are quite explicit about this. Many have told me that they have little understanding of the spirits, since they cannot be seen, and ritual speech often asks whether the spirits are present. Although the ubiquity of God might make presence less problematic for Protestants, the question persists in somewhat different form. Calvinists (already, in some sects, uncertain about their personal salvation) cannot be sure if their sermons and prayers have truly been inspired by the Holy Spirit (see Peacock and Tyson 1989). For both religions, the effort to encounter and interact with an otherwise inaudible and invisible world creates unavoidable dilemmas.

The problem of presence gives rise to another theme mentioned by both men. According to Wielenga, the invisibility of the spirit world explains the fear that permeates pagan life. The source of this fear is twofold, the human's imputation of agency to external agents (see also Dijkstra 1902), and the invisibility of those agents. Pak Kadiwangu's remarks pick up the theme of fear and, extending the point, hint at the temptation that fetishism might hold for people. Faced with invisibility, *marapu* followers turn to material objects. These objects stand for immaterial entities that should be present but whose immateriality puts this presence at any given moment into doubt. Thus, according to Pak Kadiwangu, the objects used in *marapu* ritual are in truth only signs and thus not actually fetishes—except for those *marapu* followers who do not recognize their semiotic function.

Moreover, according to Pak Kadiwangu, the use of material signs makes up for something that seems to be missing. But once people become aware that that something is not really missing, they can abandon those signs in favor of the real thing, Jesus Christ. The passage from material signs to full acceptance of the invisible is something that transpires over historical time. Material things seem to have the status of temporary stopgap measures that are now no longer necessary.[5] Once one can call them "fetishes," one is in a position to abandon them.

The historicizing view has two further implications worth noting. According to this view, the proper way to understand the material forms of religion is as signs of invisible spiritual presences. But this ultimately leaves the solution of the problem of presence to the inner faith of the beholder. For the weaker members of the congregation, the appeal of some external guarantee of divine presence is likely to persist. Protestants themselves are occasionally made aware of this temptation when they perceive the small Catholic mission to be poaching on their converts by means of the sensuous forms of masses, idolatrous statues, and priestly robes.[6] In addition, if the historicizing view is carried to its logical conclusion, it also means that the conversion to Christianity implicates the convert in more than just a new set of religious beliefs and practices. The new religion tends to be identified with an entire historical epoch; as even persistant ancestral ritualists were prone to say in the 1980s, the hallmark of the "modern era" (*masa moderen*) is that "the foreign *marapu* has won" (*taluneka na marapu jiawa*). This new era involves transformations in political economy and social organization, which may be difficult for the missionary to keep distinct from spiritual transformation in the eyes of the convert.[7]

AMBIGUOUS ANIMACY

The fetishism that missionaries ascribed to the Sumbanese takes several forms, the most apparent ones being sacralia, offerings, and the distribution of sacrifices. What I here call sacralia are objects known as "the *marapu's* portion" (*tagu marapu*; see discussion in Keane 1997a, chapter 8). Among them are bits of rare imported cloth, metal statuettes, spears, swords, gongs, old Chinese and Vietnamese trade ceramics, and, most commonly, gold ornaments of the type normally used in ceremonial exchanges. Every clan and its major divisions should possess at least one of its own *marapu* portion, which is carefully preserved out of sight in a designated house. Sumbanese often speak of these sacralia as the true inhabitants of the house, for which the human residents are only caretakers. Sacralia impose on their inhabitants specific ritual prerogatives and obligations. If the rituals are regularly performed, the sacralia remain silent guarantors of the wellbeing of the living. Should the rituals lapse, however, the living will be reminded of their presence by means of drought, fires, the illness of children, lightning strikes, and infertility. On the rare occasions when they have been transfered to another owner, people say, they have resisted. One such valuable was given away to someone who kept it in a wooden chest. But it banged around so vigorously in there that the new owners returned it to its house of origin.

Such objects have many of the characteristics of the religious fetish. They are material things to which people attribute animacy. They are treated as if they were the ancestor and normally they bear that ancestor's name. But in what exactly their personhood lies seems to be a matter of ambiguity even to the Sumbanese. The missionary Lambooy (1930: 281) reported that although they were usually identified for foreigners as the *marapu* itself,

> sometimes I ask of a Sumbanese, "is that now really the Marapoe."
> Then he looks at me indignantly, for that is not the Marapoe, only the

Tanggoe Marapoe, the possession of the Marapoe. "But what is the Marapoe then?" "We ourselves do not know the Marapoe, who for us is concealed."

In my own time, some people told me that the ancestral body was physically transformed into sacralia; others saw the objects as conventional symbols that stand for the ancestor (see also Kapita 1976: 90). When accused by Christians of idolatry, contemporary *marapu* followers sometimes respond that the valuables are merely a meeting place (like the altar), a mat of honor on which the spirit sits, or a horse for, or a reminder of, the ancestor.

In conversations with me, people most often said that the object is the "replacement" (*na hepanya*) of the ancestral body or its "sign, mark, trace" (*tada*). This suggests that the ancestor is, at best, ambivalently present in it, since both expressions presuppose an absence. For example, the son of a *ratu* "replaces" his father upon the latter's death by taking over his office. The word *tada* can refer to the owner's mark on a household possession that has been loaned to someone else, or to the token given as a promissory note in lieu of an exchange valuable. Similarly, it is only because the *marapu* are gone that the living hold onto these objects. The sacralia thus index the absence of the *marapu* at the same time that they make them present.

The various accounts of sacralia turn on the problem of invisibility and the accompanying uncertainty. One reason these accounts vary is that, since the invisible subject is unknowable, there is no way of knowing exactly how it is present in or connected to the object. Moreover, most *marapu* followers agree that it would be arrogant to say otherwise. Herein lies one of the central accusations that *marapu* followers make against Christians: that they are shamelessly brazen in pretending to know God as well as they do. More specifically, *marapu* followers often express astonishment that Christians claim to be able to speak to God without the mediation of material things and, as will become apparent below, formal speech. What Christians see as fetishistic displacements are also forms of mediation that contend not just with invisibility, but with respect for the divine.

THE TEMPTATIONS OF FLESH

Even though sacralia come closer to the classic definition of the fetish than does the sacrificial offering, in practice the latter has posed more of a problem for Christian efforts to stabilize the distinction between subjects and objects. Sacralia are easy for converts to ignore, since they remain hidden in the houses and are only rarely drawn into ritual activity. When they are brought out, they are so dangerous that only specialists are permitted to see or handle them, and the convert can avoid them. Offerings are only slightly more problematic. The problems they pose are due to the ubiquity of ritual speech events. In general, no speech is valid without the material "base" (*lata*) on which it rests. The principle extends beyond ancestral ritual, since all formal exchanges between living humans, such as those for marriages, also require that speech be grounded in objects and objects in turn be given direction by speech (Keane 1994). Thus when Christians perform ritual speech for such occasions as baptisms and thanksgivings, without making offerings, they can feel vulnerable to the accusations of impropriety laid against them by *marapu* followers (Keane 1995). This sense of impropriety turns on how one interprets the status of objects. The official Christian view of the combination of words with offerings in *marapu* ritual is expressed by a song, composed by an early Sumbanese minister, meant to ridicule pagan practices. One line ran "What good is prayer, the *marapu* words? They just use up chickens." His argument was taken up by many Christians, who justify their conversion by appeal to economics: Offerings and sacrifices are wasteful. This argument, by stressing rational calculation, also aligns the church with the contemporary Indonesian state's discourse of economic development. But in the process, *marapu* followers are quick to point out, Christians betray themselves to be vulgar and self-interested materialists. Probably the single most common argument I have heard against them is that they are greedy and lacking in the respect for ancestors and (here people turn Christian expressions against them) for the spiritual. Non-Christians never eat meat except when compelled to make offerings, and they never slaughter animals without verbally expressing to them the purpose for which the killing takes place. In contrast, Christians simply eat meat because they are hungry, driven by their own desires. In acknowledging nothing beyond the value of the animals as meat, it is Christians who are the true materialists.

In varying degrees, sacralia and offerings are relatively straightforward matters for the church. Since they usually come into play in events that are unambiguously ritual, converts could eschew the entire event. But since arriving on Sumba, the church has faced great problems with sacrifices. This is due to the inseparability of ritual from the whole range of exchange and feasting around which the bulk of Sumbanese public life is constructed. The problem of how to deal with the problem of the meat distribution after sacrifice has given rise to some of the most contentious and persistant debates both between Christians and *marapu* ritualists, and among Christians themselves (see Keane 1996).

Meat is a problem not only because of the exchange system, but because of the difficulty of establishing its semiotic character. The sacralia are easy to interpret as symbolic: Even some *marapu* ritualists speak of them as signs of the spirits, and some Christians are willing to accept them by treating them as "signs of social unity" (Keane 1997a: 199–201). As for offerings, if one does not believe in their spirit recipients, or if one does not think they actually consume the offerings, it is easy to treat offerings as signs of human intentions. But once the offering has been transformed into meat to be eaten by humans, the question becomes more complex. Unlike the token portions of the Christians' Holy Communion, sacrificial meat is conceptually hard to categorize as lacking immediate practicality and thus as purely symbolic. As a central medium by which social relations are tested and reproduced, the sharing of sacrificial meat is difficult for the convert to avoid.

Large-scale sacrifice and feasting occupy an important part of Sumbanese ritual and social life (see Hoskins 1993). Even events whose religious affiliation is ambiguous or overtly Christian, such as funerals and thanksgiving ceremonies, can involve the slaughter of scores of buffalo, pigs, or, occasionally, horses. The meat is then distributed among those in attendance. Some is cooked and consumed there. The rest of the raw meat is brought home and redistributed to people who did not attend. As a result, some meat from a large feast may end up in the hands of a substantial percentage of the households in the area.

The problem is that when the sponsors of the event are *marapu* followers or even sympathetic Christians, they offer the animals to the spirits with ritual speech before the killing. To kill animals without prayer incurs several sanctions. The spirits of the victims, uninformed of their destinations, will be lost, which may affect the fertility of the herds. Those who feast without displaying the fact that they are compelled by ritual obligations imposed on them from external sources (the ancestors) will appear to be both arrogantly willful and shamefully under the sway of their desires.

Even a Christian who does not attend the original feast might not elude the distribution of meat, and strong social pressures make it hard to reject the gift (and the debt it entails). To insist that converts refuse sacrificial meat would be to condemn them to social isolation. But to consume that meat runs against the injunction in

1 Corinthians 8 and 10 in which Paul warns against eating sacrifices as tantamount to "fellowship with devils." The issue gave rise to a series of sharp debates, evident early in this century and persisting in the 1990s. Some missionaries insisted on the letter of the scripture, some on a more liberal practicality, and a third group found a middle position, forbidding the eating of meat at the sacrificial feast but not that delivered to the house.

Some of the antiprohibitionists pointed out that the prohibitionist position carried a theological as well as social danger, since it risked crediting the power of material things. If meat really is only symbolic, it should have no effects on the souls of those who consume it. The next logical step, then, would be to work towards reinterpreting feasts as symbolic activities. This led to proposals that Sumbanese practices might take on new functions:

> The giving of food to the dead and the dead-feasts can be renewed in a commemoration speech on New Year's Eve. Harvest feasts become thanksgiving days. . . . In funerals, animals may rightly be killed but only those which are necessary to provide food for those in attendance. The custom among the Sumbanese, to bring home the meat given to the spirits, is transposed into support for the poor. (Lambooy 1932: 342)

In other words, what is required is that the outer forms of tradition be retained, but that they be endowed with new functions both expressive and practical. In order to bring this about, those functions should be portrayed in terms of the intentions of the participants. By placing a functional interpretation on the meat, Christians find themselves stressing its materiality at the expense of the spiritual dimension, something the *marapu* followers are quick to point out. But by stressing intentions, Protestants suppress the materiality of things in favor of their symbolic character, treating them as objectified expressions of immaterial meanings.

The most direct way to effect the latter transformation, the one that best eludes the threat of materialism posed by the former, is through the use of speech. As Lois Onvlee put it, writing of the proposed harvest ceremonies, the Christian should stress the disinterested character of the event: "The feast then is no longer a necessity but a gift. Not in order to influence but to thank; not 'supaja' (in order) but 'sebab' (because)" (1973a: 156–57). That is, Christians should not see the performance as *marapu* followers do, an externally imposed obligation to the ancestors, but as the outcome of choices made by persons who possess free will. In order for the will to be properly located in the person, it must be clearly distinguished from the material objects that serve as its media. This can be done by restructuring the actions performed by ritual. What had been an action anterior to an outcome ("in order" to obtain a harvest from the ancestors) must become the response to a prior action ("thank you" for the harvest conferred by God). But the physical activities of killing and butchering animals remain the same for *marapu* followers and Christians. The meat that results, as a material substance, remains silent about its possible meanings and purposes, and inherently subject to mistaken interpretations. The reconfiguration of the relation between material things and immaterial meanings, therefore, must be effected through speech.

THE SPIRIT OF THE WORD

When flesh and other material objects have been banned from the intercourse with God, what remains? How can divine presence be ascertained and what mediates between the humans in the visible world and the agents of the invisible? For one ritual specialist of my acquaintance these were serious questions. Umbu Paji had converted to Christianity, but after his wife died suddenly, while they were both still young, he returned to the *marapu* and eventually became a *ratu*. In our many conversations over the years, he continually returned to the problem of presence. Once, for example, he explained to me how he responds to Christian polemics:

> Christians say we make stones into God, but that's not so. The stone altar is where we meet. It's like if I promise to meet you, we need to have someplace to meet, right? How can we meet if there's no sign? . . . The Psalm says God exists everywhere—in the house, on the veranda, in the forest. Well, if this is so, how come when we pray [in these places] they tell us it's Satan?

By my understanding of *marapu* ritual, Umbu Paji is correct in saying that Christians misrepresent the role of stone altars. Still, Umbu Paji's experience with the Christians, who form the majority in his village, has made him a skilled casuist, and his words should not be taken to represent the views of all *marapu* followers. But he does touch on a central problem for adherents to both sides of the debate.

As the problem of meat shows, material objects, especially those subject to ordinary uses like eating, cannot unambiguously determine and delimit their semiotic and practical functions (see Keane 1997a, chapter 3). Thus such objects cannot in themselves either guarantee the autonomy of the subject or resolve the problems posed by the invisibility of the deity. They are available for too many conflicting uses and interpretations, and offer the temptations of fetishism. If the possible meanings of objects are to be constrained, they must be subjected to the reflexive powers of language, with its capacity to speak from within the act itself about what is being done and what is intended.

Language can seem to promise a way to stabilize the distinction between subject and object. This is both because of what it can say, by virtue of its own reflexivity (see Lucy 1993), and because of the intimate nature of its relationship to the speaker. For many strands of the Christian tradition, the chief mediator between material and immaterial, visible and invisible, and interior and exterior is speech (see Keane 1997b). Words, which arise from the true, spiritual locus of the will, are the spirit made manifest (Niesel 1956: 212–26). Central to the origins of the Protestant tradition was the question of the status of language. Translation of the Bible into vernaculars was to make the scriptures available to the lay reader, without the mediation of clerics. In contrast to doctrines that hold sacred words to be untranslatable (as in some understandings of the Qur'an, for example, or of Vedic mantra), the emphasis on scriptural translation tends to presuppose the transparency of language. This transparency means that it is not its sound shape, for example, that grants scriptural language its divinity, but its semantic content. Translation tends to place greater value on meaning than linguistic form.

One of the classic accounts of linguistic meaning from medieval theology (Asad 1993) through contemporary linguistic pragmatics (Grice 1957) is that words give outward expression to the inner intentions of persons. If those intentions are truly the speaker's own, and if speech truly arises from the speaker's own interiority, then that speech would be sincere. In many Protestant sects, the sincerity of prayer is the necessary condition for true communication with God. But language is in some ways exterior to its speaker. Therefore even it does not entirely unproblematically guarantee the autonomy of the subject and its separation from objects. Some Protestants discover that language presents its own temptations to fetishism. There seem to be two reasons for this; its material embodiment, and its social character. This holds not just for writing but even for the spoken word. Thus utterances, however spiritual might be their place of origin in the soul, are inescapably material. The sounds of speech are produced by mechanical action, are received by means of physical effects on the listener, are governed by linguistic conventions about form, and, what is theologically most at issue, have some degree of existence outside both speaker and listener. After all, since we can hear ourselves speak, our words once uttered come to us much as the words of others.

Our words also come to us from others ontogenically; we learn a language that exists prior to our own utterances. In speaking we display the extent to which others have entered into our own words (Bakhtin 1981). These aspects of language thus seem to pose obstacles to sincere prayer, if, as in many Protestant views, it is defined by its origin in the individual subject. If we could guarantee the divinity of the words that come from others, this might not present a problem for religious practice. But to the extent that language is social in origin, it reveals the incipient insincerity that threatens to intervene between speaker and the divine addressee.

Both the materiality of utterances and the social character of language threaten the word's association with the intentions and interiority of the individual speaker. This has led some Protestant denominations to reject liturgical speech and others to seek its radical transformation. For all their differences, for example, the silence of Quakers and joyful noise of Pentecostals share a suspicion of both ordinary and liturgical speech. Quakers seek to eliminate any but the most spontaneous speech in religious service, which should otherwise remain in silence. The marks of sincerity include austerity, often linguistically marked by a rhetorically "unadorned" style.[8] In contrast, Pentecostal services typically involve emotional display and noise, as participants try to achieve glossolalia (speaking in tongues). This is language whose very unintelligibility is the guarantee of its divine source and the sincerity of the inspired speaker.[9]

In Sumba, the parallels between the exteriority of language and that of the fetishistic object are evident in the Calvinist critiques of *marapu* ritual speech. *Marapu* ritual has two inseparable components, the offering and the speech that must accompany it. The authority of ritual speech remains very strong, even for Sumbanese Christians. Indeed, the more that ritual speech is performed without the "base" of material offerings, the more authority is invested in the speech itself. Nonetheless, the "*marapu* words" (*li marapu*), have three defining features that, for Christians, implicate them with the general threat of fetishism. For one thing, the words, by definition, do not come from the speaker but from the ancestors themselves. In addition, this origin is marked by the form the words take, for ritual speech must follow strict poetic rules and is composed of a fixed canon of couplets.

Finally, not only do the words and their formal properties come from others, the performance too is normally delegated to specialists, who speak on behalf of sponsors or other beneficiaries who themselves remain silent during the performance.[10]

Marapu ritual speech takes advantage of the material and social exteriority of language to respond to the problems of presence posed by communication with invisible addressees. By using only canonical couplets with their strict poetic form, ritual speakers return to their addressees the very words that those addressees had provided to their speakers. Although there is no certainty that the ancestors can hear these words, at least in this way ritual speech establishes its appropriateness for spanning the semiotic gap that intervenes between speaker and listener (see Keane 1995). In contrast, the linguistic forms of Protestant prayer resemble those of everyday speech. Thus, at least for the unconvinced, Protestant prayer displays no manifest evidence of its capacity to communicate to the invisible world.[11]

On the other hand, although *marapu* speech has a clear relationship to its addressee, it leaves some doubt about the relationship between words and their speaker. Since they originate with the ancestors, the words are clearly distinct from the speaker in at least some respects. Ritual speakers neither claim to be the origin of their words, nor, unlike practitioners in some religions, do they go into trance or states of possession, and thereby lend their bodies to invisible speakers. They must use offerings and verbal self-reference to establish their identities and their rights to address the spirits.

The response to *marapu* speech by contemporary Sumbanese Protestants is exemplified in their insistence on the importance of shutting one's eyes while praying. This puzzles *marapu* followers, one of whom asked me, "What are they afraid of?" adding sardonically, "Maybe they're afraid their sins are visible!" For Protestants, shut eyes help the speaker avoid the temptation of the fetishized word. They mark off the boundary between interior and exterior. One church warden explained to me that you close your eyes so that your speech will come from the heart. Pointedly he added that Catholics not only verge on idolatry by worshipping statues of the Virgin, they also pray with their eyes open. That is, unlike Calvinists, they read from the Prayer Book. Note here the explicit association between the fetishizing displacement of idol worship and that of reciting the written word.

In a 1993 sermon, one young minister criticized his main competitors in this way:

> Yes, as for Catholicism, there are often formulae. Can't go skip over or
> go contrary to the way of praying. Have to follow exactly. . . . Like in

Islam, for example, it has to be so many times.[12] We (on the other hand) are not taught like this. It's not enough, just five times. Breathing goes on and on, doesn't it?

By comparing sincere prayer to breath, this minister rhetorically endows it with the authority of natural processes. If Catholic liturgy, Islamic prayer, and *marapu* words take their authority from the distinctiveness that sets them apart from ordinary conversation, the appeal here is the reverse. The authority of Calvinist prayer lies in its sincerity, and its sincerity is marked by its ordinariness. In this way, it is identified with the full presence of the everyday, physical locus of the individuated self.[13]

The Calvinist criticisms of inauthentic prayer view it as like the fetishized object. Like the spirits inauthentic prayer addresses, it stands outside the subject, and to it the speaking subject surrenders its own capacity to act. These become apparent as the linguist and Bible translator Lois Onvlee ponders the difficulty of rendering the meaning of "prayer" in a Sumbanese language:

> I think of the word with which we render our "to prayer," viz. *parengena li'i*, which literally means to make someone hear the word, direct the word to. . . . After my use of the word in a religious service was rejected by one of the elders, we thereafter intended to be on "safe" terrain. But this "safe terrain" did not exist. Once I went along when summoned for the killing of the chicken, one of the officients was told to *parengeni li'i na manu*, in other words, make the chicken hear the word, in order that by and by the chicken intestine should then speak what the forefathers mean to say, to be able to serve as oracle. And in another context, regarding what was "hot", and thus perilous, and to be cooled, they said *parengengge li'i ne we'e*, make the water hear the word. . . . And thus I am here in the neighborhood of the magical word, which confers coercive power onto that over which the word is spoken. And now we use this word in another connection and say *parengeni li'i Mjori*, to make the Lord hear the word. Shall this word continually be clear for those who hear it? (1973b: 202)

Notice here the way in which the problem of translation leads irrevocably from speech practices to mistaken views of agency and of the kinds of beings that inhabit the world. By addressing the chicken, *marapu* speech treats as an agent that which ontologically lacks agency, and in cooling that which is hot, it falsely attributes efficacy to words.

From a Calvinist perspective, *Marapu* words are like the fetishized object in that the speaker attributes to words and their forms powers

that properly lie in persons and their intentions. *Marapu* words seek
to have effects on material things when, for Protestants, words can
only express meanings emanating from the speaker's immaterial
spirit. By contrast, the authentic prayer of the Protestant must originate within the speaker, be guided by intentions, and, since its efficacy depends on the meanings of its words and not just their forms,
refer to a world beyond itself. According to this opposition, authentic speech is primarily a form of symbolic expression. The forms it
takes are relatively arbitrary, in the Saussurean sense, in contrast to
the canonical couplets of *marapu* speech.

CONCLUSION

As Quaker silence and Pentecostal glossolalia suggest, speech cannot
be fully relied on to determine the boundaries between external objects and the interiority of subjects. In Sumba, Dutch Calvinists coun-
terpose the sincerity of expressions arising from individual and
internal sources against what they take to be *marapu* ritual's fetishistic
displacement of agency onto objectified verbal formulae. A mistaken
view of language is inseparable from mistaken understanding of the
human subject. Wrong speech thus forms an obstacle on the way to
achieving an interior state of grace. As Wielenga writes,

> whenever one has a bad understanding of "redemption," then it is
> also given that one has a bad understanding of "thankfulness." He
> shall answer the question: how shall I be thankful to God for such re-
> demption?—thank and love God. Words and nothing but words. . . .
> And it turns out that the thankfulness stands in acknowledging that he
> *says* thanks. Only seldom shall he convert it into a deed both saying
> and doing: I am your servant and will do work for you. His heathen re-
> ligion has cost him much, many pecuniary and material sacrifices. . . .
> [In *marapu* ritual] a removal of guilt must "be purchased," for all must
> be "paid for." But a Christian "*asks*" forgiveness, receives it, and
> "*says*" his thankfulness. (1923: 223)

The lack of interiority is mutually implicated with the misuse of
words. If words are deeds, a view Wielenga imputes to *marapu* followers, they would be sufficient in themselves. But if words are only supplementary to deeds, something closer to Wielenga's own view, they
lie external to the subject, and so in themselves remain unbound to
the subject's condition and acts. Inauthentic speech is then insepara-

ble from materialism, going hand in hand with the corruption that conflates economic exchange (the purchase of an indulgence) with spiritual effects (forgiveness). Wielenga's view of speech, in its very appeal to interiority, recognizes the supplementary and ambiguously external character of language, which needs some additional resources if it is to be bound to inner states and outer works.

This opens up a possibility that finds some echoes in the *marapu* followers' response to Christian criticism. *Marapu* followers frequently assert that Christians display overwhelming hubris in seeking to address the deity directly.[14] In contrast to the forms of direct address to which Protestant prayer aspires, *marapu* followers see their ritual forms not as insincere but as deferential. It is respectful modesty on the part of speakers to insist that the words they utter are not their own, an insistence displayed in the canonical forms of the poetic couplet. In contrast, *marapu* followers commonly attribute to the isolated speaker of Christian prayer an excessive willfulness that is at once dangerous and ineffective. For *marapu* followers, Christians are suspect precisely because they take the warrants of sacred speech to lie in persons rather than in the exteriority of words. That is, through its efforts at sincerity and spontaneity, Christian prayer seeks to deny that language and its powers do not originate in the individual speaker. To *marapu* followers, this means an illegitimate transfer of responsibility from the invisible world of spirits to the fleshly domain of the living. If the ultimate agents are divine, from the *marapu* followers' point of view it is as if Christians fetishize themselves.

As I have suggested, however, both sides have to contend with the problems of ambiguous presence. Their concrete practices reveal a lingering doubt: For *marapu* followers, it is about the presence of the invisible spirits; for Christians, the presence of the sincere intentions in the worshipper. What both sides share is evidence that *neither* takes the subject to be fully autonomous and self-present. Neither, then, is in an unassailable position to portray the other as the real fetishist. This may even lend force to the charges each lays against the other, since each may in turn find tempting some of the displacements and assurances offered by the other's "fetishism."

NOTES

1. All translations from the Dutch are my own. Twenty-four months of fieldwork in Anakalang (1985, 1986–1987, and 1993) and research in the Netherlands (1988) were generously funded by the Department of Education

Fulbright-Hays Dissertation Fellowship, the Joint Committee on Southeast Asia of the Social Science Research Council, and the American Council of Learned Societies, the Wenner-Gren Foundation for Anthropological Research, and the Southeast Asia Council of the Association for Asian Studies with funds from the Luce Foundation, and was conducted under the sponsorship of the Lembaga Ilmu Pengetahuan Indonesia and Universitas Nusa Cendana. An earlier version of this article was presented at the University of Amsterdam Research Group Religion and Society conference "Border Fetishisms" (December 1995). I am grateful for the comments of Adela Pinch and Patricia Spyer, and for countless Sumbanese for their conversations.

2. In addition to the axiomatic point, there is a more specific one to make as well. The Gereformeerde Kerken, the Dutch Calvinist sect that missionized Sumba, split off from the mainstream Nederlandse Hervormde Kerk in the mid-nineteenth century in part as a reaction against the latter's liberalizing tendencies. A small minority (some 8.18 percent of the Dutch population in 1899), this sect appealed to the small farmers, artisans, and small tradesmen, whose were likely to see themselves at the margins of industrial mass society (Wintle 1987).

3. Sumba is about the size of Jamaica, with a population of some 350,000. The economy is predominantly subsistance agriculture, with some trade in cattle and horses. What is most relevant to this article is the thriving and in some places hugely expensive system of ceremonial exchange (involving cloth, gold, silver, buffalo, horses, and pigs) that mediates most social relations (for details see Keane 1997a). Sumba is home to speakers of some half-dozen closely related languages, identified with distinct territories which they inhabit. These territories vary greatly in social organization, ritual, and economic structure. Nonetheless, there is enough basic similarity among them—which Sumbanese themselves recognize—that for purposes of this article, the ethnographic differences can be glossed over. Indeed, the missionary writings with which I work frequently do not specify what part of Sumba is in question. When I draw on my own fieldwork and the language used there, I am refering to the domain of Anakalang, located in the west-central part of the island.

4. The word *marapu* properly refers to the most ancient and powerful of the ancestral spirits, and the chief interlocutors in ritual. In Sumba, the word is also used to refer to the religion and its practitioners. "*Marapu* follower" is a somewhat infelicitous shorthand; one does not "follow" the *marapu* as one might a cult leader or savior. But people do say that to perform the rituals is to "follow" (*keri*) the tracks left by the ancestors. This is a better solution than to call them "*marapu* worshippers," which inaccurately assimilates the ritual relationship with *marapu* to very different sorts of religious practice.

5. Pak Kadiwangu's historicizing version of the relation between *marapu* and Christian religions shows interesting parallels (whether intentional or not I cannot say) to the typological reading of the Bible. In this hermeneu-

tic tradition, the New Testament reveals the truth which was only immanent in the Old Testament.

6. Many of the debates between Dutch Calvinists and *marapu* followers not only replay the original conflict between Protestants and Catholics, they seem at times to contain a subtext about their present-day rivalry as well. Catholic missions historically have been a much smaller presence on Sumba than those of the Dutch Calvinists (see Haripranata 1984). In recent years, however, as both missions begin to prostelytize the final and most stubborn holdouts among the unconverted, their rivalry has intensified. In particular, *marapu* followers often find Catholicism far the less onerous choice. One *ratu* told me that if he were forced to enter a church, he would choose the Catholics both because they have the older faith (next only to *marapu* ritual), and because their ritualism has some resemblance to his own. On the latter point Protestants would gleefully concur.

7. A good example of the relationship between their traditionalism and the problem of fetishism can be found in the following passage by Lois Onvlee, describing what he sees as a noble but vanishing world. After showing how people and their possessions exist in an intimate relationship, he writes: "Possessions on Sumba . . . must be seen in terms of broad social and religious relationships. These relationships are now breaking down. . . . As the Sumbanese come increasingly to regard their possessions in an economic sense, I can only hope that they will view these goods in the proper context, without which these possessions could become a dangerous and threatening power. I can only hope that the Sumbanese people will find a new control over their possessions—one that will provide a new context and a new respect" (1980: 206–207). Here a native fetishism is counterposed favorably to something very like the fetishism of the commodity (see also Keane 1996).

8. As one Quaker has pointed out to me, not every form of spontaneous speech is acceptable in meeting. What counts as spontaneous speech is subject to strict conventions, which will vary from congregation to congregation. These conventions, however, are likely to be largely tacit, and possibly unconscious. For Quaker views of language in their formative period, see Bauman 1983.

9. Pentecostals cite the Biblical gift of tongues as the precedent for their practices, but different sects vary in how they view the words of glossolalia. Some take them to be part of some ordinary human language that happens to be unknown to the speaker; others believe they are a divine language. In addition, sects differ on whether these words can be interpreted (see Goodman 1972; Samarin 1972). For a comparison of Quaker and Pentecostal treatments of language, see Maltz 1985. For language in other religions, see Keane 1997b.

10. This brief sketch is meant only to draw out the points relevant to the encounter with Calvinism. The complex topic of Sumbanese ritual speech

has been addressed at length elsewhere; see especially Kuipers 1990; Keane 1997a.

11. The Lord's Prayer was indeed taught to its speakers by its addressee, by way of Jesus Christ. Its divine origin is known, however, only by virtue of the surrounding narrative, not through its linguistic form.

12. He is refering to the Islamic obligation to pray at five specified times over the course of the day.

13. In *marapu* ritual, the apparent displacements of the intending and acting subject by ritual objects and the external word are also echoed in its participation structure and by continual reference to its obligatory character. Speaking of the delegation of *marapu* words to specialists, one Protestant put it this way: "As for *marapu* people, they don't even pay attention during the prayers, as long as they have their *ratu* doing the job for them. They don't concentrate like we do, but just chat away." As fulfillment of an obligation, the performers of *marapu* words insist that their words are not the expressions of personal intentions and volition.

14. In doing so, *marapu* followers often overlook such theological nuances as the mediation of Christ and the role of Grace in the production of sincere speech. But then so do many of the local Christians, who in this respect are perhaps more modernist than the theologians.

REFERENCES

Apter, Emily, and William Pietz, eds. (1993) *Fetishism as Cultural Discourse.* Ithaca: Cornell University Press.

Asad, Talal. (1993) "On Discipline and Humility in Medieval Christian Monasticism." In *Genealogies of Religion: Discipline and Reasons of Power in Christianity and Islam.* Baltimore: Johns Hopkins University Press.

Bakhtin, M.M. (1981) *The Dialogic Imagination: Four Essays.* Trans. Caryl Merson and Michael Holquist; Michael Holquist ed, Austin: University of Texas Press.

Bauman, Richard. (1983) *Let Your Words Be Few: Symbolism of Speaking and Silence Among Seventeenth Century Quakers.* Cambridge: Cambridge University Press.

Dijkstra, H. (1902) "Den Duivelen Offeren." *Het Mosterdzaad* v. 21. In van den End, Th., ed. 1987 *Gereformeerde Zending op Sumba: Een Bronnenpublicatie.* Alphen aan den Rijn: Raad voor de Zending der Ned. Herv. Kerk, et al.

Goodman, Felicitas D. (1972) *Speaking in Tongues: A Cross-Cultural Study of Glossolalia.* Chicago and London: University of Chicago Press.

Grice, H.P. (1957) "Meaning." *Philosophical Review* 64: 377–88.

Haripranata, H. (1984) *Ceritera Sejarah Gereja Katolik Sumba dan Sumbawa.* Ende: Arnoldus.

Hoskins, Janet A. (1993) "Violence, Sacrifice, and Divination: Giving and Taking a Life in Eastern Indonesia." *American Ethnologist* 20: 159–78.

Ivy, Marilyn. (1995) *Discourses of the Vanishing: Modernity, Phantasm, Japan.* Chicago and London: University of Chicago Press.

Kapita, U.H. (1976) *Masyarakat Sumba dan Adat Istiadatnya.* Waingapu: Panitia Penerbit Naskah-Naskah Kebudayaan Daerah Sumba Dewan Penata Layanan Gereja Kristen Sumba.

Keane, Webb. (1994) "The Value of Words and the Meaning of Things in Eastern Indonesian Exchange." *Man* (n.s.) 29: 605–29.

———. (1995) "The Spoken House: Text, Act, and Object in Eastern Indonesia." *American Ethnologist* 22: 102–24.

———. (1996) "Materialism, Missionaries, and Modern Subjects in Colonial Indonesia." In *Conversion to Modernities: The Globalization of Christianity.* Peter van der Veer, ed. New York and London: Routledge.

———. (1997a) *Signs of Recognition: Powers and Hazards of Representation in an Indonesian Society.* Berkeley: University of California Press.

———. (1997b) "Religious Language." *Annual Review of Anthropology* 26: 47–71.

Kuipers, Joel C. (1990) *Power in Performance: The Creation of Textual Authority in Weyewa Ritual Speech.* Philadelphia: University of Pennsylvania Press.

Lambooy, P.J. (1930) "De Godsnaam op Soemba." *De Macedoniër* 34: 275–84.

———. (1932) "Zending en Volksgewoonten op Soemba." In van den End, Th., ed., 1987 *Gereformeerde Zending op Sumba: Een Bronnenpublicatie.* Alphen aan den Rijn: Raad voor de Zending der Ned. Herv. Kerk, et al.

Lucy, John A., ed. (1993) *Reflexive Language: Reported Speech and Metapragmatics.* Cambridge: Cambridge University Press.

Maltz, Daniel N. (1985) "Joyful Noise and Reverent Silence: The Significance of Noise in Pentecostal Worship." In *Perspectives on Silence*, Deborah Tannen and Muriel Sackville-Troike, eds. Norwood, NJ: Ablex Publishing Co.

Marx, Karl. (1967) (1887). *Capital: A Critique of Political Economy.* Trans. Samuel Moore and Edward Aveling. New York: International Press.

Niesel, Wilhelm. (1956) (1938). *The Theology of Calvin.* Trans. Harold Knight. Philadelphia: Westminster Press.

Onvlee L. (1973a) (1969). "Woord en Antwoord, Zending en Adat." In *Cultuur als Antwoord*. Verhandelingen van het Koninklijk Instituut voor Taal-, Land- en Volkenkunde 66. 's-Gravenhage: Martinus Nijhoff.

———. (1973b) (1957). "Taalvernieuwing uit het Evangelie." In *Cultuur als Antwoord*, Verhandelingen van het Koninklijk Instituut voor Taal-, Land- en Volkenkunde 66. 's-Gravenhage: Martinus Nijhoff.

———. (1980) (1952). "The Significance of Livestock on Sumba." Trans. James J. Fox and Henny Fokker-Bakker. In *The Flow of Life: Essays on Eastern Indonesia*, James J. Fox, ed. Cambridge, Mass: Harvard University Press.

Peacock, James L. and Ruel W. Tyson, Jr. (1989) *Pilgrims of Paradox: Calvinism and Experience among the Primitive Baptists of the Blue Ridge*. Washington: Smithsonian Institution Press.

Pietz, William. (1985) "The Problem of the Fetish, I." *Res* 9: 5–17.

Samarin, William J. (1972) *Tongues of Men and Angels: The Religious Language of Pentecostalism*. New York: Macmillan.

Weber, Max. (1958) *The Protestant Ethic and the Spirit of Capitalism*. Trans. Talcott Parsons. New York: Charles Scribners Sons.

Wielenga, D.K. (1909) "Soemba: Animisme en Spiritisme." *De Macedoniër* 13: 332–40.

———. (1923) "Van de Prediking des Evangelies." In van den End, Th., ed. 1987 *Gereformeerde Zending op Sumba: Een Bronnenpublicatie*. Alphen aan den Rijn: Raad voor de Zending der Ned. Herv. Kerk, et al.

Wintle, Michael. (1987) *Pillars of Piety: Religion in the Netherlands in the Nineteenth Century*. Hull University Occasional Papers in Modern Dutch Studies, No. 2. Hull: Hull University Press.

2

From Brooms to Obeah and Back: Fetish Conversion and Border Crossings in Nineteenth-Century Suriname

Susan Legêne

In museums we see only the dead bodies of fetishes, *"die toten Hülle . . . , ihre Kadaver."* The museum catalogue accompanying the Frankfurt 1986 exhibition on African fetishes leaves us with no illusion about the change the exhibited objects underwent before reaching their current resting place in the collections of Western museums. Gone are their spiritual inner powers—their supposed inner energies. What remains are ritual objects, composed of vegetal, mineral, and man-made elements, each with a unique form.[1] To those who made them, who lived with them, the artifact and its spiritual powers are supposed to have been one and the same. As a rule, however, the Europeans—obtaining them by accident, by force, through bargaining or theft—neither understood nor accepted the communicating powers attributed to such objects in the communities within which they functioned.[2] While crossing cultural and geographical borders on their way to Europe, they underwent complex changes in meaning. But why were these objects brought to Europe in the first place to end up in its museums? Did their fetish power indeed stop there, as the Frankfurt catalogue seems to imply, leaving us with only their dead fetish bodies, or was it in fact the museum that created their fetish identity?

At stake is a complex process of both a negation and an attribution of meaning by Europeans to ritual objects that at a peculiar moment in history came to be designated as fetishes. To discuss this process, we will follow here the trip across the ocean of two Suriname obeah. In 1824 these obeah arrived in the Netherlands, where in 1873 they ended up in the collection of the Colonial Museum in Haarlem, (forerunner of the Amsterdam Tropenmuseum).[3] The negation, in retrospect, of what these obeah had once been to their owners, will be interpreted as part of an overall Dutch colonial orientation towards the fashioning of African and Creole slaves into (de-Africanised) Western Christian citizens and disciplined workers, and the creation of a distinction between these Creole Christians as belonging to "civilized society" and animistic maroons as situated outside of "civilization."[4]

Reconstructing a biography of these two obeah helps us to understand what has been called one of the paradoxes of the colonial process: the paradox that religious symbols and systems were attacked and even destroyed on location, to reappear—out of context—in European museum showcases.[5] This should not be regarded as a paradox. These obeah indeed are ritual objects from the Afroamerican *winti*-religion in which spirits and inspired objects play a crucial role. What we will see is that these objects only could become visible *as religious symbols* the very moment they were destined to disappear from their own community. Within that community, the two obeah could be regarded as "border fetishes" in a literal sense, referring here to the crosscultural process in which they were created by enslaved and displaced peoples from a variety of African ethnic and cultural backgrounds, both newly arrived in the colony and born on plantations, who lived in close contact with indigenous Amerindian and maroon communities in the rainforests, as well as with a growing number of free blacks and mulattos. Likewise Europeans certainly influenced these identities, due to their pervasive presence and power over the slaves. The focus here, however, is not directed primarily at the place of these obeah and the role of *winti* in processes of identity creation within the diaspora slave community, but instead at the role these objects played in contesting, confirming, or negotiating European control of these identities.

Taking two obeah as a starting point for a discussion on border fetishisms, I adopt a "biographical" approach that focuses not only on the "commodity status" of things but explores their "social life" as well (Appadurai 1985). Of special interest here are the effects of things' movements, of the transformations that ensue from their cultural and geographic border crossings. A slave "broom"—as it was baptised by Dutch planters in colonial Suriname—undergoes a "conversion" to become a "ritual" artifact in a Dutch museum. In the process, through colonial meaning-making on opposite sides of the ocean, its past-relationship is brusquely swept aside.[6] A biography of the two obeah after they left Suriname may provide some insight into the ways in which Dutch society became acquainted with a foreign culture that it simultaneously rejected and subsumed, exploited and feared. It may provide us with a glimpse of the colonial mechanisms and power plays on which this rejection and incorporation were based, as well as of its effects on the Surinamese communities in which the objects originated.

The two obeah can only play this role—the question of why and under what guise they entered Europe can only be answered—if we connect their biography to that of their human collector. It was he who in 1824 brought these objects to Europe, together with the information that in 1873 made them into collection items in the Colonial Museum. To him, the Suriname "brooms" were initially souvenirs to remind him of his experiences as a plantation owner in some distant place across the ocean. But once back home in Haarlem he substituted their rather homespun status with an exemplary one. It is because of this exemplary status that the objects that the Dutchman once knew as "brooms" were handed over to the Colonial Museum in Haarlem. And there they served as an illustration within a discourse about the Dutch civilizing mission among animistic maroons, one that, importantly, kept wholly silent about slavery and slave society. It was a discourse in which the slaves themselves also lacked a voice and a say, although their objects nonetheless played a role. Let me begin by introducing a Dutch plantation owner.

THE BENEVOLENT PLANTATION OWNER

In 1823 a young man traveled from the Netherlands to Suriname in order to investigate the nature of his family's property there. His mother—remarried following the death of her first husband—had in 1804 inherited her deceased second husband's shares in two plantations in this Dutch Caribbean colony: half of the Clifford Kocqshove plantation, and a 13/60th share of Kocqswoud. Gaspar van Breugel was 25 years old when he left for Suriname as his mother's representative.

He spent eight months in the colony. Back in the Netherlands, the country of Suriname and especially the issue of slavery would keep him busy for the rest of his long life.[7]

Absenteeism on the part of plantation owners was typical of the Suriname plantation system at the time. Due to inheritance laws, most plantations were parceled out among a large number of families in Holland who, in many cases, had personally very little contact with their estates. The common practice among estate owners was to entrust the plantation administration to a banking office in the Netherlands and, in Suriname itself, to engage administrators in the capital, Paramaribo, and a director with an overseer on each plantation. They were responsible for the day-to-day management and financial administration of the plantation. Being a Suriname plantation owner had, within the Dutch context, become a rather abstract, administrative concern. Van Breugel's wish as a share holder to maintain personal control over his plantation affairs was therefore exceptional. From the Netherlands, the colony was very much a faraway place.

From Gaspar van Breugel's private *Journal* and other published and unpublished notes and writings, we can piece together a picture of someone who was initially ignorant of Suriname society with all its intricate race and gender relations, and of the existing working relationships between slaves and their supervisors.[8] Despite his tender age, Van Breugel was, because of his social standing and background as well as his involvement in plantation affairs, an accepted partner in discussions with Paramaribo's ruling class on political, social, and economic issues. In his publications he poses as a real adventurer, a man who trusts local medical knowledge and dares to taste such frightening delicacies as fried grubs. This adventurous and open-minded attitude served, within the Dutch context, as a means to show his expertise. He exploited this position to defend the colonial elite whenever public criticism was voiced in the Netherlands about the poor treatment of slaves in the colony as well as to object against the emancipation of the slaves without their proper preparation for citizenship. His claim to be an authority derived from the simple fact of having been on the spot. He took this stand in favor of the colonial elite even though he himself had grown critical of their behavior during the time he spent in Suriname. As far as he was concerned, they chiefly engaged in gossip, financial trickery, lavish dinners, and the rude or brutish treatment of women (slaves).

An essential component of this self-image and self-appointed role as mediator is Van Breugel's identity as "plantation owner," a notion which only seems to apply to the landed aspect of this property.[9]

Thus, wherever Van Breugel writes about plantation ownership, any reference to the ownership of slaves is absent from the text; the term "slave owner," is never mentioned with one exception: In 1857, he uses the term in an anonymous pamphlet against Dutch abolitionists, *Slave owners and Slave friends. . . .* Here, "slave owners" has become a kind of honorary title set against those who dared call themselves the friends of the slaves but in fact proposed to bring misfortune upon them by advocating slave emancipation (Breugel 1857). "Plantation owner" was thus a euphemism for slave owner, referring to land ownership over and above the ownership of people, even though Van Breugel at the same time admitted that in the days of declining agricultural profits the value of a plantation depended largely on the size and quality of its slave population.[10]

All this does not imply that Van Breugel did not have any personal contact with his slaves in Suriname. He gleaned useful information from his peers concerning the hierarchy among plantation slaves: field slaves (subdivided between Creoles and Africans), versus house slaves (often mulattos), as well as men and women of a wide variety of descent, skin color, and "reliability." He met with the slaves who were skilled in carpentry or medicine, and with their supervisor, called *bastiaan*—who supervised the whole slave community often being their *winti* priest as well (Lamur 1985: 19), and via whom Van Breugel communicated with the other slaves. His involvement with them seems to have been marked by an ambivalence between economic and humanistic reasoning, which enabled him to learn from his slaves about their culture, hunting methods, plants, animals, and trees, while at the same time inspecting them during roll call as if they were simply a form of capital. Back home in the Netherlands Van Breugel continued to keep track of his slaves through this register. In 1832 he notes with pride a natural growth of the slave population of Clifford Kocqshove in the period 1824–1831. Given that many of these slaves were newborn children or old people however, he concluded: "And thus, this comparison, although indicating a larger number of heads, is not favorable in relation to 1831."[11] This statement reflects his ambivalent reasoning in which economics clearly prevails.

Van Breugel's calculating approach is most clear in those cases where irregularities were discovered, as in the case of a small boy who lived in the administrator's house, or the black carpenter who profited from irregular privileges. Here, however, Van Breugel ran up against emotional and family relationships which he found rather embarrassing. He discovered that sexual relations between the plantation administrators, directors, or overseers, and enslaved women was common practice. Such personal liaisons, enforced or not, were noted in his *Journal* in a veiled way, however. Only in those cases where a woman from his own workforce had succeeded in loosening the bonds of slavery, or (in one case) even in escaping from slavery, would Van Breugel go to great lengths to reconstruct the situation in order to discover whether it represented financial damage to his family. But his experienced peers in Suriname convinced Van Breugel that he should not bother himself too much with such things. They taught him not to become involved in the personal relationships between the slaves and the administrators or directors of the plantations. To avoid any misunderstandings concerning his own lifestyle, however, he testified in his travel account to his innocence, painting there a picture of himself as someone oblivious to the beautiful women who, according to his hosts, were all around him. The implication was, of course, that he never touched a slave. He even made a point of explaining to his readers that, during a directors' party where everybody got drunk, he himself drank only water and slipped away unnoticed and early at one o'clock.

This careful, dutiful, and righteous young man, who went to Suriname on a financial mission concerning the administration and prospects of two coffee plantations, returned both charmed by the overseas community and convinced that his family should sell its plantation shares as soon as possible. This is not the place to go into the economic details concerning the plantation administration and the sales (Kocqswoud was sold in 1832, and Clifford Kocqshove in 1838/9). It was with a sigh of relief that Gaspar closed his accounts after receiving the letter confirming that Clifford Kocqshove had finally been sold and at that before his mother died, thus preventing a situation in which due to inheritance laws the plantation shares would have had to have been subdivided among still more shareholders. For the Van Breugel family the sale was a purely financial decision.[12] Uneasiness about slavery, which may have troubled them and resulted in a drive to provide the slaves with everything they were entitled to according to the formal regulations, did not play an explicit role in the family's decision to sell its shares. But in the fifteen years it had taken the family to sell its shares at a reasonable price, Van Breugel had become an expert on both Suriname and slavery, as well as a dedicated activist for the propagation of Christian education among slaves. And here is where the two obeah enter the story.

Together with detailed accounts, slave registers, plantation maps, and other valuable administrative documents, Van Breugel's luggage when he returned to Holland contained a wide variety of objects: vegetable, mineral, and man-made, alive as well as dead. The papers and numerous objects—calabashes, a wooden lock, two "brooms," an apron made of beads, strings, dolls, drums—survived him. One turtle survived the ocean voyage and lived to a ripe old age in Van Breugel's house in Haarlem. It may even have survived its master. But the two brooms he had acquired underwent a transformation during their stay in the Netherlands, where they came to be recognized as fetishes.

Two Obeah From Suriname

"Donated by Jhr. G.P.C. van Breugel, Haarlem, 1873." The documentation cards of the Tropenmuseum collection corresponding to the two obeah discussed here take their moment of entry into the museum collection as the beginning of their genealogy (cf. Figure 1). One obeah is called a brush (Dutch: *kwast*) and stored together with other brooms. The other is kept with fellow obeah from various ages. Some are brand new and seem never to have been used. According to the documentation cards our two objects are rather old. They certainly come from Suriname bush Negroes, the card tells us, and before they fell into Dutch hands were probably used by a *winti* priest to chase away bad spirits during a trance dance.

As a rule, such documentation cards are the first source of information about artifacts in museum collections. In many cases they are the starting point for the researcher in search for a certain kind of object that fits a given subject. Next comes the object itself. If this is not exhibited it has to be brought up from the depot to be looked over and investigated. The documentation card, with its essential background information, inevitably influences the ensuing analysis of the object. And since ethnographical museums along with much anthropological practice have, until recently, tended to regard non-Western societies as peoples without history, ancient artifacts from non-Western cultures have all too often been registered without precise dates and with little information concerning their provenance.[13] When I came across the objects discussed here, I was not looking for *winti* and maroon obeah, but rather for Van Breugel's two slave brooms. Relying on first-hand archival sources, I spotted these brooms before I had studied the literature on these museum objects and thus before, as maroon ritual objects, they had lost their past relationship. This provided me with a

critical stance towards their museum identity, which otherwise probably would not have surprised me.

The documentation cards trace the obeah to maroon religious
culture. Recent historical and anthropological works on *winti* and on
maroon societies confirm that these objects may indeed have been
used by maroons. However, according to the Van Breugel archives the
obeah come from Clifford Kocqshove and played their role within
that specific slave community, at the beginning of the 1820s.[14] Although Van Breugel wrote a detailed collection list with a description
of each item he donated to the collection of the new Colonial Museum in Haarlem, this information was apparently lost after they entered the museum (Breugel 1842b). The genealogical relocation of the
obeah from slave to free maroon society is not without meaning. But
let us first have a closer look at the objects concerned, combining
Van Breugel's remarks with recent literature, and following the Frankfurt museum description system which distinguishes between vegetable, mineral and man-made components.

The two obeah are basically two freakish branches of a tree (according to Van Breugel these are woody grainings of a palm tree; the
documentation cards call the wood "unknown"). They end (the documentation card state) in a bundle of "a certain grass." According to
Van Breugel in the one case the bundle was taken from the top of a
date palm (Dutch: *Palmiet dadelboom*), while the other consists of the
veins of palm leaves. This seems to be a reasonable explanation.[15] A
ring of black resin should also be included in this list of vegetable elements. Mineral are the humps of kaolin chalk, on both obeah. This
white chalk, called *pemba doti*, plays a role in many *winti* rites, where
it is applied to both ritual objects and human bodies.[16] Pressed into
the *pemba doti* are rows of cowries.[17] The small brass chains on both
obeah are man-made. They are also pressed into the *pemba doti* and
seem to bind the brushes to the freakish stalks. The largest also has a
double string of small red beads on one outer side near the brush,
and a small black brass chain around the stalk at the other side, as
well as nails with round top covers, resembling drawing pins. On this
obeah, in the *pemba doti*, blue dots have been painted.[18] Both obeah
have white cotton thread wrapped around them; one has a hole in
the freakish stalk through which the thread runs.

What did Van Breugel make of the elements that made up the
obeah? What strikes us first and foremost is that he did not attach
any explicit ritual or religious meaning to them.[19] He focuses exclusively on their vegetable components, describing the palm trees and
their utility for making brooms and other household implements, as

well as food and drinks. The two obeah are for him such brooms, used to clean the plantation yard in the same way as farmers in Holland used to sweep their farmyards to keep them clean and tidy. Cowries, beads, blue dots, black resin, white cotton, brass chains—elements that anthropologists would surely focus on in investigating the obeah's ritual power—they all seem to have gone unnoticed.

I do not want to suggest that Van Breugel may not have had any notion of the ritual dimension of the brooms. To his explanation that the slaves used them to sweep the yard in front of the plantation buildings, he adds that in this sweeping they liked to draw a caricature of a visitor, or of flower motifs. His reference to the Dutch yards swept by (free, rather than slave) farmers, may have been a way of translating his experiences for an ignorant Dutch audience, but does not imply that he (and his readers) perceived this latter act of sweeping as entirely functional either. Folklore in the eastern part of the Netherlands, for instance, still has it that each Friday before dark the yard should be swept to prevent a certain mythical being from coming and punishing the lazy farmer. Decorations on old farms still depict the broom as a protective implement against thunder and fire as well as ghosts.[20]

However, we can discern Van Breugel's orientation towards the utility of everything that grew and flowered around him and that also sparked his interest, in other descriptions of objects and products. In general, the plantation owner poses as a connoisseur content to know a great deal about the uses to which trees, plants, and nests, could be or were put—as in paper, ropes, food, beverages, body decoration, aromatic fragrances—but only in passing does he mention any alleged ritual or cultural connotation of things. Let me give another example of his—at times even forced and overstated—utilitarian, noncultural approach to religious customs in Suriname. Both in his collection list and in his published *Travel Account*, Van Breugel describes the nest of a certain weaverbird, which he calls the *bananebekvogel*.[21] These birds would build numerous nests in the impressive South American silk-cotton tree which the slaves called *kankantri*.[22] In both accounts Van Breugel tells his readers (a general public in his *Travel Account*, experts in his collection list) a story about this tree. Both times he begins with the birds' nests. These hang from the branches of the tree to prevent the snakes that also live in the tree from raiding the nests. After this introduction, which seems almost to be the point of the story, he further informs his audiences that the *kankantri* is the "Idol of the Negroes." Thus they bring it offerings—food stored in concave calabashes and small bead aprons which they called *kwedjoe*. In his *Travel*

Account he connects the story about the tree to a snake-hunting trip that took place in the vicinity of a Dutch military fortress in the rain forest. The Negroes shot a huge snake from a branch of the *kankantri* and once it fell from its branch, they dealt it a final blow on the head with their gun. (Breugel 1842a: 99–100; 1842b: 1)

Van Breugel was quite correct in his characterization of the *kankantri* as a sacred tree that also was a home to birds and snakes, but something in his account does not sit quite right. We may doubt, for instance, whether his fellow black hunters were the ones to shoot the snake (which for them might have been a deity) from a sacred *kankantri*, rather than the Dutch soldiers. In his private notes Van Breugel does not mention this shooting incident, but only explains that the Negroes were very adept at *discovering* a snake that used to sleep, barely visible, on the branches of a *kankantri*. Looking and shooting are, after all, activities quite different from each other, if one is not a hunter, but he maybe saw it as just a difference in degree and thus a small exaggeration on his part. Peculiar to this improbable snake-hunting story in his travel account as well is that the author incriminates himself in having (mis)appropriated the objects he found as offerings in the niches of the trunk of one mighty *kankantri*. Not only did he take a nest of the weaver bird, but his collection also contained a concave calabash, carved with geometrical, circle-like motifs with a bird in one of the circles, and a *kwedjoe*—exactly those items that he mentioned as the offerings put under a *kankantri*. In the description of these items, however, no reference is made to any possible ritual function of these objects. Van Breugel notes merely that the objects were made and used by the slaves. Likewise, where he describes in the *kankantri* story that the Negroes prepared a ritual medicine in order to gain protection against snake venom, he does not discuss the belief in reptile spirits, but looks for comparison between the Negroes' faith in their antisnake poison and the European certainty about the effectiveness of their cowpox vaccination.[23] The tree, the birds, the snake, the offerings—they all belonged together. To Van Breugel, however, the point at stake was that birds built their nests in such a way that the snake could not eat the birds.

Not only did he not waste many words on the "irrational" aspects of Suriname slave behavior, Van Breugel also was inclined to interpret the slaves' actions as directly related to his own presence. This happened in his story about the visitor's portrait drawn with the broom in the sand, as well as, for instance, in his explanation that the slaves were most grateful that he, as their master, had taken the trouble to come and visit them. But also his egocentric rationalizing does not prove that he did not notice the religious attitudes of others and did not have any contact at all with their religious practices.[24] We only can conclude that he could not find adequate words to describe these and each time sought a refuge in rationalizing rituals and the search for Dutch equivalents. Besides, from his notes and texts, there is no indication that during his stay in Suriname he ever contested the religious beliefs of his slaves. On the contrary, as far as he was confronted with expressions of their religion, he found it rather a source of amusement.

CONTACT AND CONVERSION

We could see the objects from his small collection Surinamica as a means by which Van Breugel experienced a bond between himself and the slaves, about whom he knew very little, but who nonetheless seem to have aroused his interest. He writes about rituals in which offerings were made, and brings home to Holland a calabash and a *kwedjoe*; he explains that slaves draw a caricature of visitors with brooms, and takes such brooms home with him too.[25] At least once during his stay on the plantation, Van Breugel must have encountered his slaves "sweeping" with obeah, and have obtained these in order to show them, for whatever reason, to his relatives and friends back at home.

I am not sure whether the *kankantri* was on the plantation itself, or even whether it was from there that Van Breugel took the various offerings.[26] It was, however, very probably at Clifford Kocqshove that Van Breugel saw the sweeping movement of the dancing brooms. Twice at least during his time on this plantation, he was confronted with a dancing and singing performance by the members of Clifford Kocqshove's slave community. At the first, in November of 1834, he had allowed the people a two-day party over the weekend. During a second stay the dancing lasted for three days (March 7–10, 1824) with a fourth day of rest. (This, according to Van Breugel, was a postponed New Year's festival (Dutch: *Doe*) to which the slaves were entitled each year.) In his *Travel Account*, the two dance parties were combined into a single one. Initially, the music and dance frightened and embarrassed the inexperienced plantation owner. He draws a caricature of the witch-like poses and unbearable din he had suffered during these festivities. His private *Journal*, written during his stay in Suriname, on the other hand, has a more positive tone, mentioning as it does the "lovely music and dance of the Negroes" (March 7,

1824). Over the next few days Van Breugel continued to follow the dances, during which his slaves—much to his own amusement—also "paid him the honor" of carrying him around seated on a chair. He learned that the dances were called *banja* and *jurrie-jurrie*, asked the carpenter to carve him a miniature set of drums, and claimed that he received some instruction about certain rhythms, with which he amused his friends back home.[27] He also ordered six dolls dressed in various women's outfits, and he inquired about the preferred fabrics among slaves, so that he could ship these from the Netherlands as part of the regular supply of textiles and household utensils for the plantation.[28] And I am inclined to think that Van Breugel acquired his obeah after this *banja* as well. The *winti* priest may have thrown them away after the dancing, or given them to him, after their purpose had been spent during the dance.[29]

So not only during the roll call, but also because of the *banja, jurrie -jurrie* dances and other ceremonies, Van Breugel sought and found a certain measure of contact with some of his slaves, a contact which assumes a material form in the artifacts the plantation owner collected. These objects helped make him feel like a connoisseur of Suriname and of slave issues. As Talal Asad has stated: ". . . things have first to be constructed as symbolic, before they can become candidates for interpretation . . ." (Asad 1993: 61). Van Breugel did not question slave rituals, but took them for granted and observed them as part of the wider social life of the plantation. He ascribed to himself an important role in permitting the slaves to dance, interpreting their style of commenting on what happened around them as an honor to him (Voorhoeve 975: 17). From his writings and his selection of objects, it seems as if he sensed an implicit connection between religion, nature, objects, and the dances. It is this feeling, combined with Van Breugel's curiosity (at that time as yet unburdened by a passion to convert the slaves) that let him to carry the obeah back with him to Europa. Once there, these object acquired a new identity in European eyes.

The main reason for the interpretation of the slaves' obeah as brooms, and as we have seen, their reinterpretation from brooms into maroon obeah, is the changing attitude of the colonial elite about the slaves' religious beliefs. Van Breugel's curiosity about the slave dances and rituals was indicative of an uncontested view, shared by himself and his peers about the institution of slavery. This attitude changed however, shortly after Van Breugel arrived in Suriname. From the second half of the 1820s onwards, the issue of slave emancipation could no longer be ignored, either in Suriname or in the Netherlands.[30] The colonial elite became increasingly aware that with the prospect of emancipation imminent, the everyday life, attitudes, and perceptions of this vast, anonymous majority of the colony's population could no longer be regarded with the same indifference or casual curiosity as before. In Suriname, this change resulted in a new policy towards slave culture, and one that aimed at the slaves' conversion to Christianity. The Comaroffs' general statement that "in the context of European colonialism, 'conversion' has always been part of its apparatus of cultural coercion" certainly seems to be true for Suriname. (Comaroff and Comaroff 1991: 251) The pressure on slaves to give up their own religious and cultural practices and to convert to Christianity would become great. And it was a pressure that went together with the destruction of numerous obeah and other cult objects.

Back home, reflecting on the impossible future of slavery, Van Breugel changed his personal views accordingly, both in practice and in retrospect. A few years after his Suriname trip, he decided to become a member of the "Society for the Advancement of Religious Education among the Slaves and other Heathen People in Suriname." This organization, based in the Hague with departments all over the Netherlands and an overseas department in Paramaribo, was founded in 1828. Leading forces were members of the colonial elite, and their counterparts in the Netherlands.[31] Van Breugel adhered to the society's main target: fundraising to strengthen the religious education of slaves by missionaries of the Moravian church, the *Hernhutters* who almost a century earlier had begun their missionary work in Suriname. Up to the late 1820s missionaries had barely been permitted to enter the plantations and proselytize among slaves. Instead they had (with varying degrees of success) primarily focused their energies on maroon communities.

The *Hernhutter* brothers were supposed to teach the slaves the Bible and Christian values, in order, it was said, to prepare them for emancipation. Their religious teachings and presuppositions clashed with the ritual beliefs and practices of the slaves living on the plantations. The latter were rejected, while the reasons motivating this rejection were reported in the journal of the Dutch supporters of the Moravian mission. It is in this journal, *Berigten uit de Heiden-wereld* (*Reports from the Heathen World*) that Van Breugel, a dedicated activist and subscriber, would have read the brothers' explanation about the obeah, the *kankantri*, and the worry that gripped the poor slaves because they feared death and lacked an understanding of the hereafter.[32] The missionaries reported discussions they had had with the slaves on the subject of idolatry and how they had cast obeah into the local rivers. In the journal's many success stories about slave

Figure 1.   Two Surinamese obeah, acquired by Jhr. G.P.C. van Breugel in 1824—donated to the Colonial Museum in Haarlem in 1873. Length: 65 cm (left) and 52 cm (right). Collection Tropenmuseum / Royal Tropical Institute, Amsterdam; collection number H 2965 (left) and H 2966 (right). (Photo: Lo Lange)

conversion, one favorite theme was how slaves had been persuaded to reject and destroy these idols and witchcraft objects *themselves,* and this was seen as a true act of embracing the Christian creed.[33] "Many of the Negroes' potential cultural-historical and religious values were destroyed," concludes the Surinamese Hernhutter minister and historian Zeefuik, who characterizes the early missionaries' approach as "bulldozing." Music and dance were misunderstood and suppressed; the Afroamerican blacks were forced to renounce their own beliefs (Zeefuik 1973: 42–46, 187).

With their acceptance of colonial relations, their preaching of Romans 13 and of Paul's lesson about the slaves' duties towards the master and the master's duties towards the slaves (I Corinthians 7: 20–24), the *Hernhutters* did not seem to pose a serious threat to the colonial elite. They were regarded as the most appropriate group to teach the slaves and to make them over according to the Christian norms and values of work, discipline, and family life. But not only did the *Hernhutters* instruct the slaves regarding obedience to authority, they also tried to convince the slave owners that their slaves deserved to be treated humanely. More important than the freeing of slaves, teaches Paul, is their baptism. The slave was a servant of God and thus a sacred being and a brother of any white Christian.[34] It was this message that Van Breugel even transferred to the title page of his *Travel Account.* There he poses pointing to heaven and explaining to a slave that there is a place in heaven for everyone. As I have already said, this Dutchman left us with little evidence that in Suriname he really discussed such matters with his slaves. His publication from Holland, of course, did not address slaves either. Van Breugel's raised finger in fact warned his fellow members of the plantation-owning circle to see to it that their slaves were properly educated and converted into civilized Christian people. Having sold his plantation it is easier for him to take his position. His is a manifesto, arguing for the humane treatment and conversion of slaves in order to prepare them to become citizens of their own country.

Not surprisingly, in Suriname the *Hernhutter* mission did not meet with universal approval. Many an administrator and director rejected the idea of the religious education and conversion of slaves. According to Zeefuik (1973), opposition to this idea arose because these people did not accept its basic implications: that black and white people would be equal before God. I am inclined, however, to suppose that Zeefuik with this explanation overestimates the theological capacities of nineteenth-century plantation administrators. Van Breugel was shocked when he wrote to his own administrator telling him to invite

Hernhutters to his plantation, and received a reply full of objections at a very mundane level, concerning obedience, leisure, the extra costs involved in housing the missionaries, etc.[35]

The conflicts in Suriname between some administrators and directors and the Moravian mission led to a highly critical article in "Reports from the Heathen-World." This publication contained a completely opposite interpretation of Gaspar van Breugel's own pleasant *doe* experience of 1824. In the crucial year of 1848 Nils Otto Tank, the enlightened Norwegian president of the Suriname Moravian Church, wrote a furious account of a dance festival that had been organized by administrators who wanted to provoke the *Hernhutters*. The poor slaves, according to Tank, were misused and misled during this disgusting party in which they danced like crazy, and took some honor in being ordered to carry the whites around on their chairs, while the whites became completely drunk and raped young girls. Tank rejected the attitude of the white colonial elite, stated that the conditions of slavery in Suriname were the worst he knew, and urged the plantation owners in the Netherlands to take responsibility and correct their employees' behavior. He thus connected the issue of the decent treatment of slaves and their religious conversion to a struggle over the interpretation of slave rituals (in his view slaves were misused for the amusement of the white overseers).[36]

The now fifty-year-old Gaspar, a subscriber to the journal, reading this article, would most likely have been reminded of his own bachelor nights at Clifford Kocqshove, of which he had written such innocent accounts about being carried around on his chair, abstaining from alcohol and retiring early to bed. It provided another context for his souvenirs from Suriname as well. His own conversion into a dedicated worker for the support of the Moravian mission, with the goal of preparing the slaves for an orderly and disciplined life, provided him with a new frame of reference to understand slave life and colored his public writings about his Suriname trip, including his own behavior at a slaves' dance party. In public he denounced the music that in private he had enjoyed, and brought home through the obeah and other objects.

THE FETISH AS MUSEOLOGICAL OBJECT, THE MUSEUM OBJECT AS FETISH

"Changing religious identity, itself a highly complex problem of meaning and action, is always an element of more embracing historical transformations" (Comaroff and Comaroff 1991: 250). This statement is certainly true for Suriname in the nineteenth century, and the two obeah illustrate this. From material objects imbued with multiple significance and put to a range of ritual and nonritual purposes, they became representations of the everyday life of slaves bereft of any reference to local religious practices and beliefs. Half a century later, they reappeared as ritual objects associated now with maroons. By that time the slaves had been emancipated and Christianized, with the help of the *Hernhutters*. To paraphrase the words of the twentieth-century *Hernhutter* author Van der Linde: The slaves had been freed from their West-African religious bonds with gods and deities which prevented them from attaining a true human existence; the missionaries made them enter history in general and the history of salvation in particular.[37]

In the process of making the slaves "enter history", many of their obeah were destroyed. The two obeah under discussion here escaped the missionaries, but disappeared from history, to reemerge exhibited in the colonial museum as fetishes. Here for the first time Europeans arrived at an explicit religious interpretation of the objects. But their separation from the calabashes, the *kwedjoe*, and other objects, and also from the archival and documentary sources that had accompanied them, washed these obeah ashore in the timeless, history-less space in which the maroons were said to live, with the documentation cards as their birth certificates.

This can be illustrated by looking at the first catalogues in which the obeah appeared. The 1899 Colonial Museum catalogue introduces the Suriname population to the Dutch public, distinguishing, in the following order, between: Indians, bush Negroes, Chinese, Javanese, British-Indians and Negroes. These Negroes, the catalogue explains, were imported into Suriname as "workers" (the term "slavery" is avoided). The majority of the Negroes belong to the Moravian church, but some are Roman Catholic. "In many respects, one can find substantial progress in civilization among them, since 1863." The museum catalogue makes no reference at all to other "religious" beliefs among the Negroes. Bush Negroes, on the contrary, are said to believe in *winti* and to use obeah. Taking our two obeah as an example (calling them sometimes obeah and sometimes "brush," or "broom"), the catalogue explains that such obeah are difficult to acquire, "unless one happens to be around at the very moment the owner decides to accept the Christian faith."[38]

The obeah on display were thus presented as the relics of a rejected animistic religion. They had been obtained from someone who, with a gesture of relinquishment, denounced his old beliefs and converted to Christianity. This is a remarkable echo of the missionaries' own success stories in their fundraising "Reports of the Heathen-World," centering around slaves who themselves were said to have destroyed their obeah in a true act of conversion. The obeah thus became symbols of conversion and at the same time "a mark of otherness," to quote Pietz—the otherness not of the slaves who according to the museum catalogue had become free Christian blacks, but of the maroons.[39] Whereas the Church had taken responsibility for the new free workers of the colony, at home, in the Netherlands, slave society had been ignored by its main protagonists: slave owners, bankers, and (the majority of the) politicians, and was forgotten as soon as slavery was abolished.

It was as part of this process that objects from slave plantation life entered the museum, with their status changed from a unique into an exemplary one. The founders of the museum were the very same people who had owned slaves, controlled their lives and collected these objects. To them the museum provided a new stronghold, a place to construct and interpret the world. One could wonder whether Van Breugel's small-scale drums, his winnowing tray for preparing cassava, wooden lock, *kwedjoe*, or any of the other artifacts in his luggage—that still have their place in the museum—can be regarded as "fetishes." Each object contains a story, related to the slaves' material culture and to the collector's perceptions, which can be distilled from his works and writings. Each object represents a moment of contact between two worlds. And what is more, in Europe, to the present day, these things have been made to play this "contact role" as collection items exhibited to an ever-changing public, and accompanied by continually updated explanations for subsequent museum-going generations.

Nevertheless, I am here inclined to reserve the concept of border fetishism for the obeah themselves instead of expanding it to the museum collection as such. As (silenced) ritual objects, the obeahs refer to a religion that—notwithstanding the Dutch fervor about conversion and the straightforward repression of *winti*—continued to exist among Creoles and maroons. It is a religion still practiced in Suriname and for some decades now in the Netherlands as well—whether integrated with Christian faith or not. The obeah as museum artifacts, more than the other objects from Van Breugel's collection, are literal border fetishes. They emerged as fetishes as an aftereffect of having crossed borders. As such they can inform the conversation about the effects of European perceptions and representations of Otherness regarding slave culture and Creole identity in Suriname—and also tell us something about Dutch identity as a Christianity-motivated civilizing power.

NOTES

1. Thiel 1986, p. 12, 65, 69, 117, 164.

2. Eugene A. Nida, in Smalley, 1978, p. 15, defines fetishes as "objects in which a communicating power exists."

3. The Frankfurt museum uses "fetish" as a common denominator, expecting that the modern anthropological museum will have left behind the fetishes' pejorative meaning that such museums formerly had helped to establish. (p. 37–39. See also Clifford, 1988, p. 199.)

According to the *Encyclopedie van Suriname*, the word *obia* is derived from *obeye*, an Akan-word indicating healer/priest. Thoden van Velzen/Van Wetering (1988) give the following description in their study of religious cults of Ndjukas (Surinam maroons): "Obeah or obia is the name given by Ndjukas to those parts of supernatural forces that have become available to mankind." (p. 17), distinguishing between various types of obeah, related to gods, people, objects and ritual devices. B. Thoden van Velzen recognized the obeah that are discussed here as *awidja's*. I am very grateful for his comments on the draft of this article.

4. I take this word from Siwpersad, p. 272. In his conclusion about the Dutch political debate on emancipation (1824–1863), he states that the colonial elite, supported by the Netherlands, promoted a policy to de-Africanise the black masses, in order to have them assimilated within a European social and cultural framework.

5. M. Anderson and A. Reeves, "Contested identities. Museums and the nation in Australia." In: Kaplan, 1994, p. 88.

6. Since the word "biography" has been declared applicable to things, I suppose that to this end Pococks "past relationship", that is the "specialised dependence of an organised group or activity within society on a past conceived in order to ensure its continuity", could be borrowed as well. (J.G.A. Pocock, "The origins of the past: A comparative approach." In: *Comparative Studies in Society and History* IV, 1961, pp. 209–246). In looking for transformation in the metropole, of the meaning of objects from colonial society, I follow Edward Said's statement on imperialism and culture. The development of (in our case) Dutch society in the nineteenth century cannot be isolated from the emerging imperialism. In cultural and ideological respect this imperialism can be traced within Dutch society as well. The ethnographical museum is one of the institutional forms to be studied as such.

7. The involvement of Van Breugel (1798–1888) in the two Surinamese coffee plantations is well documented in the Van Breugel archives and his

publications deposited in the library of the Royal Tropical Institute (KIT) in Amsterdam. In 1873 he donated these archival sources to the Colonial Museum in Haarlem, together with his modest collection of ethnographical objects and books on Suriname. Besides, many personal Van Breugel documents can be found in the archives of the "Society for the Advancement of Religious Education among the Slaves and other Heathen People in Suriname", deposited in the archives of the Moravian Mission in the Rijksarchief Utrecht. Because of their dispersion over two separated archival institutions, the connection between the two archives has been lost. Even within the Royal Tropical Institute, the connection between the written sources stored in the library and the collection items stored in the museum depot seems to have been lost sight of since the beginning of this century.

8. Van Breugel's relevant publications quoted here are: *Journal van mijn vertrek naar, verblijf te en terugkomst van de kolonie Suriname in de jaren 1823–1824, de minuut dag aan dag in de kolonie bijgehouden.* (Further quoted as *Journal*); *Intime berigt . . .*, an archive about the plantations, with 14 chapters, ca. 1806–1840; *Dagverhaal eener reis naar Suriname* (1842– further quoted as *Travel Account*, Breugel 1842a); *Lijst, vertrouwelijk geschreven, van Aardigheden door mij uit de Kolonie Suriname in 1823 aangebracht* (Confidential List of curiosities collected in 1823 and brought from Suriname), 1842. (Further quoted as Collection *List*, Breugel 1842b); *Slavenhouders en slavenvrienden. Eene stem uit Suriname beantwoord door een stem uit Holland.* ("Slave owners and slave friends; a voice from Suriname and a Dutch reply") Adiussi Massera [G.P.C. van Breugel] Haarlem, 1857. These sources can all be found in the library of the Royal Tropical Institute in Amsterdam.

9. For instance *Travel Account* p. 1, 44, 54–56, 76; 59, 66

10. Naipaul captures this same euphemistic use of words in the following statement by the Trinidad governor General Hislop, made in a conversation with Francisco Miranda in 1806: "Now, General, you have been following the debates about slavery and the slave trade in England. And I don't have to tell you that when planters talk about 'property' and 'the free transfer of property' and 'a free supply', they are simply finding a way of not saying 'Negroes' or 'slaves'. They are not even talking about land. Most of them got the land free when they came. . . ." (V.S. Naipaul, *A Way in the World. A Novel*. New York, 1994, p. 280). Teenstra (1844) writes that the slave owner should feel embarrassed to be known as such by his own friends. (p. 2)

11. *Intime berigt*, staat 9.

12. "Thank God, I am released, after having performed a difficult administration from 1823 to 1838, that is 15 years . . ." written in Dutch in pencil under the final letter of the new owner, dated 14-06-1839. *Intime berigt*, staat 14.

13. The obeah-collection numbers are: H 2965 and H 2966 (length 65 cm and 52 cm). In this respect anthropological museums and art museums have different backgrounds, reflected in distinct exhibition styles. Notions of time-change-progress that are crucial in art history make information about pro-

venance and artists essential in art exhibitions. The exhibition on non-Western fetishes in Frankfurt (1986) and on European devotion pieces in the Rijksmuseum in Amsterdam (1994) are two cases in point. See also Leyten, "Non-Western art in anthropological museums", In Leyten (ed.) 1993, p. 17; and S. Price, "Anonymity and Timelessness" in Price, 1989 pp. 56 interalia.

14. Thoden van Velzen/van Wetering (1988), Scholtens *et al.* (1992), S. and R. Price (1980), R. Price, 1990, etc. Wooding (1972) traces many *winti* rituals to slave societies.

15. The explanation could correspond to the *printa-sisibi* (a broom from the veins of palm tree leaves) and the *prasara-sisibi* (its blossom) mentioned in Wooding (1972) in relationship to *winti* in the Suriname Para-region.

16. Thoden van Velzen/Van Wetering p. 37; Wooding passim; Goslings p. 29; According to the *Encyclopedie van Suriname* the name is derived from the western Bantu word *mpemba*. See also Thiel 1986: 80. Here the white mud, (German: *weisse Flusserde*) in relationship to African ritual objects, is connected to the water, as the element of the ancestors; Van Capelle, has interpreted this use of white chalk as a reference to the search for purity.

17. One obeah has 21 cowries, the other 29. Wooding p. 403 and 404 also mentions and interprets the number of 21 cowries for a certain obeah. Thiel 1986:74 connects the number of cowries on a fetish with male and female elements.

18. Wooding 1972: 431 refers to blue dots on a healing obeah. These blue dots are related to *bakru*, a lower bush spirit.

19. I refer to the Collection *List* 1842b number 28 and 29, p. 12–13.

20. I learned these old Dutch folklore stories in my youth. See also J. and E. Jans, *Gevel en stiepeltekens in Oost-Nederland.* Enschede, 1974, pp. 13–18 on "Donderbezems" (thunder brooms) which have been stylized in protective ornaments on farms. Years later, in Amsterdam, an English friend gave me a new broom, when I moved house, to chase away the old ghosts belonging to former inhabitants of my new house.

21. Collection *List* 1842b number 3, p. 1. *Encyclopedie van Suriname*: *Banabeki* weaverbirds (*Icteridae*) of which some 14 species occur in Surinam.

22. *Encyclopedie van Suriname*: *Kankantri Ceiba pentandra*, L. gaertn. fam. Bombacaceae. Thoden van Velzen/Van Wetering: *Kankantri* is the holy dwelling of Agedeonsu (p. 37); Wooding (176–177) as well as Thooden van Velzen/Van Wetering (p. 40) connect the tree with reptile spirits.

23. Interesting for our search for the meaning of the two brooms is that Van Breugel here claims that the blacks used cowries (*papamonnie*) to prepare their antidote. He mistakes these cowries for "a certain herb". This misunderstanding, however, may be an indication that he has seen a medical obeah with cowries on it, maybe a *sisibiwiwiri*, a vegetable obeah with a brush, used in purification rites (as described in Wooding p. 140–141). See also Voorhoeve

975: 52 on the Papawinti-reptile spirits. The calabashes are described in the Collection *List* 1842b number 23 p. 10 (collection numbers H2552 and H2553); the *kwedjoe* is number 36, p. 14 (collection number H 2466). In the Collection *List* they are attributed to slave society; the *Travel Account* suggests that he took them from a *kankantri* near Groningen, which implies that they could come from Saramaka maroons. This, however, I doubt. Van Breugel would not have been unique in stealing offerings. See for instance Benoit 1839: 55.

24. Van Stipriaan (1993b), quoting among others Van Breugel, concludes that during the first decades of the nineteenth century, the white colonists did in fact know and see very little about the inner lives and religion of their slaves. The slaves hid this from white eyes, retreating into an inner world; the planters only saw the outward expressions and very often did not know how to interpret these, or even did not realize that they should perceive these expressions in another way. To me, however, it is not clear what we should expect to see within the early nineteenth-century context about what Van Stipriaan calls the "knowledge" and "understanding" of "the other". Not only the suppressed slaves, but also their conventional, class-conscious and authoritarian masters lived both an inner and outward life. A globetrotter like Van Breugel, behaving as he was supposed to do, thus established contact with the outer world of the slaves. What he himself made out of it is also difficult to find out. I am inclined to interpret Van Breugel's dedication, once back in the Netherlands, to have the slaves converted into Christians, as a means to try and establish contact between the inner worlds of civilized Europeans and uncivilized slaves.

25. See also the Comaroffs' explanation of commodity fetishism, concerning the relationship between people as dictated by the relationship between objects. (p. 23)

26. On the plantation map (Tropenmuseum collection serienumber 3728, nr 531, 690–692) I cannot find the tree, whereas the trees that border the alley from the river to the plantation house all are drawn. But the absence of the tree on the map does not prove that this "idol" did not grow on or near the plantation.

27. On *banja* dance see Voorhoeve/Lichtveld 1975: 15–17; Wooding 1972: 272–274; Van Breugel 1842a: 63.

28. The drums I have traced in the museum collection are a *Poeja* (number H 2913) and a *Kroema* (H 2911) Others mentioned by Van Breugel are *Mandron, Kwakwa Bangi, Saka* and *Fluti negri*. One doll was donated by Van Breugel as well, but still has to be traced.

29. A strong indication of this is that Van Breugel listed, among the instruments that were played during the *banja* two *Kroema Tiekie*. This could refer to the *krom tiki* (the freakish branches) of the obeah. Van Stipriaan 1993b discusses the various instruments and dances of slaves, relying on Van Breugel as well.

30. Siwpersad (1979, p. 87) has characterized this period as a turning point—a period in which slavery was still undisputed, but from which many social, economic and cultural changes would originate.

31. Here I can not elaborate on this organisation, which in my view, was initiated by the colonial elite, in order to keep government at a distance by showing its dedication to prepare the slaves for future emancipation. cf Zeefuik 1973.

32. Rijksarchief Utrecht 25.246 Subscribers *Berigten uit de Heiden-wereld.*

33. *Berigten uit de Heiden-wereld* 1847: 15, 16, 26, 57, etc.

34. Zeefuik (1973: 41, 139) whose study is written within a *Hernhutter* theological context, criticizes the missionaries of that time because of their biblical attitude.

35. Letters between Hans Klint (Surinam administrator of plantations) and Van Breugel, 1833–1834. Klint, by the way, was himself a member of the Paramaribo Department of the Society for the Advancement etc . . . [Rijksarchief Utrecht 25.376 EBG buiten Zeist 1833–1824.] See also Lamur 1985: 46–48 on Klints action against missionary work at Vossenburg plantation 1859.

36. *Berigten uit de Heiden-wereld* . . . 1848 nr. 5: 66–70. Th. Bray drew a picture of such a scene in 1844, entitled *Le nouvel an à l'habitation*. Collection Tropenmuseum/Royal Tropical Institute; see also Brommer, p. 112. Tank also published a questionnaire, circulated among absent plantation owners, in order to get permission from the Netherlands to contact slaves on plantations. Opposition against Tank in the colony became strong, however, and he was replaced by another *Hernhutter*. In 1848 slavery was abolished in the French colonies; the communist manifesto of that year stated that proletarians had nothing to loose, except their chains. Colonial circles within the Netherlands and in Suriname succeeded in postponing the question of slave emancipation for another 15 years.

37. J.M. van der Linde, p. 31–32; like Zeefuik, Van der Linde expresses his scepticism about the motives of the adherents of the "Society for the Advancement etc.", but he praises the results of the *Hernhutter* mission.

38. Catalogue 1899, p. 30–31; 32, 70, 75. (my translation). Also *Gids* 1902: 79 and Goslings 1934: 28–30, 45–46.

39. Pietz, quoted in Clifford, p. 219

REFERENCES

Appadurai, A., ed. (1988) *The Social Life of Things: Commodities in Cultural Perspective*. Cambridge. (Cambridge University Press)

Asad, T. (1993) *Genealogies of Religion: Discipline and Reasons of Power in Christianity and Islam*. Baltimore. (Johns Hopkins University Press)

Benoit, P.J. (1839) *Voyage à Surinam. Description des possessions Nèerlandaises dans la Guyane.* Bruxelles (Société des Beaux Arts).

(1834–1848) *Berigten uit de Heiden-wereld, uitgegeven door het Zendeling-genootschap, te Zeist.*

Breugel, G.P.C. van (1842) *Dagverhaal eener reis naar Suriname.* Amsterdam. (C.G. Sulpke)

———. (1857) *Slavenhouders en slavenvrienden. Eene stem uit Suriname, beantwoord door een stem uit Holland.* Haarlem. (C. Zwaardemaker)

Bruining, C.F.A., en J. Voorhoeve (1977) *Encyclopedie van Suriname.* Amsterdam. (Elsevier)

Clifford, J. (1988) *The Predicament of Culture: Twentieth-Century Ethnography, Literature and Art.* Cambridge/London. (Harvard University Press)

Comaroff, J. and J. (1991) *Of Revelation and Revolution: Christianity, Colonialism, and Consciousness in South Africa.* Chicago. (University of Chicago Press)

Gids voor de bezoekers van het Koloniaal Museum te Haarlem, met plattegronden en vele illustraties. (1902) Amsterdam. (De Bussy)

Goslings, B.M. (1934) *Gids in het Volkenkundig museum XIII. De Indianen en boschnegers van Suriname.* Amsterdam. (Koloniaal Museum te Haarlem)

Kaplan, F.E.S. (ed.) (1994) *Museums and the Making of "Ourselves": The Role of Objects in National Identity.* London (Leicester University Press) New York (St. Martin's Press)

Koloniaal Museum te Haarlem (1899) *Catalogus der Nederlandsche West-Indische Tentoonstelling te Haarlem 1899.* Amsterdam (De Bussy)

Lamur, H.E. (1985) *De kerstening van de slaven van de Surinaamse plantage Vossenburg, 1847–1878.* Amsterdam (Universiteit Van Amsterdam)

Leyten. H. and B. Daamen, eds. (1993) *Art, Anthropology and the Modes of Representation: Museums and Contemporary Non-Western Art.* Amsterdam. (Royal Tropical Institute KIT-Press)

Linde, J.M. van der (1953) "De emancipatie der negerslaven in Suriname en de zendingsarbeid der Moravische broeders." *West-Indische Gids* 34: 23–37.

Price, S. (1990) *Primitive Art in Civilized Places.* Chicago. (University of Chicago Press)

Said, E. (1993) *Culture and Imperialism.* New York. (Alfred A. Knopf)

Scholtens, B., G. Wekker, et al. (1992) *Gaama Duumi, Buta Gaama. Overlijden en opvolging van Aboikoni, grootopperhoofd van de Saramaka Bosnegers.* (With a summary in English.) Paramaribo. (Surinaams Museum/ Minov)

Siwpersad, J.P. (1979) *De Nederlandse regering en de afschaffing van de slavernij (1833–1863)*. Groningen. (Bouma's Boekhuis)

Smalley, W.A., ed, (1978) *Readings into Missionary Anthropology II*. (enlarged 1978 edition). South Pasadena. (William Carey Library)

Stipriaan, A. van (1993a) *Surinaams contrast. Roofbouw en overleven in een Caraïbische plantagekolonie 1750–1863*. (KITLV Caribbean Series 13). Leiden.

―――. (1993b) " 'Een verre verwijderd trommelen . . ." Ontwikkelingen van Afro-Surinaamse muziek en dans in de slavernij." In,: T. Bevers, A. v.d. Braembussche, B.J. Langenberg, eds., *De Kunstwereld. Produktie, distributie en receptie in de wereld van kunst en cultuur*. Hilversum, (Verloren) pp. 143–73.

Teenstra, M.D. (1844) *Bijdrage tot de ware beschouwing van de zoo hoog geroemde uitbreiding des christendoms onder de heidenen in de kolonie Suriname, toegewijd aan alle philantropen*. Amsterdam. (M.H. Binger)

Thiel, J.F. (1986) *Was sind Fetische?* Frankfurt-am-Main. (Museum für Völkerkunde (Roter Faden zur Ausstellung 9).)

Thoden van Velzen, H.U.E. and W. van Wetering (1988) *The Great Father and Danger: Religious Cults, Material Forces, and Collective Fantasies in the World of the Surinamese Maroons*. (KITLV-Caribbean Series 9) Dordrecht. (Foris Publications)

Voorhoeve, J., and U.M. Lichtveld (1975) *Creole Drum: An Anthology of Creole Literature in Surinam*. New Haven and London. (Yale University Press)

Wooding, C.J. (1972) *Winti; een Afro-Amerikaanse godsdienst in Suriname. Een cultuur-historische analyse van de religieuze verschijnselen in de Para*. Meppel (Krips Repro b.v.)

Zeefuik, K.A. (1973) *Hernhutter zending en Haagsche Maatschappij 1828–1867. Een hoofdstuk uit de geschiedenis van zending en emancipatie in Suriname*. Utrecht. (Elinkwyk)

3

Your Money, Our Money, the Government's Money: Finance and Fetishism in Melanesia

Robert J. Foster

Introduction: Cargo and Fetish

Talk about cargo cult(s) permeates the fetish discourse associated with Melanesia. Lindstrom (1994)—doing for "cargo cult" something like what Pietz (1985, 1987, 1988) did for "fetish"—recently traced the genealogy of the term while trying to account for its continuing currency within and beyond anthropological circles. He asks:

> Could it be, then, that we are entranced by cargo cults because we are, at heart, commodity fetishists? That cargo cults are so titillating and seductive because we imagine the natives to be exercised by our own secret desires? We want cargo but we know also, at heart, that the moral connections that dominant capitalist rhetoric narrates between hard work and material success are fraudulent and ultimately illusory (Lindstrom 1994: 9).

Lindstrom's questions point to how the construction of and delight in cargo talk tentatively reveals a range of otherwise hidden doubts, fears, and desires: doubts about the connections between labor and wealth; fears of an unsatisfied "endless yearning" (1994: 9); and desires for a world of instant and unlimited abundance delivered without the necessity of labor. In this view, the attraction of cargo cult lies in the projection of Our secret fantasy onto Them.

Pietz's work suggests a related way in which cargo cult discourse sustains an uneasy separation between Us and Them, namely, by indulging Our lingering Enlightenment fantasy of a world without fetishes. Cargo cult discourse validates the conceit of a critical acuity acquired from living in a world where the real and true value of material things is self evident and irrefutable. It is this conceit, I suggest, that organized official cargo cult discourse in the context of post-WWII Australian colonialism in Papua and New Guinea. And it was this conceit that, in the context of Australia's role as administrator of a U.N .Trust Territory, inevitably prompted a campaign of native education, a process whereby They would learn the truth and so become like Us.

I begin this paper by first examining some of the means used by the postwar Australian Administration to educate the people of Papua and New Guinea about money and wealth. I go on to look at other subsequent instances of discourse about money in postcolonial Papua New Guinea (P.N.G.), focusing on the way in which constructions of money become entailed in constructions of both nation and state. I ask: How did the fetish discourse identified by Pietz as originating in the intercultural space-time of fifteenth-century West Africa erupt in the intercultural space-time of late twentieth-century Melanesia? What specific forms did "the problem of the fetish" (Pietz 1985) come to assume for various agents encountering each other along the final frontiers of European expansion?

My reply rehearses the themes of fetish discourse singled out by Pietz: the irreducible materiality of objects; the composite fabrication of heterogeneous elements; the nonuniversality (and hence social constructedness of value); and the power of fetishes over human bodies. My aim is to show how the moral educational projects of first the Australian colonial state and then the national state of P.N.G. effectively though differently sustained a fetish discourse through explicit teachings about money and wealth. I demonstrate how the peculiar difference between money as an abstract medium of exchange, on the one hand, and metal coins and paper notes as gross matter, on the other, defined an arena for contesting and conjoining disparate conceptions of "the nature and origin of the social value of material objects" (Pietz 1988: 109). In conclusion, I propose how some indigenous Melanesian understandings of money might furnish a critique of both commodity and state fetishism while at the same time construing money and indigenous wealth objects as material media that articulate diverse value codes.

YOUR MONEY: FEAR OF FETISHISM AND COLONIAL EDUCATION

Lindstrom traces the first written appearances of the term "cargo cult" to the pages of the news magazine *Pacific Islands Monthly* (*PIM*), more specifically, to a three-sided debate among expatriate planters, colonial administrators, and Christian missionaries over the future of the natives in Papua and New Guinea in the wake of WWII. Norris Mervyn Bird, described by *PIM* as an "old Territories resident," initiated the debate in print with a 1945 article that invoked the government anthropologist's authority to argue that " 'ill-digested' religious teaching" was the main cause of cargo cult. The following year, Bird responded to the letters of several missionaries who criticized the labor practices of the planters. His letter exposes in all its ugliness the underbelly of cargo talk in Melanesia during the immediate postwar years:

> My views on the acceptance of primitive natives into a civilised society are well known, but as Mr. Inselmann [an American Lutheran missionary] has raised the subject, in his letter, I challenge him with one question: Is he prepared to accept, as an equal in civilised society, the New Guinea native in his present state of development? Would, in fact, Mr. Inselmann be prepared to allow the average New Guinea native to marry his daughter or sister? I have asked other would-be reformers this question and the stock answers are:
>
> - Having neither sisters nor daughters the question does not apply. But would have no objection to these savages marrying other people's sisters or daughters.
> - Would not try to influence the women either way, but would rely on their good taste and innate decency to prevent their making a decision that they may later regret.
> - A long and pointless dissertation on the equality of man in the sight of God.
> - Ditto on the inadvisability of mixing the races (i.e., the "colour line" with reservations supported by quotations from the Bible) (Bird 1946: 45, quoted in Lindstrom 1994: 21).

Lindstrom's (1994: 21) observation is worth underscoring: "Breakouts of cargo cults and miscegenation are both directly predicted if comfortable structures of colonial inequality are permitted to decay."

Here surely is fear of fetishism. For like the offspring of a "mixed race" union, the fetish is composite: a novel identity of "articulated relations between otherwise heterogeneous things" (Pietz 1985: 8). Cargo cult and miscegenation are elided inasmuch as both are taken to be cognate forms of confusion, of radical heterogeneity and unacceptable coupling.

If miscegenation described the unacceptable mixture of racially distinct bodies, then cargo cult described at bottom the transgression of hierarchically distinct statuses. It is this sort of social confusion against which educational campaigns about cargo cult were directed, even though these campaigns often presented themselves as targeting an *intellectual* confusion—the presumed incapacity of the native mentality to sort out cause from effect and so to unite promiscuously different value codes. Hence, for example, "How You Get It," a column that appeared in the *Papua and New Guinea Villager*, a newsletter produced in English by the Australian Administration during the 1950s for the small population of literate natives. Each month, the column took it upon itself to answer questions like these:

> When you go to the store and buy a packet of tea, do you ever wonder how the tea got into the packet?

> Most of us eat rice. We like to go to the store and buy a bag and take it home. How does the rice get into the store?

Having posed the question, the column would go on to describe the processes of production that got the tea or rice from India to Australia and, finally, to Papua and New Guinea. The column apparently presumed that what required explaining to the natives was the unseen production of things rather than their manifestly unequal distribution. So, for example, the "How You Get It" column dealing with money explained the procedures for designing and minting metal coins and printing paper notes. The implicit concern of the whole exercise was thus to dispel the dangerous idea that things, including money, were *not* produced, but rather somehow delivered ready-made—say, by benevolent ancestors or by potent magic.

The unarticulated assumptions of this educational effort became explicit in later joint attempts by the Administration and the Reserve Bank of Australia to provide the natives in the Territory "with an understanding of the management of money" (Australia 1962: 34). In June 1961, "financial booklets" were produced by the Bank in English, Pidgin, and Motu; they were distributed throughout the Territory, mainly to secondary school students. The titles included: *Prices, Savings Clubs, What Is Wealth?*, and *Your Money*. Film versions of the last two booklets were also commissioned by the Reserve Bank for showing to native audiences (Reserve Bank of Australia 1964a, 1964b). Audiences in Australia were informed of the project by a brief notice in the government publication, *Australian Territories*. Here is how the notice describes the first booklet, *Your Money*:

> This explains the use of notes and coins in everyday transactions, and lays stress on the value of the individual's personal savings in planning a well-ordered and productive life. It also stresses the need for the health and growth of the co-operative enterprises so widespread now throughout Papua and New Guinea (Australia 1962: 34).

It is in the attempt of *Your Money* to explain money to the natives that one can glimpse the colonial strategy for preventing fetishistic couplings, namely, the strategy of assimilation—of replacing the old with the new, the primitive with the modern:

> In this country, metal coins and paper notes are replacing things such as shells, clay pots, feathers and pigs, which earlier were used to buy things which men and women needed. This change has occurred in other countries in the past and is still taking place in parts of the world other than Papua and New Guinea (RBA 1961a).

This strategy begins by identifying "money" (notes and coins) with specific wealth items such as shells and pigs; but having done so, it then discounts these wealth items as inferior forms of money due to their irreducible materiality and localized or nonuniversal recognition as valuable.

The irreducible materiality of wealth items impedes their capacity to discharge the function of money as means of payment: "Can you imagine the difficulty of exchanging at a shop or a store a pig for a radio set or guitar? Even if you could bring the pig to the shop or store which had the radio set or guitar for sale, the shopkeeper might not want a pig." (The film version of *Your Money* includes the protracted scene of a man futilely trying to exchange shell valuables in a tradestore.) Money, by contrast, is "small and easy to carry" and, moreover, allows one to get what one desires in a single exchange, whenever one so desires. Money therefore reduces the materiality of the pig into that of the guitar, just as its own reducibility from note into coin allows it to measure differences between the values of material items (such as pigs and guitars). Thus, the shopkeeper would always accept money.

Not only would *that* shopkeeper accept money, moreover, *any* shopkeeper *anywhere* in the country would accept money: "Money can be used in all parts of a country for buying and selling, but other things can not always be conveniently used." In other words, money is recognized translocally; the social recognition of it as acceptable extends beyond the localized society of the village, the archipelago, or the valley system. The portability and spatial extensiveness of money are of a piece.

In the same way, the essential and translocal immateriality of money makes it a superior standard and store of value. Yes, the booklet does point out how "Money does not decay or go bad like such things as taro, sugar or tobacco." But this is somewhat beside the point that money transcends its materiality, and not only with respect to the convertibility of paper notes and metal coins: "Even when notes become soiled or worn, they can always be exchanged at a bank for clean and fresh ones." Thus, money's spatial extensiveness is paralleled by a deep temporal extensiveness. (It is the space-time defined by money that practically defines "the country" of Papua and New Guinea, a silhouette of which graces the covers of both *Your Money* and *What Is Wealth?* But this definition is problematic, inasmuch as the money in question is *Australian* money, which was also used in the Territory from after WWII until independence in 1975; see below.)

Both materiality and locality of wealth items, then, make them less convenient than "money," and it is convenience above all that accounts for the replacement of wealth items by money (a point also argued by Adam Smith): "Money, then, has come to replace most of the older ways of making payments, because it is much more convenient to use." The evolution toward "money" is thus imagined as inexorable and natural, a consequence of the search for more efficient ways of discharging the presumably universal functions of money. The replacement of wealth items by money is an index of Papua and New Guinea's inevitable participation in this unilinear evolutionary progress toward a life of greater efficiency and convenience—"a well ordered and productive life."

The problem in and for this strategy of colonial education lay in communicating to the natives that the matter of money does not matter (Pietz 1985: 15). In other words, the challenge of colonial education lay in teaching a mode of symbolization in which money could be apprehended as a signifier referring beyond itself (ibid). To what? Work. Accordingly, the explanation of the "properties" of money in *Your Money* gives way to a section called "How We Get Money." It is here that one can sense the fear of cargo cult/fetishism emerging anew—the fear that the natives will embrace money not as a signifier that transcends its materiality, but as a substance whose intrinsic material properties underpin its efficacy:

> You have been told that the coins and notes are issued for the Government. You may wonder why much more is not issued and given to us so that we need not have to work, grow crops, or perform a service for it (RBA 1961).

The answer to this hypothesized puzzle involves revealing what money "really" represents: work.

> When people buy things with money they have earned, they are really paying with their work or their goods or services which are stored up in the money they have earned.

> People who are paid with money are really paid with work and, as we have said before, money can be either metal or paper, but it still represents the value of the work or goods which people bring into existence by their efforts (RBA 1961).

Accordingly, education about money required teaching the double lesson that money is *a form* of wealth and all wealth is not (in the form of) money.

Both the booklet and the film titled *What Is Wealth?* are lessons in a labor theory of value and an ethics of industry and frugality that seem drawn directly—like the stuff about money's convenience—from *The Wealth of Nations*. The film version opens with a staged scene of natives lined up on a beach, bowing and waving leaf wands to the sea in an apparent attempt to summon the cargo. Ismael To-Mata, Vice President of the Gazelle Peninsula Local Government Council, announces an anticargo message: "This is ignorance and foolishness. . . ." He goes on to assert that wealth comes from work, and, explains how he went to Australia and saw that people there have more wealth because of their work. Thus, in a stroke, this particular labor theory of value takes care of the problems of production *and* distribution. The booklet asks: How does a man get wealth? Answer: Wealth can only be created by someone's work. The booklet asks: Why are some people richer than others? Answer:

> Some people in Papua and New Guinea will never be very wealthy but every person can, by hard work and saving, become better off than he is now. The man who wastes all the money he earns will always be poor. The man who saves money whenever he earns some, will gradually improve his standard of living (RBA 1961a).

And so the booklet catechizes along the lines of what Lindstrom (1994:9) refers to as the "dominant capitalist rhetoric," narrating "the moral connections . . . between hard work and material success." "Why cannot we be given Motor Cars, etc.?" Answer: "You will see that it costs a lot of money to make a motor car and the people who buy cars must pay a big enough price for each one so that the people who own the factories can get back all the money they have spent [paying for work and materials]." (Note: profits here means "reward" and payment for "risk.") "Why cannot we make such things as Motor Cars, Radios and Refrigerators in the Territory?" Answer: "People in Papua and New Guinea do not yet have enough money to buy machines and materials to set up factories . . . " And so forth.

I will return presently to the implications of the Australian Reserve Bank's program in moral education for enforcing a particular notion of personhood—that of the modern individual. For the moment, however, I would like to concentrate on a tension in the program surrounding the attempt to dematerialize money, that is, to render money as no object. This tension derives, I suggest, from the dissonance between the ideological explanation of money, on the one hand, and the immediate practical goal of the Administration, on the other. That goal was to get natives to put their money in one of the four Australian trading banks operating in the Territory and thereby to accumulate capital locally for financing the development of the Territory. Accordingly, the educational campaign emphasized the virtues of saving, of "growing" money in a savings bank (see P.N.G.V. 1954: 69). At the same time, the booklets and films raise the specter of losing money, especially paper money, not through improper consumption, but through its material dissolution: "Paper money not put into a BANK may be eaten by rats or other pests, or, if there is a fire, it can be burned." Even ordinary conditions might prove disastrous for notes which "might be spoilt over a long period because the paper can deteriorate in hot and humid climates." In other words, in order to motivate natives to deposit their money in a bank, the educational campaign emphasized the fragile materiality of money. This emphasis,

I suggest, potentially fanned the flames of fetishism by making out of money not a signifier that referred beyond itself, but a material object that was intrinsically mysterious and potent.

The clearest evidence of this potential is *The Luluai's Dream*, commissioned by the Reserve Bank as one of three films made for showing to native audiences. *The Luluai's Dream*, however, is distinctive in that it presents its case in the form of a dramatic narrative enacted entirely by New Guinea natives. (There is anecdotal evidence that New Guineans also collaborated with the film's producer, Maslyn Williams, in writing the script.) The story revolves around the attempt of John, a sophisticated young agricultural officer, to persuade Tengen, an old untutored rustic and the government appointed "chief" (*luluai*) of his area, to stop keeping his money in an old tobacco tin and instead to put it in a bank. Tengen is depicted as a man who, rather like Dobbs in *The Treasure of Sierra Madre*, is obsessed with his money, that is, his actual notes and coins. Tengen inspects his tin frequently; he counts out his money again and again; and he lays with his money at night.

The climax of the film is a dream sequence in which Tengen's spirit leaves his sleeping body. This immaterial Tengen runs to a burning village. An ethereal voice urges him to hurry or his money will be cooked. But Tengen arrives too late and discovers his house and money on fire. Waking suddenly, Tengen reports his dream to John and vows to change his ways. John accompanies Tengen to a bank in Rabaul, the district headquarters, where Tengen deposits his money and receives in exchange a bankbook, the use of which the narrator then explains. The end.

The Luluai's Dream precisely depicts Tengen's money as his fetish, in the specific sense that Tengen surrenders his autonomy, his self-control, to the force of his money-objects. Here we encounter one more of Pietz's themes of fetishism: the subjection of the human body to the irreducible materiality of the object. The film represents Tengen's struggle as one of overcoming the influence or control over his body exerted by a powerful external organ: his money.

Perhaps we can characterize this film as strategic fetishism. In order to compel the natives to use banks, the film draws upon the power of the fetish—even if this means suggesting that the matter of money does, after all, matter. (Likewise, the film depicts banks primarily as secure places in which to store money, physical repositories of money-objects.) In the end, though, Tengen does manage to establish his autonomy by bringing his money-fetish under control, indeed, by reducing the materiality of the money-objects into that of a bankbook. This is the trade-off that the film makes: Money's fetishization facilitates projecting the image of a progressive, self-disciplined individual—an image that returns us to the sort of moral education implied in the Reserve Bank's program.

Who is the "you" addressed in *Your Money*? It is first of all a singular you, a you that presupposes a certain kind of individuated, self-contained person, in short, an individual externally related to its (his) possessions. It is this modern individual that the Reserve Bank's educational campaign at once presupposed and naturalized in claiming that each individual's security and status depends upon his relation to money, not to other people. Consider this parable from the *Papua and New Guinea Villager* (1954: 69):

> Let us imagine a young man who has just got a job. He works at that job until he is 50 years old, but he never saves any money. He spends it all on himself. The time comes when he cannot work. His family have to look after him. That is very hard on the family, and not very fair.

And consider this advice from the booklet *Your Money*: "A man with money in a BANK is a more important man. People know he is a sensible man and respect him." Both of these declarations presuppose a world of individuals defined not through their relations to each other, but prior to and independent of those relations and hence definable only in terms of a common external standard, the standard of wealth in the form of money. Indeed, there is a surprising openness—almost crassness—about this state of affairs in the Bank's campaign. In the booklet *What Is Wealth?*, it is suggested that if a man "puts most of his money in a bank, he can show his friends how wealthy he is by letting them see his bank book." And so at the end of *The Luluai's Dream*, Tengen can be seen displaying his bank book to some interested onlookers, advertising thereby his identity as measured in pounds and pence. But the outcome is indeterminate: Does not the irreducibly material bank book itself take the place of Tengen's notes and coins as his new fetish?

OUR MONEY: FROM COLONY TO NATION

The bank book-*cum*-identity card marks one of two moments in a single strategy of moral education fitfully pursued by agents of Christian colonialism in Papua and New Guinea. It indexes the moment of individuation, the creation of individuated persons (individuals) as the primordial units of modern society. The second moment, then, is that of aggregation, the bringing together of individuals to form a society or "community." This community, in turn, is imagined as a collective individual, the corporation formed out of many singular individuals—some of whom might be unknown to each other. It is in this second moment of the educational process that one sees the connection between the Administration's talk about money and wealth and its U.N.-mandated program for nation building.

The Reserve Bank's effort to explain the nature of money and wealth was bound up with its concern to accumulate capital in the Territory. Discussions of hard and efficient work as the source of an individual's wealth often merged into discussions of "community wealth": "The wealth of any community includes the total of all the wealth owned by individuals in the community, together with a great many other things which are owned by the community or the country as a whole" (RBA 1961b). Such things include schools, aid posts, roads, airstrips, and wharfs. The acquisition of these things was beyond the means of any one individual, and therefore required the association of individuals each of whom would contribute a small amount of money. Of course, the most usual way of building up community wealth was through paying taxes to the government (or Native Local Government Council) (1961b). But other sorts of novel voluntary associations, such as women's clubs and cooperative societies, were also vehicles for accumulation. As the narrator of the film *What Is Wealth?* puts it: "Small amounts of money collected together make it possible for a group of people like yourselves to do big and important things."

My point here is that colonial education conjured not only the singular "you" in your money, but a collective "you" as well. This collective "you" was imagined as a community of ownership composed of discrete individual owners, such as "a village." But at the most encompassing level, this community designated the country: "Beyond the village, we think of the wealth of a country—things which belong to all the people of the country. They all share in the ownership of these things, even though they may never have seen them" (RBA 1961b). This country is the collective "you" imagined by the colonial state. When such imaginings become those of the colonized themselves—a process that Anderson (1991) has deftly outlined— assertions of Your Money become nationalist counter-assertions of Our Money. And it is in the context of such counter-assertions that fetish discourse about money and wealth items—pigs, pearlshells, and clay pots—becomes transformed.

In the Territory of Papua and New Guinea, Australian notes and coins (first pounds, shillings, and pence, then dollars and cents) circulated in the post-WWII years, replacing the specially minted Territorial coinage and printed currency in use in New Guinea during the interwar years. After the proclamation of internal self-government in 1973, planning began for the name and design of the future coinage and paper currency of Papua New Guinea. The then Minister for Finance (now Prime Minister), Mr. (now Sir) Julius Chan, announced that the new currency would be distinctly Papua New Guinean, with designs that reflect "the spirit and feeling of Papua New Guinea" (quoted in Mira 1986: 139). The following year, Chan proposed to the House of Assembly a format (denominations, size, weight, etc.) for P.N.G. coinage and currency that was broadly similar to that of Australian currency, but with significantly new names for the basic monetary units:

> I therefore propose that the name of the dollar equivalent should be Kina, and the name of the cent equivalent should be toea. The word Kina is found in both the Pidgin and Kuanua languages. In pidgin it refers to the valuable pearl shell used widely in the Highlands as a traditional store of wealth. It is probably the source of one of the terms for pearl shell in the Mount Hagen Melpa language, Kin. The fact that this shell is traded into the Highlands from coastal areas far afield makes it an appropriate national name for one of the basic units of our new currency.

> The word toea is a Motu word meaning valuable arm-shell. The toea has had a wide traditional use in coastal Papua for trading and bride-price payments. One bride-price recorded about 70 years ago consisted of 43 toea, three pigs, and 100 dogs' teeth. I am not sure whether there has been inflation or deflation since then. The combination of these two names should help to preserve a valuable part of our cultural traditions, drawn from as broad a spectrum as possible of the whole of Papua New Guinea (quoted in Mira 1986: 140–41).

In April, 1975, the new currency was issued. After a year-long "dual currency period," during which Papua New Guinea became an independent state, the new currency officially supplanted Australian dollars and cents.

Chan's proposal indicates two ways in which state officials constructed the new money, and by the same token (so to speak) the new nation itself, as a fetish—that is, a fetish in the sense of a composite fabrication, a coming together of heterogeneous elements. First, the money was to be understood as a synthesis of elements drawn from different locations within the borders of the territorial state, thereby expressing both the unity of the nation as a whole and the parity of its constituent parts. Considerable attention appears to have been given to devising a monetary symbolism that would mediate some of the major cleavages emerging within the new nation, especially cleavages between the Highlands and the Islands, between Papua and New Guinea, and between Motu speakers and Pidgin speakers. (Special mention also seems to have been given to Kuanua (the Tolai) speakers, an important and potentially secessionist ethnic group during the time of independence.) Not only the names of the major monetary units, but also the iconography of the paper currency was conceived with this mediation in mind. The back of every note of each denomination depicts items of traditional wealth—cowrie shell necklaces, clay pots, and so forth (figures 2 and 3). Taken together, the

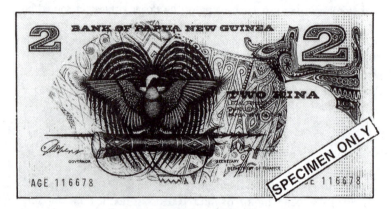

The front of a K2 note.

The back of a K2 note.

Figure 2.   Design of P.N.G. 2 kina note. (Source: Papua New Guinea, 1987, p. 11.)

notes depict items from all of the administrative districts (now provinces) within the nation.

The second way in which Chan's proposal indicates a familiarly postcolonial sort of fetish discourse for the nation lies in its invocation

Figure 3.   Designs of P.N.G. 5, 10, and 20 kina notes. (Source: Papua New Guinea, 1987, p. 12.)

of "cultural traditions." The following statement of Sir Henry ToRobert, once Governor of the Bank of P.N.G. and before that a member of Chan's 1973 Currency Working Group and Manager of the Port Moresby Office of the Reserve Bank of Australia, makes the point concisely:

> In preparation for political independence, currency in Papua New Guinea on 19 April 1975 took on its own unique form and emphasis. Physically the needs of a modern world and a desire to maintain the country's heritage came together to give meaning to our notes and coins (Mira 1986: ix).

The coins and currency of Papua New Guinea are, in this view, seen as the material embodiment of an encounter between the past and the present, tradition and modernity. But the upshot of this encounter is not, as in the colonialist rhetoric of RBA's booklets, the replacement of the former by the latter. There is no assumption here of a process of total assimilation to the imported but irresistibly superior media of modernity. Rather, what is emphasized is the continuation of the past in the present, the resilience of tradition or heritage in the modern world. Thus, for example, a grade six school textbook used throughout Papua New Guinea as an introduction to the topic of money tells its readers that:

> Early Papua New Guinean money is shown on our present banknotes. The drawings on our banknotes show valuable traditional things that have always been used as money (P.N.G. 1987: 4).

The point I wish to make in this regard is that the threatening fetish of colonial times—the irreducibly material and locally restricted wealth item—has been rehabilitated as an emblem of cultural identity. But this rehabilitation (or revaluation) is also a form of domestication, for the wealth items now indicate not an alternative and competing value code, but rather a nonthreatening if apparently different mode of cultural identity. In other words, what takes the place of assimilation—the replacement of the primitive with the modern—is juxtaposition, a complementarity of differences made viable by a new structural equation: Modernity is to tradition as economy is to culture. Let me illustrate how this trope of juxtaposition makes itself present in a range of images, all of which play self-consciously on the visual dissonance of bringing "cultural traditions" within the same frame as the "modern economy."

The following figures are taken from a modest coffee-table book published in 1970 by Maslyn Williams, producer of the RBA films and numerous other documentary films for the Australian government. Pictures 1 and 2 form a pair (figure 4); they are captioned: "Housewife—1960" and "Housewife—1970," respectively. The message seems to be that a major change has taken place; an old and primitive version of "the housewife" has been replaced by a new and modern one in the short span of ten years. Such, I suggest, is the colonialist reading of the trope, *In One Lifetime*, the title of the book of photographs (compare the subtitle of the popular autobiography of Sir Albert Maori Kiki: *Ten Thousand Years in a Lifetime*.) In this reading, what is emphasized is the process of replacement, that is, the radical difference between the before and after pictures.

Picture number 3, however, lends itself to a different reading (figure 5). It is captioned: Highlanders shopping in a self-service supermarket. Here the contrast is not that of before and after, but rather between heterogeneous elements of the same present—a contrast within the now, as it were. It is not a process of replacement that is emphasized, but rather an instance of juxtaposition. From one point of view, the photo can be read as a transitional moment and thus placed after picture 1 as a step on the way to picture 2. But from another point of view, the photograph can be read as depicting what Julius Chan and Henry ToRobert were imagining, namely, the timeless coexistence of cultural tradition and modern economy. In this latter reading, indigenous cultural practices are not replaced, but rather repositioned, indeed, reclassified as tradition or heritage—as Culture. These repositioned cultural traditions then become the basis for defining a unique and distinctive national-cultural identity in a homogeneous modern world economy.

The ambiguity of picture 3—its intelligibility within both colonialist and postcolonialist readings—disappears in the self-consciousness of pictures 4 and 5 (and, of course, the P.N.G. paper notes). Picture 4 forms the cover of *Money*, the community life pupil book for grade six used in community schools throughout P.N.G. (figure 6). A diagonal line bisects the cover. In one section, there is an image of a woman (as usual) paying a cashier at the checkout counter of a supermarket; in the other section, an arrangement of shell wealth items. The cover is a composite, a coupling of tradition and modernity—but *not* a promiscuous mixing: Tradition and modernity each occupy discrete domains. It is juxtaposition, not blending, that organizes the image.

The same can be said for picture 5, a 1995 advertisement taken from P.N.G.'s daily newspaper, the *Post Courier* (figure 7). Here the text

Figure 4. "Housewife—1960" and "Housewife—1970." (Source: Williams, 1970, p. 53.)

Figure 5. "Highlanders shopping in a self-service supermart." (Source: Williams, 1970, p. 70.)

of the ad makes explicit precisely what is at stake in the displacement and juxtaposition of visual markers of local and premodern life: the construction of a new national cultural identity. Pepsi is not a threat to Papua New Guinea national culture, but on the contrary an active supporter of this culture in its sponsorship of the annual Port Moresby Show, a state fair–like event highlighted by its prize competitions in traditional dance and self-decoration among emerging ethnic groups. Indeed, the marriage of Pepsi and "cultural heritages" yields a "new generation" for P.N.G.: not the once-feared offspring of "mixed-race" unions, but instead a nation of Papua New Guineans (rather than Trobrianders or Tolai) whose identity derives from the ever present,

Figure 6.　　Cover of the textbook *Money*, produced for community schools in Papua New Guinea. (Source: Papua New Guinea, 1987.)

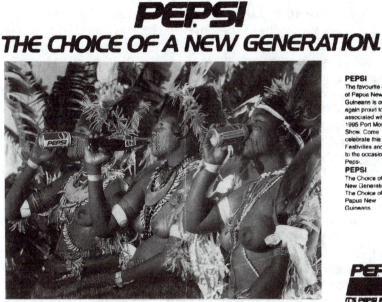

Figure 7.   Pepsi advertisement. (Source: *Papua New Guinea Post Courier*, 1995.)

infinitely repeatable encounter of tradition and modernity. The national Us that crystallizes from this imagery is indeed a composite one: not so much a composite of diverse ethnicities—"unity in diversity," Indonesian style—but a composite of past and present, indigenous and exogenous, traditional and modern (see Foster 1995). Like its coin and currency, then, the nation of P.N.G. embodies—now and forever—an encounter between radically heterogeneous elements; the nation-form here mimics the fetish-form.

THE GOVERNMENT'S MONEY: STATE FETISHISM IN P.N.G.?

The rhetoric of the Australian Reserve Bank's financial booklets insisted that the notes and coins called "money," because "they are issued for the Government, . . . are always good." In other words, "the Government" is the ultimate source of all the money circulating in the Territory (and Australia, too). Conversely, "the Government" is responsible for collecting a portion of all the money in circulation, through taxes paid by individuals in money, in order to build up "community wealth." Money, then, is the mundane instrument through which "the

Government" asserts and legitimates its holistic existence and reality. It is this entity and being—"the Government"—as much as it is work or labor that is the something beyond itself to which the material signifier of money refers. Put otherwise, money is what "the State" designates as its mask, as the material form that gives shape to an insubstantial but powerful fiction (Taussig 1992).

The grade school book *Money* likewise deploys a rhetoric that animates the matter of money with the idea of the independent state of Papua New Guinea. In its iconography, P.N.G. currency represents the nation-state as the totality holding together the ethnic/cultural diversity of "the country." Thus, the national emblem, a bird of paradise perched on an hour-glass drum, appears on the front of almost *every* coin and *every* note (figure 2). The backs of the coins and notes vary, however (figures 2 and 3). Coins depict various fauna—crocodiles, a cuscus, and so forth; notes, as already mentioned, depict wealth items associable with different regions of the country—"different kinds of traditional money," as the school book puts it.

The exception is the one kina coin, the largest of all the coins and the only one with a hole in the center, enhancing its portability by making it easy to carry on a string looped around one's neck. This coin bears instead of the national emblem a "specially designed figure of a Bird of Paradise [which] is the symbol of the Bank of Papua New Guinea" (Papua New Guinea 1987: 13). The text book, in a section titled "The Government's Money," explains:

> Every country has its own bank to look after the country's money business. The bank of Papua New Guinea does this for us. It plans how much money people will need to carry on the country's business. . . . All the other banks get banknotes and coins from it.

In this representation, the Bank of Papua New Guinea ("the Government's" bank?) is the ultimate source of all the money in the country. The Bank is also the storehouse of "the nation's wealth" in the form of gold (the text book thus includes a photograph of dozens of bars of gold stacked in a vault). It is the Mother of all banks, the bank to which not only all other banks, but all individuals who use money are simultaneously and necessarily connected.

In other words, the coinage and currency of Papua New Guinea—like that of many other states—are inscribed with visible traces of state. Yet, coinage and currency "work" efficaciously—in P.N.G. as elsewhere—only when these traces are erased from consciousness, that is, subsumed under an implicit fiction that the coinage and currency as signifiers depend upon nothing (whether labor or the state) beyond themselves, upon no signified. Or as Taussig (1992: 138) puts it, "The fetish absorbs into itself that which it represents, erasing all traces of the represented. A clean job." Under such conditions, the matter of money—including its iconography—really (i.e., practically) does not matter. Under such conditions, the connection between money and the state goes without saying and so goes unsaid.

Do such conditions prevail in Papua New Guinea? Hardly, I think. But I don't mean to suggest that such conditions prevail elsewhere, either. Take, for example, the recently publicized militia movement in the United States, a complicated discursive field that engages, among other things, attacks on the Federal Reserve Banking System. In a pamphlet called *Why a Bankrupt America?* published by Project Liberty (1993), the question of what is money is taken up as part of a critical inquiry into the nature of the Federal Reserve. The pamphlet seeks to establish that the Federal Reserve is a private company and not the U.S. government. It also seeks to demonstrate that only gold and silver, not paper, are money (thereby reviving a debate that gripped many Americans in the last century; see Michaels 1987, Shell 1982):

> Precious metals such as gold and silver have been the most highly prized means of monetary exchange for many centuries. They are honest money. By mining the Earth, one exchanges his God-given talents and resources for wealth. That wealth can, in turn, be exchanged for the goods and services honestly produced by another's talents and resources.

After citing the United States Code at Title 12, Sec. 152, to the effect that lawful money of the United States shall be construed to mean only gold and silver coin, the pamphlet draws its conclusion:

> What we really see from these definitions is that paper cannot be money. What we carry in our pockets—Federal Reserve Notes—are disqualified as money, because they are notes. A note is an IOU—an evidence of debt. It is not money! Why, then, do we call it money? Have we been tricked?

We have been more than tricked, as it turns out; for close scrutiny of the image of the seal on the back of every U.S. one dollar bill will reveal the motto of the devilish conspiracy in which the Federal Reserve participates: *novus ordo seculorum*, new order of the ages—the New World Order of global government ruled by the United Nations.

My point follows accordingly: if one looks hard at and takes seriously the material form of money—especially the statish iconography of coin and currency—then one can recover money's erasure and question the connection between one's self and the state. Such inquiry is happening in Papua New Guinea, where the idea of "the government's money" is taken very seriously. But in P.N.G., the main issue is not whether paper currency is somehow less real or less valid than metal coinage. In fact, I doubt that this problem has ever been a problem for most Papua New Guineans, mainly because most Papua New Guineans have historically understood money (coins and paper notes) as the material token of a social relationship, a relationship of power between themselves and some radically alien Other. The first of these Others were the Germans, who were compelled in 1900–01 to issue ordinances forbidding the use of shell money (*diwara*) in transactions between Europeans and natives. Then came the Australians, who were also compelled in 1920 to issue the Native Currency Ordinance, which stipulated that: "no European or any other person having the status of a European and any coloured person in the employ of such European, shall sell, exchange, give or take in payment, or use as a means of barter or exchange any of the earthenware saucepans which are commonly used in currency by the Siassi group of Islands, nor earthenware articles similar in nature to such saucepans" (Mira 1986: 29). The Japanese imposed their money during WWII, and the Australians reimposed their money afterwards. It is not surprising, then, that I heard men in rural New Ireland narrate a history of colonialism in terms of currency shifts: First we had marks, then shillings, then dollars.

During the last currency shift, around the time of Independence, many people, especially in the Highlands, felt uneasy about converting their Australian dollars and cents to Papua New Guinea kina and toea. The P.N.G. Government was compelled to extend twice the deadline for free conversion of Australian money due to the large amounts being withheld in rural areas (Mira 1986: 143). This widespread hesitation to convert Australian currency bespoke widespread anxiousness about political independence and the fortunes of Papua New Guinea apart from Australia. It also bespoke the fate of the newly independent state, namely, to be cast as the latest in a long line of Others with whom diverse indigenous local populations entered into contested relations of power.

Because, then, Papua New Guineans have always understood money as the index of both "the government's" power over them and its ability to supply desired goods to them, criticism of the P.N.G. government today is articulated through criticism of its money. Several New Ireland men complained to me that their money was not as strong as it was before independence; they equated the diminished purchasing power of their money with the weakness and mismanagement of the P.N.G. government compared with that of Australia. Jeffrey Clark (1997: 81) reported a similar, but more specific complaint from Pangia in the Southern Highlands: "It is believed in Pangia that Australian money was made by the Queen, Papua New Guinea currency made by [Sir Michael] Somare [former Prime Minister] in Port Moresby (people prefer the K2 note because it is most like the one pound note)." Here the invidious comparison of P.N.G. with Australia entails a personification of the state with Somare and an identification of Somare with P.N.G. currency. These equations are not unpersuasive, given that the recently issued K50 note bears the images of both Sir Michael himself and the National Parliament building. The main Parliament building, moreover, was built in the singular shape of a "spirit house" (*haus tamberan*) from the Sepik area, Somare's place of origin.

Clark's point is that Pangia people imagine the P.N.G. state as a classic Melanesian "big man" whom they follow *if and only if* the big man remains bound by moral obligations of reciprocity and redistribution. My point is different. I want to stress that people in Papua New Guinea can accept as eminently plausible the claim that money *is* the government's money. Indeed, they verify the claim with reference to the iconography of the money, thereby uncovering a connection that the fetish-power of money ordinarily obscures. But having accepted the claim, Papua New Guineans are then free to develop its implications into a critique of the government, to apprehend the P.N.G. state as an Other with whom nothing less than an egalitarian, reciprocal relationship is morally proper. Hence the consternation of one New Ireland man at the depictions of wealth items on P.N.G. bank notes. When I pointed out to him the image of a masked figure (*dukduk*) from nearby New Britain and southern New Ireland, he immediately observed: "that's not **our** *kastam* [tradition]." The P.N.G. state, despite its deliberate efforts, failed to represent (in both senses of the term) him; "the government's money" was not, in this instance, "our money."

CONCLUSION: NEW MONEY, OLD FETISHISMS

There are other ways in which to qualify or subvert the claim that money is the government's money. I conclude by considering two of them. Both ways recall the critical remarks made by New Irelanders

and Pangia people about P.N.G. money in that they take the matter
of money seriously. That is, they reevaluate money—notes and
coins—and/or wealth items in terms of material properties—in aesthetic terms—and in so doing accomplish what colonial educators
sought to prevent: They create material media capable of traversing
and articulating diverse value codes.

The first way, which I will call after Nihill (1989) "the contextual
demonetization of money," is illustrated by the ceremonial uses to
which Anganen men (Southern Highlands) put twenty kina notes.
Nihill reports that Anganen liken twenty kina notes to pearlshells
(*kina*) and use the two interchangeably in certain exchange contexts
in which men accrue prestige. This perceived similarity does not extend to all money, but rather only to the twenty kina notes. First of
all, Anganen regard paper money as "male," and coins as "female."
Moreover, they associate small denominations of paper money (two
kina and five kina notes) with mundane productive activities (wage
labor, coffee selling), on the one hand, and acts of consumption
(buying cigarettes and beer, paying taxes) in which money is "lost."
This association also metaphorically links small denomination paper
notes to women, who grow and sell coffee, and, in the eyes of men,
"eat" cash by channeling it into wasteful consumption.

By contrast, twenty kina notes—new, red notes—are unequivo-
cally associated with the masculine realm of exchange. They are, according to Nihill, "like male-oriented groups (clans, subclans)" in
their capacity to integrate "power and value into a single entity
which should then be directed to purposeful" and socially reproductive ends (1989: 153). They are like the intact pearlshell crescents that
men esteem and care for, "applying red ochre to renew their 'skin'
(152). Men display these pearlshells in prestations made in respect of
bodies—prestations undertaken to alleviate illness, compensate
death, or combine a woman's "womb blood" with her husband's
semen and thereby create children. And herein lies the analogy that
underwrites the spectacular substitutability of pearlshells and twenty
kina notes:

> The stress on presentational excellence also suggests why the Anga-
> nen emphasize the newness or crispness of paper money in a manner
> parallel to the renewing of shells through red colouration. They may
> even go so far as to swap old notes for new at savings banks in Mendi.
> Like pearlshells, new notes have an aesthetic quality all their own
> which gives their display a value that older notes cannot achieve. An
> analogy with human bodies is not misplaced here: tight, shiny skin or

brilliant body decoration, bright red pearlshells and crisp, pristine 20-
kina notes are all of inherent merit and beauty. (Nihill 153–54).

The display of money thus has an iconic quality to it; the twenty
kina notes at once evince and ensure the ends of social reproduction:
strong and beautiful bodies. Hence, as Nihill points out, the cultural
good sense with which one Anganen man named his son and daughter Kina and Toea, the basic units of P.N.G. money.

All this was probably not what the Australian Reserve Bank had
in mind when it assured the natives that soiled notes could always be
exchanged for fresh clean ones. In fact, the use of twenty kina notes
in Anganen exchanges seemingly realizes the worst fear of the Reserve Bank: the (noncommodity) fetishization of money. The fetish-
power of twenty kina notes consists in their capacity, like that of
pearlshells, to evince the regeneration of social relations and perforce
the reproduction of healthy bodies. New money becomes fetishized
on old grounds, animated with the life-giving qualities that distinguish pearlshells as wealth items of the highest order. But this fetishization is unstable; for despite their "contextual demonetization,"
twenty kina notes are always at risk of remonetization, of being frag-
mented into smaller denomination notes and coins and "lost" in
un(re)productive consumption. The fetish-power of crisp red twenty
kina notes thus depends upon sustaining a separation between two
realms: the realm of socially reproductive ceremonial exchange
among male transactors, and the realm of wasteful and multiple retail transactions where women and lesser men circulate dirty money
(see Bloch and Parry 1989).

A similar (though ungendered) dichotomy is entailed in a second
way in which indigenous strategies have implicated state issued
money in old fetishisms. In this instance, however, old wealth items
become (re)fetishized on new grounds. I am thinking in particular
about the famous "shell money" of the people of the Gazelle Peninsula (East New Britain), called *tabu* or *tambu* by Tolai and *diwara* by
Duke of York Islanders. This shell money has been the subject of discussion by missionaries, government officials, and anthropologists
for over one hundred years—mainly because it has impressed outsiders as a "true money," that is, a medium of exchange, and a measure and store of value. Its material properties lent themselves well to
all these functions:

Shell money . . . consisted of small cowrie shells (*nassa camelus*) strung
onto strips of rattan and counted either individually or measured on

> the body in standard lengths. . . . Continuously spliced, these strips
> could be arranged in large wrapped and sometimes decorated coils
> containing hundreds of fathoms (Errington and Gewertz 1995: 54).

These same outsiders were equally impressed with the sheer perva-
siveness and unambiguous centrality of shell money in the life of the
Tolai and Duke of York Islanders. Neumann (1992: 186) claims that
today not only must shell money be used to purchase magic and
commission dance performances, but also that "At the village level
nearly all other goods that can be bought with kina can also be
bought with *tabu*—which makes *tabu* in that sense the 'truer' of the
two currencies used on the Gazelle." Errington and Gewertz (1995:
54) add that

> shell money was the single standard by which not only everything but
> everyone was distinguished. The differences in the amount of shell
> money that an individual owned and used in public ceremonies dis-
> tinguished a person of importance from one of mere respectability
> and the latter from one of no consequence. Shell money was funda-
> mental to the prestige system and to the ordering of social life.

Yet while outside commentators have sought to identify shell
money with "real" money—a curious parallel, perhaps, to the Anganen effort to identify twenty kina notes with pearlshells—inside commentators have sought to maintain a clear contrast. This contrast is
drawn in terms that recall the Anganen distinction between twenty
kina notes and other lesser forms of money:

> [S]hell money was frequently described by Duke of York Islanders in
> terms of an essentialized contrast to money: Shell money was extolled
> as "heavy" (*mawat*)—as substantial and significant—as capable of
> generating the activities on which both male and female reputations
> were built and social order rested; money was denigrated as "light"
> (*biaku*)—as flimsy and inconsequential—as incapable of creating or
> sustaining personal worth or enduring social relationships (Errington
> and Gewertz 1995: 58).

Here again we see the world divided into two realms, one where
money flits away in the purchase of "easily broken, imported goods"
(58), another where shell money circulates indefinitely, generating
further exchanges. But in this version of the dichotomy, the difference between the two realms parallels a valenced opposition between

Them and Us in which They—Europeans—are construed as being like Their money: morally inferior.

This particular version of the contrast between shell money and money emerged out of the long history of encounters between Tolai/Duke of York Islanders and Europeans. As I have mentioned, German colonial administrators were compelled to ban shell money in certain transactions in order to limit *their* dependence on the natives and force the natives into the cash economy. The official annual report for 1900–01 noted that:

> It was often very difficult for the European firms to obtain the shell required to purchase copra etc. In this respect they were completely dependent on the natives, and at times the exchange rate for shell money was forced up absurdly high . . . (translated by Sack and Clark 1979: 220; cited in Errington and Gewertz 1995: 58).

But it is also important to note, as do Errington and Gewertz (1995), that this history of encounters includes the exercises in colonial education exemplified by the Reserve Bank's financial booklets. These booklets can thus be regarded as instances of what Carrier (1995) is pleased to call "occidentalism," the self-representation of the modern West in terms of an essentialized contrast with some nonmodern Other ("the East," though not necessarily in a geographical sense). Accordingly, contemporary Tolai/Duke of York understandings of money as "light" and inconsequential must be themselves understood as in dialogue with an occidentalism promulgated first by the colonial state and then, in a revised form, by the independent P.N.G. state.

Looked at this way, local understandings of shell money on the Gazelle can be seen, at least potentially, to do two things. First, they designate shell money as a cultural icon. In this way, people accept the official postcolonial evaluation of wealth items as emblems of both "tradition" and "ethnic" identities contained within a unifying national-cultural framework. Hence the successful effort of one prominent Tolai government official to stop the export of shell money on the grounds that it is (national) cultural property (see Errington and Gewertz 1995).

Second, local understandings devalue European money as an inferior form of shell money, thereby inverting the moral of the Reserve Bank's teaching. Unlike European money, shell money can be displayed in the form of accumulated coils that are sometimes cut apart and redistributed in mortuary exchanges that enact the reproduction of matrilineal social relations. But the devaluation of European money is plausible precisely because shell money has become and continues to be used everyday in all contexts as a universal currency. Indeed, Errington and Gewertz (1995: 59) report that in parts of East New Britain, it is now possible to do what the Germans and Australians explicitly outlawed: pay taxes with shell money—a brilliant assertion of how to build up "community wealth." The "culturalization" of shell money as a marker of collective identity has gone hand in hand with its spread as a medium of exchange into new transactional contexts. And it is this duality—its suitability for both short term commercial (commodity) transactions and long term kinship (gift) exchanges—that makes shell money superior to European money (as well as both P.N.G. state-issued money *and* other indigenous currencies no longer in use). Thus one of the underlying objections to the foreign export of shell money for display in European museums and collections was that the exporters were "buying large amounts of shell money in order *not* to use it" (Errington and Gewertz 1995: 68). That is, the exporters threatened to fetishize shell money on the wrong cultural grounds.

The Anganen use of money and the Tolai/Duke of York use of shell money are two versions of how to articulate different value codes with different forms of one material medium: notes and coins, on the one hand, coils and "loose" shells, on the other. Anganen reserve new twenty kina notes for ceremonial exchanges and circulate coins and soiled small denomination notes in mundane transactions. Tolai and Duke of York Islanders reserve their precious coils of shell money for mortuary displays and distributions while they use small strips of cane or unstrung shells for everyday purchases. Anganen money and Tolai/Duke of York shell money, in other words, are two versions of the unacceptable coupling or miscegenation that inhabits the fetish. They bring together what colonial and postcolonial administrations hell-bent upon modernization, with or without a nod to local culture, have been at pains to keep apart.

Whether one should regard this articulation of value codes as "resistance" is another question. After all, the Anganen use of twenty kina notes in ceremonial exchanges puts the whole system of exchange at risk; and the celebration of shell money as a local cultural icon for Tolai/Duke of York Islanders masks the rapidly emerging class lines within those "communities." What is certain, however, is that the colonial encounter not only introduced Marx's fetishism of commodities across the borders of Melanesia, but also cleared new grounds and furnished new means for reenchanting home-grown ideas about the social value of material objects.

ACKNOWLEDGMENTS

This paper was written for presentation at the international conference on Border Fetishisms, Research Centre Religion and Society, University of Amsterdam, Dec. 9–11, 1995. I thank the conference organizer, Dr. Patricia Spyer, for inviting me to participate. I thank the P.N.G. Dept. of Education, the Bank of P.N.G., and Maslyn Williams for kind permission to reproduce their illustrations. The research on which the paper is based was supported by grants from the Australian-American Educational Foundation, the American Council of Learned Societies, the University of Rochester, and the Spencer Foundation. The data presented, the statements made, and the views expressed are solely the responsibility of the author. This paper is dedicated to the memory of Jeffrey Clark.

REFERENCES

Anderson, B. (1991) (1983) *Imagined Communities*. 2nd ed. London: Verso.

Australia. (1962) "Banks aid education drive." *Australian Territories* 2(5): 34–35.

Carrier, J., ed. (1995) *Occidentalism*. Oxford: Oxford University Press.

Clark, J. (1997) "Imagining the State, or Tribalism and the Arts of Memory in the Highlands of Papua New Guinea." In T. Otto and N. Thomas, eds., *Narratives of Nation in the South Pacific*. Amsterdam: Harwood Academic Publishers.

Epstein, A. L. (1992) *In the Midst of Life: Affect and Ideation in the World of the Tolai*. Berkeley: University of California Press.

Errington, F. and D. Gewertz (1995) "Duelling Currencies in East New Britain: The Construction of Shell Money as National Cultural Property." In *Articulating Change in the "Last Unknown."* Boulder, CO: Westview.

Foster, R. (1995) "Print Advertisements and Nation Making in Metropolitan Papua New Guinea." In R. Foster, ed., *Nation Making: Emergent Identities in Postcolonial Melanesia*. Ann Arbor: University of Michigan Press.

Lindstrom, L. (1993) *Cargo Cult: Strange Stories of Desire from Melanesia and Beyond*. Hawaii: University of Hawaii Press.

Michaels, W. (1987) *The Gold Standard and the Logic of Naturalism: American Literature at the Turn of the Century*. Berkeley: University of California Press.

Mira, W. (1986) *From Cowrie to Kina: The Coinages, Currencies, Badges, Medals, Awards and Decorations of Papua New Guinea*. Sydney: Spink and Son.

Neumann, K. (1992) *Not The Way It Really Was: Constructing the Tolai Past*. Hawaii; University of Hawaii Press.

Nihill, M. (1989) "The New Pearlshells: Aspects of Money and Meaning in Anganen Exchange." *Canberra Anthropology* 12 (1&2): 144–59.

Papua New Guinea (1987) *Money. Community Life Pupil Book*. Port Moresby: Department of Education.

Parry, J. and M. Bloch, eds. (1989) *Money and the Morality of Exchange*. Cambridge: Cambridge University Press.

Pietz, W. (1985) "The Problem of the Fetish, I." *Res* 9: 5–17.

Pietz, W. (1987) "The Problem of the Fetish, II." *Res* 13: 23–45.

Pietz, W. (1988) "The Problem of the Fetish, IIIa." *Res* 16: 105–123.

Project Liberty (1993) *Why a Bankrupt America?* Arvada, CO: Project Liberty.

Reserve Bank of Australia (1961a) *Your Money*.

Reserve Bank of Australia (1961b) *What Is Wealth?*

Reserve Bank of Australia (1962a) *Your Money* [Film Version].

Reserve Bank of Australia (1962b) *What Is Wealth?* [Film Version].

Shell, M. (1982) "The Gold Bug." In Money, Language, and Thought: Literary and Philosophical Economies from the Medieval to the Modern Era. Berkeley: University of California Press.

Taussig, M. (1992) "Maleficium: State Fetishism." In *The Nervous System*. New York: Routledge.

Territory of Papua and New Guinea (1950–60) *Papua and New Guinea Villager*. Department of Education, Port Moresby.

Williams, M. (1970) *In One Lifetime*. Melbourne: Cheshire.

4

The Spirit of Matter:
On Fetish, Rarity, Fact, and Fancy

Peter Pels

This essay is an attempt to use the concept of fetish for an inquiry—begun elsewhere (Pels n.d.; Van Dijk and Pels 1996)—into the place of materiality in present-day cultural and social theory. The fetish is a good guide in such explorations, because, ever since it emerged from the cultural tangle of West African trade, it has signposted an untranscended materiality and beckoned its students to sojourn in the border zones that divide mind and matter, the animate and inanimate. The fetish foregrounds materiality because it is the most aggressive expression of the social life of things: not merely alive, it is an "animated entit[y] that can dominate persons" (Taussig 1980: 25). Fetishism is animism with a vengeance. Its matter strikes back.

My inquiry is divided in two parts. The first addresses the way in which "fetishism" can be distinguished from other expressions of the social life of things through a discussion of Arjun Appadurai's seminal essay on the subject. In particular, this section addresses the difference between fetishism and animism in terms of what I call the spirit *in*, as opposed to fetishism's "spirit *of*" matter. Next, Appadurai's positive evaluation of the alterity of the fetish leads to a discussion as to what extent the fetish is an "other thing" in cultural and social theory. It addresses the paradox that the fetish is commonly regarded as something negative, a denial of an accepted reality or "normal" hierarchy of values, yet also is made to function within this normality in some way. Thirdly, I will argue that Appadurai's focus on commodities leads away from the questions of materiality raised by the fetish, and discuss what concept of materiality will accommodate the contradictions sketched in the preceding sections. This theoretical part reflects the way in which the fetish functions to question the boundaries between things and the distinctions they are held to delineate (cf. the introduction to this volume).

Abstract theory, however, is never sufficient to counter the threat posed by the fetish's materiality and historicity. The second part of the paper, therefore, investigates the possibilities for advancing another mode of argument by suggesting a historical contextualization of the first, theoretical part, a contextualization that I feel is essential for a proper understanding and use of fetish. By linking the discourse on fetish to the, historically synchronous, discourse on rarities, and both these discourses to the emergence of Western notions of "fact" and "fancy," I hope to show that the possibility of thinking of an untranscended materiality of things is historically contingent on the emergence of a global trade in objects, in which "fetish" was the derogatory term of a pair of which "rarity" was the appreciative one (both being, in a sense, the "others" of the commodity). The persistent idealism of a Western discourse of representation that emerged afterwards, during the Enlightenment, subsumed this untranscended materiality to orders of classification, and made it into something of an occult quality of Western philosophy. As such, it points to a theory of signification that cannot be thought from within an intellectual tradition that is still heavily inflected by Enlightenment thought. Since that is also my provenance, the essay doesn't really have a conclusion: It disrupts and unsettles rather than clarifies. If that lack of conclusiveness isn't caused by my lack of mastery of these issues (and it may very well be), we can always blame the fetish. It wouldn't be the first time in its history for it to be declared guilty of confusion.

METHODOLOGICAL FETISHISM

Arjun Appadurai formulated the methodological prerequisite for the analysis of the social life of things as follows:

> Even if our own approach to things is conditioned necessarily by the view that things have no meanings apart from those that human trans-

actions, attributions and motivations endow them with, the anthropological problem is that this formal truth does not illuminate the concrete, historical circulation of things. For that we have to follow the
things themselves. . . . [E]ven though from a *theoretical* point of view
human actors encode things with significance, from a *methodological*
point of view it is the things-in-motion that illuminate their human and
social context. No social analysis of things (whether the analyst is an
economist, an art historian, or an anthropologist) can avoid a minimum level of what might be called methodological fetishism. (1986: 5;
emphases in original)

This profound and puzzling paragraph rules out the possibility for
any independent "life of things" in its first sentence ("things have no
meanings apart from . . . human transactions" etc.), but allows
"things-in-motion" sufficient independent activity to "illuminate
their human and social context" further on. This struggle for primacy
between people and things may be clarified by setting Appadurai's
"methodological fetishism" within the context of the genealogy of
the fetish.

Appadurai assumes that the theory that says things have no
meanings except those that humans endow them with is a "necessary
condition" of "our" approach. At the same time, he posits a methodology that assumes that human life cannot be understood without
the illumination provided by things-in-motion. He thereby inverts
the relationship of continuity between theory and method of normal
science, where theory provides hypotheses that method translates
into research practice. Instead, Appadurai seems to use method here
to obtain an alternative or counterpoint to a theory that, for the understanding of the "concrete, historical circulation of things" stands
in our way. But why cultivate such an incongruity?

I feel this can be clarified by zooming in on the genealogy of the
fetish. William Pietz has beautifully shown how, in the seventeenth
century, the fetish emerged from the hybrid wilds of West African
trade, allowing Dutch merchants to name those aspects of their trading relationships with Africans that could not be understood in terms
of mercantile ideas of the rational calculation of value (Pietz 1985;
1987; 1988). Merchant ethnographers like Willem Bosman transformed the *fetisso*—an object functioning within African trading relationships—into the fetish—the central feature of "African" religion.[1]
This essentialization of the fetish tends to obscure that it was, in a
sense, an uncontrollable object that burst the bounds of capitalist calculation. Even though European ethnographers try to bring its hybrid
inexplicability under control by making the fetish into something

essentially "African," this same discourse gave the fetish a life and a career that eventually allowed it to migrate from Africa and (un)settle down in two of the most important intellectual landscapes of Western modernity, Marxism and psychoanalysis. Even in this diaspora, it retained parts of its original identity: Whether as "African" religion, as the overvaluation of Western commodities, or as a specific articulation of sexual desire, the fetish remained an object of *abnormal traffic*.

Appadurai's injunction to be methodologically fetishist, therefore, seems to call for an "abnormal" traffic in information, in which the norm to be deviated from is obviously given by the theory—providing "necessary conditions"—that says "meanings" cannot but come from humans. The answer to the question about Appadurai's intended relationship between theory and method could then be that "methodological fetishism" is a reversal of the commonly accepted hierarchy of facts and values in social and cultural theory, which says that things don't talk back. Or, better, that says that those people who say that things talk back may be dangerously out of touch with reality.

Now, there are two ways of saying that things talk back, of which one seems more out of touch with this commonly accepted reality than the other. Things can talk back because they are animated by something else, or they do so because of their own "voice." The first possibility is in fact what Appadurai means: The sentences that I left out of the quotation given above say that the meanings of things are inscribed in their forms, uses, and trajectories and that we can only understand how human traffic "enlivens" them by analyzing these trajectories (Appadurai 1986: 5). The notions of "inscription" and "enlivening" indicate that, whatever things can do in this way of thinking, their agency is derivative. In contrast, one can also say that things act, emit messages and meanings on their own. The first attitude is animist: a way of saying that things are alive because they are animated by something foreign to them, a "soul" or, in the evolutionary anthropologist Edward Tylor's words, "Spiritual Being" (Tylor 1873, I: 424): a spirit made to reside *in* matter. Animism, as applied to things, transcends their materiality by saying that the perception of the life of matter is only possible through an attribution of a derivative agency. In contrast, fetishism says things can be seen to communicate their own messages. The fetish's materiality is not transcended by any voice foreign to it: To the fetishist, the thing's materiality itself is supposed to speak and act; its spirit is *of* matter. As I see it, Appadurai's social life of things is more properly the life of the ventriloquist's dummy, a "methodological animism." A call for a "methodological fetishism" would entail something more radical, for it would indicate a relationship in which such transcendence of materiality by human intention or artifice is not possible.

An obvious objection at this point seems to be that one can only come to such a theoretical distinction by ignoring the actual "life" of a thing, its biography in which, at a certain point in the thing's career, it is inscribed with human intentions, while at a later moment it may appear, fetishistically, as a *Ding an Sich* emitting the messages of such inscriptions on its own. In such a view, the fetish would be merely an isolated, phenomenological moment within a culturally and historically encompassing process. However, there is a danger of tautology if such an argument is used within the context of Appadurai's methodological propositions, which are meant to "illuminate . . . the concrete, historical circulation of things" (1986: 5). These propositions define materiality as contingent while positing human intentionality and artifice as transcending that contingency, thus introducing the terms that need to be explained as facts into the explanation. A crucial point of the different discourses on fetishism is precisely to outline the possibility that the materiality of things can stand in the way of, and deflect, the course of human traffic ("when the fetish comes to life, . . . some process has been suddenly interrupted," Freud 1950: 201).[2] Defining this human traffic as the transcendence of materiality and contingency theoretically outlaws the fetish before it has been given a chance to unfold its otherness.

THE FETISH AS OTHER THING

By discussing the fetish animistically, Appadurai appears to reconcile his call for the abnormal traffic of things with the theoretical primacy of human intention and artifice. This coupling of social determination by humans with "fetishism" is something Appadurai owes to his emphasis on commodity fetishism. Commodities occupy front stage in Appadurai's argument, and an astonishing range of commodity fetishisms appear in his text (1986: 50–56). Yet Appadurai's use of "methodological" fetishism is quite unusual, as a further examination of Appadurai's relationship to the discourse on fetish will show. Appadurai significantly departs from most uses of fetishism in refusing to deploy it simply as "a critical discourse about the *false* objective values of a culture from which the speaker is personally distanced" (Pietz 1985: 14, emphasis mine). His call for a useful methodological fetishism partially reverses this negative judgment. At the same time, Appadurai's derivation of the life of things from human agency (for which, in my terms, a methodological animism would seem to be conceptually sufficient) downplays the actual *danger* posed by talk of the fetish: its threat to overpower human beings by its materiality.

Appadurai's use of a methodological fetishism retains fetishism as an "other" of existing theoretical assumptions, yet reverses its valuation as something "false." This move can be understood as being analogous to the ways of rationalizing difference of many anthropologies: "this custom may seem weird, but it is not as strange, irrational or useless as it appears on the surface." There are two primary ways of thus demystifying curious customs: the *comparison* with things done by "us" that turn out to be similar, and the demonstration that a curious custom actually fulfilled an active *function* in social survival. In the case of fetishism, demystification by comparison (which often implies a reenchantment of "our" world) is used by Michael Taussig in juxtaposing a Latin American "fetishism" with the Western commodity variety;[3] or by Appadurai in juxtaposing the different commodity fetishisms arising from Chicago stock exchanges and New Guinean cargo cults (1986: 50 ff.). This debunking use of "fetishism" goes back to Marx, who both rehabilitated West African fetishism and reenchanted capitalism by applying "fetishism" to the world of commodity production and exchange (Pietz 1993). It is important to bear in mind that, while such positive assessments of fetishism are unusual, all the examples given are regarded as seminal moments in the development of social and cultural theory.

The second demystification—rationalizing fetishism by showing it has a social function—is even more unusual within the discourse on fetish. It is a part of Appadurai's reasoning to the extent that his methodological fetishism leads him to propose, in the wake of Baudrillard and others, a rehabilitated, that is, social, relational, and active notion of consumption (Appadurai 1986: 31). Appadurai translates Baudrillard's critique of the Marxian emphasis on production into a theory of *demand*, which is no longer seen predominantly as a passive false consciousness but also as an active intervention in the world by consumers: Now, they do not just suffer but also make the market (cf. Miller 1987). Whether this critique of Marx is completely justified is a moot point: Marx's own account of the fetishization of capital can serve to show consumption's potential importance for understanding fetishism. Capital is fetishized by the process of valorization by labor, the realization of that value by market circulation, and the accumulation of realized value through capital investments. The last part of the process can be interpreted as the fetishistic consumption of capital by the capitalist, for it "becomes identified as wealth itself," "the very embodiment of desire" (Pietz 1993: 147). This process is, therefore, simultaneously a fetishization of capital, and an investment of it that may set in motion further cycles of valorization, realization, and accumulation—that is, its motivation is *both "false" and functional*, both "subject to" and "subject of" culture, both product and producer. Similarly, we can say that less privileged consumers are both passively subject to, and active subjects of, fetishized commodities: Under capitalism, their demand—which is both determined by, and determining, social and economic forces (Appadurai 1986: 31)—more often than not takes the form of the fetishized commodity. Nothing brings out the inevitability of this contradiction as well as the story of Marx's overcoat, the fetishized commodity that, in a fully capitalized world, was a necessary material condition for the production of the book that would "unmask" the fetishization of commodities (Stallybrass, this volume). This "double attitude" of the fetishist, the simultaneity of affirmation and denial of reality (Freud 1950: 202–3) helps to explain why fetishism has been such a successful exemplar for understanding ideology, and why it can be easily inserted within arguments that endorse the thesis that any regime of truth is a regime of power and vice versa. This bringing forward of a more "positive" conception of the otherness of the fetish is, I feel, the most valuable element of Appadurai's approach.

Of course, fetishism is not Appadurai's main topic and he uses it merely instrumentally, as a counterpoint to an over-emphasis on the causative role of human traffic. That means that his interesting departure from the traditionally derogatory notion of the fetish is subordinated to a theory that proclaims the opposite: that things are ultimately and necessarily subject to human traffic. This does not sufficiently acknowledge the central importance of the "untranscended materiality" of the object that Pietz argues is crucial to the discourse on fetish (1985: 7). Appadurai's elevation of fetishism from the status of a falsehood to that of a method for understanding object relations addresses the dimension of fetishism that defined the fetish as the "other thing" of the commodity, thus making (African) fetishism into an irrational (that is, noncapitalist) attribution of value; while at a later, Marxian stage, criticizing the capitalist attribution of value itself as being fetishistic. But Appadurai's theoretical interests steer him away from the other side of the fetish's genealogy: the fact that the Dutch merchants of the seventeenth century not only defined the fetish as the other thing of the capitalist commodity, but also as an alternative to their own Protestant Christianity.[4] In contrast to the

idolatrous others of Christianity, who were thought to worship material *representations* of false spirits, the worship of the fetish implied
revering the terrestrial and material object's presence itself (Pietz
1993: 131). This powerful object remained, in the discourse of fetishism, underdetermined by a system of commensurable human values:
Any "trifle" that "took" an African's "fancy" could become a fetish or
object of worship (mark the active tense of "to take"). I shall return
to this notion of "fancy" below, where I discuss an aesthetics in
which the positive power of an object to influence a human being is
coupled to its underdetermination by a system of (rational) human
values. Suffice to say here that this untranscended materiality provided the Enlightenment with a radically novel, because atheological
conception of religion (Pietz 1993: 138).

This threat of the fetish to undercut the primacy of human signification by the materiality of the object is not sufficiently recognized
by Appadurai's account of the social life of things, because he con-
centrates on the spirit of the commodity, which is its exchangeabil-
ity (Appadurai 1986: 13). By concentrating on the commodity phase,
commodity candidacy or commodity context of the thing (1986:
13–15), Appadurai highlights its systematic social life, its transcendence by a system of human exchange values, while downplaying
the way in which fetishism insists that the fetish is an object that has
the quality to singularize itself and disrupt the circulation and commensurability of a system of human values. This capacity to singularize itself in relation to an ongoing process, and thereby to arrest it, is
what makes the fetish into an "other thing." It is "other" in relation
to accepted processes of defining the thing by its use and exchange
value. The fetish is one of the "other kinds of worth" that, according
to Igor Kopytoff, are "attributed to commodities after they have been
produced, and this by way of an autonomous cognitive and cultural
process of singularization" (1986: 83). However, its singularity is not
the result of sentimental, historical or otherwise personalized value:
The fetish presents a *generic* singularity, a unique or anomalous quality that sets it apart from *both* the everyday use and exchange *and* the
individualization or personalization of objects. The fetish presents a
general difference from the everyday valuation of objects, for a fetish
can be a commodity at the same time—be it an "other" commodity,
like velvet or fur (Freud 1950: 201), lace (Pinch, in this volume), or
blue jeans (Miller 1990). The fetish may be commoditized (in the
broad sense of being exchangeable against something else: Appadurai 1986: 9, 13), but even then its system of circulation is different
from the everyday: an exchange of things already used, as with shoes

or underlinen (Freud 1950: 201); pawning, as with Marx's overcoat (Stallybrass, this volume); the theft of a piece of lace (Pinch, this volume). Unlike souvenirs (Stewart 1993: 132ff.) or foodstuffs (Kopytoff 1986: 75), the fetish is not singularized by being absorbed into the person or history of the consumer: although it is often close to the body, it maintains an aesthetic value that radically distinguishes it as a material object from the subject it confronts. In this confrontation, the fetish always threatens to overpower its subject, because—unlike our everyday matters—its lack of everyday use and exchange values makes its materiality stand out, without much clue as to whether and how it can be controlled.

MATERIALITY?

Thus, we can see that one of the possibilities provided by the discourse on fetish is the existence of objects—"other" things—that disrupt everyday valuations, and thereby raise doubts about the ability of human beings to maintain control over their meaning. Again, an untranscended materiality impresses itself upon the argument. One of the aims of this paper is to show why the discourse on fetish serves as a continual reminder of that materiality—why, in fact, talk of untranscended matter has such a fetish-like attraction in Occidental discourse. But we cannot address that cultural and historical question without first asking what we might be speaking of when we discuss materiality.

Most cultural and social theorists that address the issue will agree that in using "matter" or "materiality," we cannot be talking of a *Ding an Sich*, let alone a thing that, like a fetish, has an independent agency, capable of making and breaking human beings. Yet that does not necessarily imply that one has to affirm the eventual transcendence of the materiality of things by human intentionality and artifice.[5] Daniel Miller has argued that there is a "physicality" which carries over certain forms of signification from one context of human behavior to another.[6] This would imply attributing at least a minimum capacity for transcendence to material objects, although, since they are artifacts, this transcendence is achieved by human intentionality and artifice, and matter remains an empty signifier, a *tabula rasa* on which humanity inscribes meanings differentially. But despite reinstating this primacy of human intentionality and artifice, this first step enables Miller and Van Beek to argue—rightly—for a recognition of materiality in social process, by systematically treating materiality as a quality of *relationship* rather than of things. Van Beek has recently formulated this in terms of materiality as an "ontological commitment" of human beings, their acceptance of the autonomy of the things with which they come in contact (1996: 18ff.). Yet, Van Beek's critique that Miller's theorizing of a dialectic of objectification addresses the theory of culture in general rather than the specifically material (1996: 9; see also Miller 1996: 27) seems equally applicable to his own argument, for "ontological commitment" implies that human beings *attribute* an autonomous materiality to a thing, not that there is anything specifically material about the relationship between people and things. Instead, I would suggest that the materiality of human interaction with things is best studied in terms of *aesthetics*: the material process of mediation of knowledge through the senses (Eagleton 1990: 13).

Such a step is supported by recent studies arguing for the crucial contribution of different sensory regimes to the construction of social knowledge. These studies have opposed a predominantly visualist, Occidental sensory regime to oral/aural (Fabian 1983), tactile (Pels 1998) and even olfactory registers (Classen 1993). However, such a separating out of different senses is itself a discursive construction, just as the distinction and ranking of five senses is peculiar to "the West" (Classen 1993; Howes 1991). Moreover, there is nothing "natural" about senses whose functioning is constantly changing under the influence of developments in human technology.[7] Yet, despite this constructedness of human perception, there is a level at which it becomes useful to distinguish a material, nonreflective politics of sense-perception from the way it is talked about (Van Dijk and Pels 1996). At this level, one can recognize ethnographically how a certain training of the senses and a certain construction of material culture come together to deflect, halt or change the rhythm of an ongoing social process (Seremetakis 1996). This happens, for instance, when the "stillness" of a souvenir or monument suddenly changes our everyday rhythm, to connect it with a memory or a history that is commonly absent; or simply when a cup of coffee reminds us of a necessary break in the work process (Seremetakis 1996: 12, 14–15). It also happens—and this will become more important below—when we are confronted with the difference from everyday life presented by strange museum objects or other curiosities.

This implies, however, that we recognize that materiality is not some quality distinguishing an object from a subject—that one should, in fact, question the slippage from the epistemological to the ontological notion of "object" which undergirds arguments like Miller's (1987). Also, it implies that the "material" is not necessarily on the receiving end of plastic power, a *tabula rasa* on which signification is conferred by humans: Not only are humans as material as the material they mold, but humans themselves are molded, through their sensuousness, by the "dead" matter with which they are surrounded.[8] It is in this way that I understand fetishism—which confers a measure of plastic power to things—as providing an argument against idealism. In a Hegelian perspective, fetishism was associated with sensuous determination, which could never attain categorical universality and therefore obstructed the liberation by *Geist* (Michasiw 1992: 80; Pietz 1993: 140). Such atheological worship, of a thing "untranssubstantiated into the signifier or allegory of a concept or ideal" could not be honoured with the name of "religion," just as Africa as a whole could not be admitted into "history" (Pietz 1993: 140; 1985: 7, note 10). Marx turned this on its head: Although he, too, identified fetishism as the "religion of sensuous desire," he thought it was closer to reality than monotheism (Pietz 1993: 140). This allowed the double movement of rehabilitating fetishism and reenchanting capitalism which I mentioned above, in an explicit anti-idealist critique.

Marx's formula of fetishism as the "religion of sensuous desire" recognized the notion of materiality implicit in fetishism, and took its threat to elevated spiritualities like Hegel's seriously. It recognizes that human passion—both of possessing and of being possessed, of greed and fancy—emerges within a material dialectic between human sensory routines and material objects. Marx himself shows how difficult it is, within this dialectic, to demarcate subject from object and determine the direction of their mutual influence:

> To be *sensuous*, i.e. to be real, is to be an object of sense, a sensuous object, and thus to have sensuous objects outside oneself, objects of one's sense perception. To be sensuous is to *suffer* (to be subjected to the actions of another). (quoted in Pietz 1993: 144)

This conception of materiality and reality no longer excludes the possibility brought forward by the discourse on fetish, that to be sensuous is "to be subjected to the actions of another *thing*."

The fetish, therefore, is both discursive creation and material reality (Pietz n.d.), something that emerged historically to designate a process in which objects constitute subjects. It points to an aesthetic sensibility in which the direction of mutual influence of human subject and thinglike object can be reversed; in which we cannot only think animistically, of anthropomorphized objects, of a spirit *in* matter, but also fetishistically, of human beings objectified by the spirit *of* the matters they encounter. The greed or fancy evoked by the fetish constitutes humans as sensuous, and therefore suffering, beings, as both subject and object of a historical configuration of desire in which neither humans nor objects possess a predetermined primacy.

However, the exploration of the possibilities which the discourse on fetish opens up is fairly recent, fed by, among other things, a more consistent attention paid to consumption, where the immanence of the object plays a more independent role than it does in the study of production (which privileges human agency) or exchange (which emphasizes the transcendence of a system of commensurability). Why this recent emergence of the materiality of things, and of the fetish in particular? The fetish has been a possibility in Occidental discourse since the seventeenth century. Since then, similarly hybrid objects like caste, totem, and taboo have arisen, without having an impact in the West equal to that of the fetish.[8a] The fetish somehow possesses an intellectual force that makes one wonder whether it is sufficiently served by a theoretical discussion like the preceding, that turns it into a general human trait (whether one calls this an aesthetic sensibility, or a cognitive process, or something else). Such theoretical exercises, although useful, will never "tame the beast" of fetishism (cf. Ellen 1988: 220), for such domestication implies that it is possible to arrest the continual, paradoxical movement that most uses of the concept entail. Any merely *intellectual* attempt to go "beyond" fetishism (see also Miller 1990) fails to recognize that fetishization is both "false" and functional, a form of misrecognition *as well as* recognition of reality; that it implies a "double attitude" (Freud 1950: 203) or "double consciousness" (Pietz 1985: 14) on the part of the fetishist. As (part of) an aesthetics of untranscended materiality, fetishism tells us to move in, rather than escape, the sensuous border zone between our selves and the things around us, between mind and matter. In the remainder of this paper, I will argue that the aesthetics that produced the—predominantly "false"—fetish was also the source of—predominantly "functional"—commonplaces of Western objectivity like "rarity" and "fact," and that this gives us a reason why the fetish has so preoccupied European minds. So let us shift from metaphor to metonymy and go back to the period in which the fetish first materialized.

SINGULARITY, CHANCE, AND THE SHUFFLE OF THINGS

The seventeenth century, wedged in between the first (De Marees 1604), and the most widely read ethnography of the West African fetish (Bosman 1702), was also the heyday of the curiosity cabinet and the object displayed in it, the so-called "curiosity" or "rarity." I think it can be argued that the rarity—in Francis Bacon's words, "whatsoever the hand of man by exquisite art or engine has made rare in stuff, form, or motion; whatsoever singularity, chance, and the shuffle of things hath produced; whatsoever Nature has wrought in things that want life and may be kept" (1594, quoted in Impey and MacGregor 1985: 1)—is the twin of the fetish: It was not just born at about the same time, but also duplicated its mercantile features, if with a European complexion. Since the rarity is an important source of the Western notion of objectivity, this comparison sets the fetish within the history of Western objectivity, and gives us another angle from which to consider the reasons why a majority of (post-) Enlightenment scholars shied away from its untranscended materiality.

Like the commodity (Appadurai 1986: 16), the rarity can only be understood as a thing in motion, a thing being "shuffled." Unlike the commodity, however, the rarity's motion makes it into a marvelous object, something that stands out as "curious" and "rare" from the everyday world of commodities, something that possesses a generic singularity over and against everyday commodities that we also found with the fetish. The rarity stands somewhere between a magical or miraculous substance like a relic—an object with power of its own—and the modern museum object, which represents some broader concept or reality other than itself. The rarity substantiates categorical transformations, things that confuse the everyday, like natural mimicry, nature's freaks, or exotic imports. The categorical mobility of the rarity is above all manifested in a specific performance: The arousal, in its spectators, of a sense of *wonder*, the feeling of being in the presence of the extraordinary, out-of-place, or radically different. This sense of wonder was an attitude as applicable to the marvels of natural magic, the meditations of Protestant pietist science, or the novelties of exotic artifacts, flora, or fauna.

Curiosity cabinets or *Wunderkammern* are often regarded as the origin of the museum, and of course they provided many museums now extant with a collection with which to start. According to stereotype, these "not-yet" museums were deficient in order and not as publicly accessible as one might have wished, yet "in terms of function, little has changed" (Impey and MacGregor 1985: 1). In such views, the curiosity cabinet is taken to be an ordered display of things, a "collection" which erases the context of origin of its objects, to make them dependent on principles of interior classification, organization, and categorization (Stewart 1993: 153). Such taxonomic collecting is thought to characterize the curiosity cabinet, even if some of its orderings were symbolic rather than functional, and for private display rather than public education (Olmi 1985: 5–7).[9] However, it is doubtful whether this story can be upheld. The museum order of arranging objects in such a way that they form a collection representing "history," "nationality," or "nature" only comes up as taxonomy in the eighteenth, and as series in the nineteenth century (Bennett 1994). It is characterized by a discourse of representation, based on the idea that the things displayed "stand for" something else (Mitchell 1991; cf. Stewart 1993: 152). In contrast, sixteenth- and seventeenth-century curiosity cabinets do not display an order or system of that kind (Olmi 1985: 15). Some argue they are "not even a vague or half-formed gesture" toward the museum (Mullaney 1983: 41). Instead, it might be better to avoid the museological and taxonomic discourse of representation as much as possible, and look upon the sixteenth- and seventeenth-century *Wunderkammer* with a theatrical metaphor, as a place for the production and performance of aesthetic difference.[10]

This may be clarified by the relic, for despite their mutual differences, both the rarity and the relic stand on one side of a divide that separates them from the museum object. The late Medieval relic collections of the great religious houses and the Renaissance curiosity cabinets were, in content at least, related: While the former included "secular" rarities like giants' teeth and bones, or natural marvels like "thunderstones" (prehistoric stone implements; MacGregor 1983b: 70–71), curiosity cabinets sometimes included relics and statues of saints (Daston 1994: 256; MacGregor 1983a: 21). This correspondence in content is reinforced by the fact that both relic and rarity were not meant to *represent* anything (if that is understood in terms of being a sign that stands for an absent referent). The relic did not represent but *was* the saint, and this identity proved itself by the performance of a miracle (Geary 1986). Similarly, a rarity demonstrated its identity by evoking "wonder" in its spectator, a feeling of being in the presence of the extraordinary and marvelous. The performance of the wondrous or marvelous also covered the miraculous, and that explains the presence of relics in a rarity collection, although the performance of wonder meant, as we shall see, much more than the kind of miracle commonly expected from a Medieval relic.

An important difference between the relic and the rarity is that the singularity of the former was personalized: The relic was, properly speaking, a saint. In contrast, the singularity of the rarity was, like that of the fetish, generic rather than individual. The rarity collections did not represent the world because "they ignored 99.9 percent of it in favor of the singular and anomalous" (Daston 1988: 458), and this departure from the accepted categories of the everyday was an important reason for their selection *as* rarities, objects meant to produce astonishment in their audience. Rarities and curiosities were not held together by a classification imposed on them before or after the fact, their character was based on their criteria of entrance in the collection: They were *selected* so as to "defy classification in principle" and "break the rules of the normal and predictable" (Daston 1988: 458). Rarity collections included magical substances like bezoar stones and unicorn horns (only later "disenchanted" as the horn of the narwal whale), substances expected to perform miraculous cures and regarded as preternatural, a category that was always "wondrous" but only *sometimes* a sign or representation of something else (like a religious lesson or satanic influence; Daston 1994: 256). But they also included collections of antiquities, meant to reproduce the atmosphere of the classics (Evans 1956); or works of art, for as long as genres like the still life—often depicting rarities—had not yet secured the nobility of painting (Foster 1993: 255); or the magic of mechanical innovations like the automatons of Inigo Jones and Salomon de Caus (Yates 1972: 39–40). Most importantly, they were dominated by exotic objects, first brought by Columbus and his successors to the cabinets of the Medicis and other Southern noblemen, and later by Dutch and English traders to those of Northern collectors.

The performance that the curiosity cabinet was meant to achieve, therefore, ranged from the magical through the classical, artistic, and scientific, to the exotic, and it was theatrical in the widest sense of the word. The sixteenth-century Italian, and the early seventeenth-century English curiosity cabinet and garden were private *theatrum naturae*, arranged according to the conventions of the art of memory (Laurencich-Minelli 1985: 19; also, Boström 1985: 100–101; Hunt 1985: 198). These conventions derived from the rhetorical practice of memorizing speeches by furnishing an imaginary architectural trajectory through a "memory palace" with the symbols needed for the narrative sequence of the speech (see Spence 1985; Yates 1966). The speech could then be given by passing through each room or corridor in sequence, retrieving the symbols that evoked that specific section of the speech required. Thus, the sections of the memory palace's display did not represent so much as produce an oral performance aimed at the persuasion of an audience; a presentation of otherness, rather than a sign of its absence. Similar productions of affect among the audience were what was aimed at in the itineraries produced by Italian and English landscape designs (Hunt 1985; see also Paulson 1975: 19ff.) It is significant that both John Tradescant's rarity collection and

Shakespeare's plays were thought to fall under the College of Revels, which controlled such performances. Both performed the "fullness of the world," the former in his house, The Ark, the latter in his theatre, The Globe (see Hunt 1985: 198; MacGregor 1983a: 20; Mullaney 1983).[11] The Ark and The Globe were "theatres of the world" (Yates 1969: Fucíková 1985) in the sense that theatre also meant "conspectus" or "collection" (Hunt 1985: 197).

As Frances Yates has shown, the idea of a "theatre of the world" was common to what she called the Rosicrucian Enlightenment, the work of a set of innovative practitioners of natural magic and Hermetic philosophy (1969; 1972). For these scholars, the art of memory symbolized the possibility of a knowledge of the world that could lead to truly miraculous performances (Yates 1966; 1969). However, the idea of the rarity collection as theatre goes beyond the sphere of the Rosicrucians, and connects them with Protestant pietist critics and the main protagonists of the "Scientific Revolution" that were otherwise critical of magic and its aura of demonic persuasion. Early cabinets in Italy and England were often the property of an aristocracy, or of the scientific, clerical or technical personnel they employed or protected, and often displayed a perception of the world in terms of Rosicrucianism. Later Protestant owners of curiosity cabinets in Northern Europe, like the members of the Royal Society, and Dutch and Scandinavian mayors, bankers, scientists, and merchants may or may not have been hostile to Rosicrucianism, but many of them substituted the architectonic imagery of the art of memory with the two-dimensional block- and tree-diagrams popularized by the philosopher Petrus Ramus and his followers (Stagl 1995; Yates 1966), an epistemological shift that was necessary for the idea about the representation of the world through taxonomy of later philosophers of "universal language" (Knowlson 1975; Slaughter 1982).[12]

However, until the urge towards taxonomy came into its own in the eighteenth century (along with the work of Linnaeus, Buffon, and the creation of the first museums), the idea of a theatre of the world, and more particularly, of the role of wonder as the essential performance of the rarity, was not displaced. Despite the growing suspicion of the leaders of the Scientific Revolution towards rarity collections and marvelous performances, major collections (such as those of the Royal Society and of the University of Leiden) were made more, rather than less marvelous, during the seventeenth century (Hunter 1985: 164–165; Olmi 1985: 14; Schupbach 1985: 171). Dutch collectors spoke as easily of the "theatre of wonders" of their cabinets as their Italian predecessors (Amsterdams Historisch Museum 1992:

89). The University of Leiden perfected a display that—though clearly opposite in intention to the magicians' *hubris* implicit in Rosicrucianism—did not in the least undermine the power of the rarity to arouse wonder: The *anatomie moralisée* of the summer display of skeletons and rarities in the anatomy theatre, where, instead of the winter performances of dissection, visitors could now be impressed by the lessons of worldly *vanitas* conveyed through these palpable images of mortality and human insignificance (Lunsing Scheurleer 1985: 120; Schupbach 1985: 169). The display was copied widely (Oxford, Hunter 1985: 160; Copenhagen, Schupbach 1985: 172). As the Dutch collector Swammerdam, writing to a Parisian colleague in 1678, shows, "moral anatomy," Protestant piety, and wonder went very well together:

> I present you herewith the Almighty Finger of God in the anatomy of a louse; in which you will find wonder piled upon wonder and God's Wisdom clearly exposed in one minute particle. (quoted in Lunsing Scheurleer 1985: 120)

Similarly, the wonders of God's creation were meditated upon by Protestants through, for instance, their collections of shells (Lunsing Scheurleer 1985: 116). And this piety did not prevent more mundane uses of wonder, as in Swammerdam's apothecary, where the display of tortoise shell, alligator skin, or rhino horn would advertise his mastery of the secrets of medicine (George 1985: 186). Such moral imagery of objectivity would endure well into the nineteenth century (Daston and Galison 1992). However, since morality was something following on wonder rather than inherent in it (according to Descartes and Spinoza: Greenblatt 1991: 24), such moralizing was already an attempt at controlling wonder's potential insubordination.

WONDER, FACT, AND FANCY: THE RARITY AS FETISH

In fact, the wonder aroused by the displays of theatres of the world was, from the late Medieval period up to the Enlightenment, regarded as a primary passion, and the fount of all knowledge. It was an experience that seemed "to resist recuperation, containment, ideological incorporation," and this may be why Descartes and Spinoza suspected the suspension of categories that it entailed, and the "freezing" or "paralysis" of the subject that an excess of wonder brought about (Greenblatt 1991: 17, 20, 24). Of course, the most perfect wonder was one that was also a material reality (1991: 36). Descartes' scepticism as far as rarity collections was concerned may be explained by his suspicion of an excess of wonder, yet he regarded wonder as the fount of all science (Daston 1988: 459). Francis Bacon suffered from a similar scepticism, yet he regarded the rarity as a necessary possession of the philosopher, for in his conception, the wondrous provided a novel sense of "fact."

It has been recognized that rarity collections are related to the Scientific Revolution in the sense that they raised the classificatory quandaries that bore fruit in the eighteenth-century work of Linnaeus, Buffon, and Lamarck (George 1985: 179). They provided a "granular view" of the world that facilitated the eighteenth-century disposition of things in the slots of a taxonomic scheme (Daston 1988: 462, 465). But the bizarre, rare and monstrous are not usually included in the history of science, despite the crucial role they play in the history of Western objectivity (Daston 1988: 453). Rarity collections, in bringing together automatons and natural freaks, helped assimilate art to nature and prepare for a mechanistic philosophy (Daston 1988: 464; Hunt 1985). Most important, they created a sense of factuality separate from scholastic "natural philosophy" (Daston 1988: 465). Despite Bacon's scepticism about the frivolity of the curiosities on display, he also regarded "singularity, chance, and the shuffle of things" as essential contributors to philosophy. He could use "marvels" in order to break down the distinctions between artificial and natural, and between natural and preternatural, and criticize natural philosophy by asking it to also explain the "singular instances" that, particularly in the case of the preternatural, it had defined as being out of its bounds (Daston 1994: 261).

> This is why the first scientific facts retailed in the annals of the Royal Society and the Paris Académie des Sciences were often such strange ones, for natural philosophy required the shock of repeated contact with the bizarre, the heteroclite, and the singular in order to sunder the age-old link between a "datum of experience" and "the conclusions that may be based on it"; in other words, to sunder facts from evidence. (Daston 1994: 261–62)

The cabinet of curiosities, that "museum of the preternatural" (1994: 256), provided that shock through wonder, aroused by preternatural freaks of nature, exotic objects from overseas, works of art, or the products of human technical or artistic virtuosity. Thus, rarities helped promote our familiar sense of the word "fact" as a datum of experience separate from the conclusions we may base on it (Daston 1991: 345). The word entered the English language in this sense in the early seventeenth century, when Bacon praised the rarity cabinet and De Marees disparaged the fetish.

Thus, the seventeenth-century career of the rarity suggests its pivotal role within an aesthetics of wonder that concentrated on the singular instance or anomalous "fact." This aesthetics dominated the thinking of a European intelligentsia that was rich, cosmopolitan, and prone to travel, and could, at times, disregard incipient divisions between magic and science or between religious denominations in the name of knowledge and curiosity (Daston 1988: 455).[13] While in the new science, one could talk of a "new creed of particulars" that opposed anomalies and singularities to the commonplaces of everyday life (or the *topoi* of the rhetoric of natural philosophy; Daston 1991: 341), in other fields of European culture, one can speak of an aesthetics of the fragment and the quotation that is often subsumed under "Mannerism" or "Baroque" (Bunn 1980; Olmi 1985: 9, 14). This aesthetics is apparent in the "metonymic or synecdochic tabulation of objects" of Dutch still life (Foster 1993: 259); its affinity with scientific culture appears in the label of an "art of describing" (Alpers 1983). James Bunn identifies this aesthetic as "mercantile," for to him it thrives on displacement, on the removal of a form or figure from its context or ground, to make it stand on its own. The curio collection is the soul of this aesthetic (Bunn 1980: 303). Like its artistic cousin, the seventeenth-century still life, it displays little taxonomic logic, but presents things as having a "power of their own" (Foster 1993: 255). Within this aesthetics, the things themselves call for an immediacy of description that cannot be assimilated to the narrative conception of art that emerged in fifteenth-century Italy and dominated art history's major analytic strategies (Alpers 1983: xix–xx). Mercantile aesthetics, whose "ultimate principle of order . . . may well be the imperial market" (Foster 1993: 259) presents things without a narrative connecting them, or, better, with the homogeneous and empty space of global exchange forming their only connection.

Hal Foster links this aesthetic to fetishism through the Dutch still life, but despite noting the historical convergence of ethnographies of the fetish and depictions and collections of "rare commodities," his analysis is largely metaphorical, treating the still life "as if" it is fetishistic. It is as important, however, to emphasize the metonymic, historical link between fetish and rarity—for which one has to acknowledge that the still life did not just depict rarities, but was in itself a rarity, to be included in a collection. James Clifford has hinted at this congruity of fetish and rarity when he argued that, in order to undo the effects of power of the taxonomic museological regime, we shall have to return to the museum objects their "lost status as fetishes" (1985: 244)—while he was patently referring to a museum, the Pitt Rivers, in which the status lost would rather be that of rarities, at least partly derived from the Tradescants' cabinet (Williamson 1983). Rarity and fetish are easily confused because both are objects "close to being sui generis" (Daston 1988: 456). Rarity, fetish, and still life all present objects with a "power of their own," displaced from the economies in which they functioned and that Dutch merchants encountered in the course of the expansion of the global market; objects that therefore appear "not alive, not dead, not useful, not useless," in "eerie animation" (Foster 1993: 257), promoting the conceit that they have a factual presence of their own. Just as the fetish emerged, as an object, out of the trading relationships established by Dutch merchants on the West African coast, so too was the rarity to a large extent the result of the import of exotic products and artefacts. As the rarity collector John Tradescant asked West African traders, he desired "Any Thing that is Strang" (Macgregor 1983b: 20), that is, anything that was set apart from existing systems of signification. Of course, a West African fetish was itself "strang" enough to be included in a rarity collection. But I am suggesting that rarity and fetish are twins—one bright, the other of a darker hue—born on the shipping routes frequented by European merchants, and christened as either outlandish fact or bizarre fancy. The rarity was "any thing that is strang"; the fetish—according to William Smith's account of 1744—"any thing [the Guinea Pagans] fancy" (Pietz 1987: 41). Both strangeness and fancy combine the positive power of an object to fascinate with its underdetermination by the systems of signification with which the subject is familiar.

My interpretation of the rarity's "wonder" as the inversion of the fetish's "fancy" is reinforced by the fact that, as "wonder" became subordinated to the taxonomic urge of the Enlightenment, the rarity was increasingly described like the fetish, in terms of "fancy," or related terms like "trifle" or "bric-a-brac." As "fact" separate from systems of interpretation became an accepted category, and the clamor for systems of classification of such facts increased, "wonder" became a threat rather than a liberation. No longer serving as an escape from scholasticism, the rarity's singularity became suspect, and redefined as a thing insufficiently controlled by subjective discipline. Already in the seventeenth century, suspicions towards the "fancy" that could lead to the erroneous acceptance of evidence from miracles accompanies attempts to naturalize the preternatural (Daston 1994: 265); just as Descartes and Spinoza suspected the "paralysis" of the subject which wonder could effect. The Enlightenment replaced wonder with doubt, and questioned the naming of things by drawing up ever-perfected systems of classification (which, among other things, declare fetishism, the religion of materiality, to be the most primitive expression of mankind). By the early nineteenth century, Samuel Coleridge could describe the often riotous category transgressions of the rarity and the curio as an "epistemology of fancy" (Bunn 1980: 319). "Fancy" was the way in which Victorian culture reacted to a form of collecting that was too passionate, too subject to the article collected, too *feminine* to measure up to the discipline and rigour of contemporary male collecting and its model, the museum. This "other" kind of collecting was domesticated in the "fancy fair" (Dolin 1993). Even Bunn, in describing the aesthetics of the rarity, mostly adopts a depreciative tone, the style being one of "bric-a-brac," "randomly purchased knickknacks," a "prodigious yet patternless" Baroque (1980: 303) that apparently still threatens the subjective discipline of art history, just as its kind of collecting was felt as a threat overburdening the island by late eighteenth-century British intellectuals (1980: 316). Present-day museologists' negative assessment of the rarity cabinet, as a museum deficient in order, can be traced to this eighteenth-century suspicion of the unordered object.

But note that such a negative assessment of a perception of and dealing with objects that is "developing out of the hands" of seventeenth and eighteenth century artists and thinkers (1980: 303), that this disparagement of an *uncontrollable* aesthetics, builds on this aesthetics itself. It does not deny its truth as much as it displaces it by the idealism of an epistemology of classification. The threat of mercantile aesthetics may have had to be contained in such a way because "wonder" is such an easily democratized attitude, one difficult to discipline within any "style" or "taste." To restore hierarchy, wonder had to be domesticated as kitsch, "fancy," or "bric-a-brac," objects collected—at home, by women and children—without order or use. But as such, these unordered objects still recall a period in which their riotous independence was functional; when the falsity of fetish and fancy emerged together with the functionality of rarity and fact, and the displacements effected by the globalizing market made them all appear as *Dinge an sich*, with an "eerie animation" of their own.

Fetish and the Limits of Representation

Thus, we see the fetish is not the only substantiation of the spirit of matter: Its emergence coincides with that of "fact" and "rarity," two other ways of discussing an untranscended materiality. Moreover, it seems this spirit of matter is largely released by the dominance of market relationships. In the same tentative and exploratory mode of the rest of this paper, one might suggest that this is also a step towards explaining why consumption and fetishism are again at the center of attention in cultural and social theory, for this resurgence seems to coincide with global developments that have given market ideology a new lease of life. However, this paper was meant to suggest that the fetish is not merely a symptom of, but also a challenge to some of the ways of thinking that characterize the present; just as, at other moments in its genealogy, the fetish threatened to disrupt everyday processes of human signification. In particular, it sits uneasily with the new magic of constructionism, which tends to treat the social as nothing but a human product and to see the materiality of social life as just an empty carrier or representation of human intention and artifice. The fetish, or the spirit of matter in general, militates against this idealism and suggests a counterbalancing materiality. The fetish provides an alternative to those theories that say everything is representation, if representation is understood as a process in which a material signifier is made to stand for an absent signified defined as a mental category or human process of construction. Already at the point of its first emergence, the fetish's material *presence* was opposed to the idol as *representation* of a (false) spirit (Pietz 1993: 131). In conclusion, I want to suggest that the fetish still occupies a similar position today: that of an occult counterpoint that marks the limits of a dominant discourse of representation.

Of course, I do not deny that fetish can itself be a representation. It has, for example, long "stood for" something typically "African" (whether "religion," or something pre-religious in its stead). Twentieth-century anthropological consensus, however, has branded this representation of Africa as false, since it did not and does not accord with West African practice (cf. MacGaffey 1994).[14] Pietz's genealogy of the fetish has shown that its discourse does not represent (West) Africa. Rather, it marks "a space of cultural revolution" (1985: 11). The fetish, like the rarity, indicates a crossing of categorical boundaries, a border zone where one cannot expect the stability of meaning that is routine in everyday life. Even more: Whereas in everyday life, we can usually supply the meaning of things, by giving either their use, or a description of their place in life, such a distinction between the thing and its meaning, symbol and referent, or representation and represented is subverted by fetishistic relationships: The fetish erases the distinction between signifier and signified on which the present-day discourse of representation is based (Ellen 1988: 226). It is too powerful a presence to be a mere re-presentation of something else.

The discourse of representation is idealist in so far as it maintains the Saussurian distinction between a material signifier and an ideal signified, and assumes the former is given meaning by the latter. Such a theory makes human intention and artifice—communication on the model of human consciousness—a prerequisite of signification, excluding all other forms of natural interaction (cf. Eco 1976: 14–15). Saussure *re*discovered this relationship of material signifier and ideal signified, for it was forged in the seventeenth, and became dominant by the eighteenth century (Foucault 1973: 67). This emergence of the modern concept of the sign is directly related to the systems of classification that subsumed the formerly unruly Baconian "facts" and that helped to label collections gathered without such classifications as "fanciful." The prime example of the modern concept of the sign's binary relationship with the signified was the map or diagram (Foucault 1973: 64), and this shows its affinity with the "diagrammatic reduction of thought" characteristic of eighteenth-century taxonomic schemes (Fabian 1983: 116).[15] The modern discourse of representation, the modern concept of the sign, and the systems of classification that subsumed the uncontrolled objects released by market relationships, were all products of the Enlightenment. This is the historical provenance of the systems of meanings that, in Appadurai's words, "encode things with significance" (1986: 5), the "necessary condition" of the primacy of human traffic that Appadurai mentioned as the context for his methodologically fetishist counterpoint.

The aesthetics of order and taxonomy that displaced the fetish and the rarity to the margins of occidental thought has made them into occult qualities, things that live hidden lives in demonic or domesticated form. Yet they are necessary for the order of representation to pretend to extend itself over a surface of chaos that needs to be disciplined. But this universal extension of the sign "precludes even the possibility of a theory of signification" (Foucault 1973: 65). The fetish foregrounds the basic problem of signification that the idealist theory of representation has attempted to submerge in the binary model of the material signifier and the ideal signified: that our only way to know of a distinction between material and ideal, or actual and virtual, is through an actual material sensation. On the one hand, the fetish is a material presence that does not represent but "takes one's fancy," making us suffer sensuously. On the other, it is only fanciful to us because it reminds us of a displacement and signals a loss or denial. Thus, the fetish shows the limits of representation by disrupting the continuity of reference and replacing it by a substitution (not a re-presentation but a presentation of something else). Yet at the same time it asks how we can know the substituted by the signals emitted from what substitutes for it; or how we can know the virtual if that can only be conveyed through the material itself. This is the poststructuralist question of how we know of "codes" or "encoding" *without* such entities or operations being, practically speaking, present. It may also be the first step that makes a theory of signification possible.

NOTES

This essay was written while I enjoyed the hospitality of the University of Michigan's International Institute and Department of Anthropology as Netherlands Visiting Professor for the 1995 fall term. I thank Fernando Coronil and Nick Dirks for their critical comments on an earlier draft, the participants in the "Border Fetishisms" conference for their lively reactions to the presentation of the paper, and Patricia Spyer for her acute editorial remarks. I alone can be held responsible for the result.

1. Such essentializing movements, in which a practical relationship between unequal (groups of) people is translated into an "essential" difference between subject and object, are constitutive to ethnography. In order to understand its operation, however, one has to acknowledge that ethnography was a genre of and for colonial relationships from the inception of early modern colonization and trade (Pels and Salemink 1994; 1998).

2. See also Daniel Miller's account of Marx's idea of objectification as rupture (1987: ch.3).

3. "If they can see the maintenance or the increase of production under capitalism as somehow bound up with the devil and thereby make a fetish of the productive process, do we not also have our own form of fetishism in which we attribute to commodities a reality so substantial that they acquire the appearance of natural beings, so natural in fact that they appear to take on a life of their own?" (Taussig 1980: 30).

4. "Fetish could originate only in conjunction with the emergent artic-ulation of the commodity form that defined itself within and against the so-cial values and religious ideologies of *two* different types of non-capitalist society" (Pietz 1985: 7: my emphasis), that is, the Iberian, Catholic Christian, and the West African.

5. As the work of Appadurai shows, the implication of this distinction is to avoid the question of materiality in favor of a concern with commodity and use values.

6. "The importance of this physicality of the artifact derives from its ability thereby to act as a bridge, not only between the mental and physical worlds, but also, more unexpectedly, between consciousness and the uncon-scious" (Miller 1987: 99). One might add that objects can also transfer form—and consequently, signification—from one historically or culturally distinct context to another.

7. Cf. the changes in human sensory regimes under the influence of the technologies of the linear perspective, the lens, the camera (Jay 1993), or the telephone (Van Beek 1996: 8).

8. "Dead" in this context, means little more than "without intention," but in semiotics, intention is no longer regarded as a prerequisite for signifi-cation (Eco 1976: 14–15).

8a. The complete genealogies of these concepts on the lines of what William Pietz did for the fetish remain to be written, but they will surely reveal that they are similarly placed in a context of "cultural revolution": caste, as an originally Portuguese term inflected by colonialism in India and orientalist imagery to denote a human group other than class or no-bility (see Dirks 1992); totem, as a North American term domesticated by anthropology to denote an improper understanding of the relationship be-tween the human and natural realms; and taboo, as an Oceanic term in-flected to give European languages a nonlegal and nonreligious notion of prohibition.

9. Susan Stewart's otherwise brilliant observations on the collection (1993: 151ff.) fail to recognize the difference between taxonomic collections and curiosity cabinets; the latter are closer to the collections of the pack rat (1993: 153) than to those governed by a "narrative of interiority." See also below, on the "entrance criteria" of the curio collection.

10. This is a paraphrase of Steven Mullaney's description of the curio cabinet in terms of a "rehearsal" of cultural difference (1983: 42, 48). De-spite a number of agreements in our argument, I have avoided the term "re-hearsal," to counter any association with a preexisting script being interpreted. However, if I understand Mullaney rightly, he, too, means a repetition of the same production, rather than the representation of an ab-sent original.

11. The rarity collection of the Rosicrucian Jesuit Kircher in Rome was actually meant to recreate the contents of the Ark (George 1985: 186); a shop for rarities in Paris was called "Noahs-Arke" (Macgregor 1983b: 91).

12. Given the general association of magic with Catholicism, Rosicrucianism might be expected to have found few adherents in Northern Europe. However, the origin of the term Rosicrucian at least needs to be sought in Reformation Germany (Yates 1972), and while many Northern rarity collectors were Protestants (such as the Dutch: Lunsing Scheurleer 1985: 117; Amsterdams Historisch Museum 1992), they were not necessarily hostile to Rosicrucian thinking (like the Swede Hainhofer (Boström 1985). Hostility to Rosicrucianism was more likely to be found among those scholars who wanted to replace the magical worldview of Rosicrucianism by taxonomic thinking (Knowlson 1975; Vickers 1984).

13. See also Marie Louise Pratt on the "continental, transnational aspirations of European science" in the early eighteenth century (Pratt 1992: 25).

14. To interpret Freud's theory of fetishism as saying first of all that the fetish represents the mother's phallus is, I feel, as silly as saying that the fetish is a typically "African" thing (cf. Freud 1950: 199).

15. Another important model is the disparity between the book and the text, where material form is easily separated from ideal content in a similarly binary model (cf. Stewart 1993: 22–23).

REFERENCES

Alpers, Svetlana (1983) *The Art of Describing: Dutch Art in the Seventeenth Century*. Chicago: The University of Chicago Press.

Amsterdams Historisch Museum (1992) *De wereld binnen handbereik. Nederlandse kunst- en rariteitenverzamelingen, 1585–1735*. Zwolle: Waanders Uitgevers/Amsterdams Historisch Museum.

Appadurai, Arjun (1986) "Introduction: Commodities and the Politics of Value, in: A. Appadurai (ed.), *The Social Life of Things: Commodities in Cultural Perspective*. Cambridge: Cambridge University Press, pp. 3–63.

Bennett, Tony (1994) "The Exhibitionary Complex, in N. Dirks, G. Eley, S. Ortner (eds.), *Culture/Power/History: A Reader in Contemporary Social Theory*. Princeton University Press, pp. 123–54.

Boström, Hans-Olof (1985) "Philipp Hainhofer and Gustavus Adolphus's *Kunstschrank* in Uppsala," in: O. Impey and A. MacGregor (eds.), *The Origin of Museums: The Cabinet of Curiosities in Sixteenth- and Seventeenth- Century Europe*. Oxford: Clarendon Press, pp. 90–101.

Bunn, James H. (1980) "The Aesthetics of British Mercantilism," *New Literary History* 11: 303–21.

Classen, Constance (1993) *Worlds of Sense: Exploring the Senses in History and Across Cultures*. London and New York: Routledge.

Clifford, James (1985) "Objects and Selves," in: G.W. Stocking (ed.), *Objects and Others: Essays on Museums and Material Culture*. History of Anthropology vol. 3. Madison: University of Wisconsin Press.

Daston, Lorraine J. (1988) "The Factual Sensibility," *Isis* 79: 452–70.

———. (1991) "Baconian Facts, Academic Civility, and the Prehistory of Objectivity," *Annals of Scholarship* 8: 337–363.

———. (1994) "Marvelous Facts and Miraculous Evidence in Early Modern Europe," in: J. Chandler, A.I. Davidson, H. Harootunian (eds.), *Questions of Evidence: Proof, Practice and Persuasion across the Disciplines*. Chicago and London: The University of Chicago Press.

Daston, Lorraine J., and Peter Galison (1992) "The Image of Objectivity," *Representations* 40: 81–128.

Dirks, Nicholas B. (1992) "Castes of Mind," *Representations* 37: 56–78.

———. (1996) "Reading Culture: Anthropology and the Textualization of India," in: E. Valentine Daniel (ed.), *Culture/Contexture: Explorations in Anthropology and Literary Studies*. Berkeley: University of California Press.

———, and Dolin, Tim (1993) "*Cranford* and the Victorian Collection," *Victorian Studies* 36: 179–206.

Eagleton, Terry (1990) *The Ideology of the Aesthetic*. Oxford: Blackwell.

Eco, Umberto (1976) *A Theory of Semiotics*. Bloomington: Indiana University Press.

Ellen, Roy (1988) "Fetishism," *Man* (N.S.) 23: 213–35.

Evans, Joan (1956) *A History of the Society of Antiquaries*. Oxford: Oxford University Press for the Society of Antiquaries.

Fabian, Johannes (1983) *Time and the Other: How Anthropology Makes its Object*. New York: Columbia University Press.

Foster, Hal (1993) "The Art of Fetishism: Notes on Dutch Still Life," in: E. Apter and W. Pietz (eds.), *Fetishism as Cultural Discourse*. Ithaca and London: Cornell University Press.

Foucault, Michel (1973) *The Order of Things: An Archaeology of the Human Sciences*. New York: Vintage Books (orig. French 1970).

Freud, Sigmund (1950) "Fetishism," in: *Collected Papers* vol. V, ed. J. Strachey. London: The Hogarth Press.

Fucíková, Eliska (1985) "The Collection of Rudolf II at Prague: Cabinet of Curiosities or Scientific Museum?", in: O. Impey and A. MacGregor (eds.),
*The Origin of Museums: The Cabinet of Curiosities in Sixteenth- and Seven-
teenth-Century Europe.* Oxford: Clarendon Press, pp. 51–61.

Geary, Patrick (1986) "Sacred Commodities: The Circulation of Medieval
Relics," in: A. Appadurai (ed.), *The Social Life of Things: Commodities in
Cultural Perspective.* Cambridge: Cambridge University Press, 169–91.

George, Wilma (1985) "Alive or Dead: Zoological Collections in the Seven-
teenth Century," in: O. Impey and A. MacGregor (eds.), *The Origin of
Museums: The Cabinet of Curiosities in Sixteenth- and Seventeenth-Century
Europe.* Oxford: Clarendon Press, 179–88.

Greenblatt, Stephen (1991) *Marvelous Possessions: The Wonder of the New
World.* Chicago: The University of Chicago Press.

Howes, David (1991) *The Varieties of Sensory Experience: A Sourcebook in the Anthropology of the Senses.* Toronto: University of Toronto Press.

Hunt, John Dixon (1985) "*Curiosities* to Adorn *Cabinets* and *Gardens*," in: O.
Impey and A. MacGregor (eds.), *The Origin of Museums: The Cabinet of
Curiosities in Sixteenth- and Seventeenth-Century Europe.* Oxford: Claren-
don Press.

Hunter, Michael (1985) "The Cabinet Institutionalized: The Royal Society's
'Repository' and its Background," in: O. Impey and A. MacGregor
(eds.), *The Origin of Museums: The Cabinet of Curiosities in Sixteenth- and
Seventeenth-Century Europe.* Oxford: Clarendon Press.

Impey, Oliver, and Arthur MacGregor (1985) "Introduction," in: O. Impey
and A. MacGregor (eds.), *The Origin of Museums: The Cabinet of Curiosities in Sixteenth- and Seventeenth-Century Europe.* Oxford: Clarendon
Press.

Jay, Martin (1993) *Downcast Eyes: The Denigration of Vision in French Twentieth-
Century Thought.* Berkeley: University of California Press.

Knowlson, James (1975) *Universal Language Schemes in England and France
1600–1800.* Toronto and Buffalo: University of Toronto Press.

Kopytoff, Igor (1986) "The Cultural Biography of Things: Commoditization
as Process," in: A. Appadurai (ed.), *The Social Life of Things: Commodities in Cultural Perspective.* Cambridge: Cambridge University Press, p.
64–91.

Lunsing Scheurleer, Th.H. (1985) "Early Dutch Cabinets of Curiosities," in: O.
Impey and A. MacGregor (eds.), *The Origin of Museums: The Cabinet of
Curiosities in Sixteenth- and Seventeenth-Century Europe.* Oxford: Claren-
don Press.

MacGaffey, Wyatt (1994) "African Objects and the Idea of Fetish," *Res* 25: 123–31.

MacGregor, Arthur (1983a) "The Tradescants as Collectors of Rarities," in A. MacGregor (ed.), *Tradescant's Rarities: Essays on the Foundation of the Ashmolean Museum.* Oxford: Clarendon Press, pp. 17–23.

———. (1983b) "Collectors and Collections of Rarities in the Sixteenth and Seventeenth Centuries," in A. MacGregor (ed.), *Tradescant's Rarities: Essays on the Foundation of the Ashmolean Museum.* Oxford: Clarendon Press, pp. 70–97.

Michasiw, Kim Ian (1992) "Nine Revisionist Theses on the Picturesque," *Representations* 38: 76–100.

Miller, Daniel (1987) *Material Culture and Mass Consumption.* Oxford: Blackwell.

———. (1990) "Persons and Blue Jeans: Beyond Fetishism," *Etnofoor* 3: 97–111.

———. (1996) "Why It's Safer to Build on Concrete Than Epistemology. A Comment on 'On Materiality' by Gosewijn van Beek," *Etnofoor* 9: 25–27.

Mitchell, Timothy (1991) *Colonizing Egypt.* Berkeley: University of California Press.

Mullaney, Steven (1983) "Strange Things, Gross Terms, Curious Customs: The Rehearsal of Cultures in the Late Renaissance," *Representations* 3: 40–67.

Olmi, Giuseppe (1985) "Science-Honour-Metaphor: Italian Cabinets of the Sixteenth and Seventeenth Centuries," in: O. Impey and A. MacGregor (eds.), *The Origin of Museums: The Cabinet of Curiosities in Sixteenth- and Seventeenth-Century Europe.* Oxford: Clarendon Press, 5–16.

Paulson, Ronald (1975) *Emblem and Expression: Meaning in English Art of the Eighteenth Century.* Cambridge, Mass.: Harvard University Press.

Pels, Peter (1998) *The Microphysics of Colonial Contact: Interactions between Catholic Missionaries and Waluguru in Late Colonial Tanganyika.* Chur Switzerland: Harwood Academic Publishers (forthcoming).

———. (1998) "Introduction: Locating the Colonial Subjects of Anthropology," in: P. Pels and O. Salemink (eds.), *Colonial Subjects: Essays in the Practical History of Anthropology.* Ann Arbor: University of Michigan Press (forthcoming).

Pels, Peter, and Oscar Salemink (1994) "Introduction: Five Theses on Ethnography as Colonial Practice," *History and Anthropology* 8: 1–34.

Pietz, William (1985) "The Problem of the Fetish, I," *Res* 9: 5–17.

———. (1987) "The Problem of the Fetish, II: The Origin of the Fetish," *Res* 13 (1987): 23–45.

———. (1988) "The Problem of the Fetish, IIIa: Bosman's Guinea and the Enlightenment Theory of Fetishism," *Res* 16: 105–23.

———. (1993) "Fetishism and Materialism: The Limits of Theory in Marx," in: E. Apter and W. Pietz (eds.), *Fetishism as Cultural Discourse*. Ithaca and London: Cornell University Press.

———. (1998) "The Fetish of Civilization: Sacrifical Blood and Monetary Debt," in: P. Pels and O. Salemink (eds.), *Colonial Subjects: Essays in the Practical History of Anthropology*. Ann Arbor: University of Michigan Press (forthcoming).

Pratt, Marie Louise (1992) *Imperial Eyes: Travel Writing and Transculturation*. London/New York: Routledge.

Schupbach, William (1985) "Some Cabinets of Curiosities in European Academic Institutions," in: O. Impey and A. MacGregor (eds.), *The Origin of Museums: The Cabinet of Curiosities in Sixteenth- and Seventeenth-Century Europe*. Oxford: Clarendon Press.

Seremetakis, C. Nadia (1996) *The Senses Still: Perception and Memory as Material Culture in Modernity*. Chicago: The University of Chicago Press.

Slaughter, Mary M. (1982) *Universal Languages and Scientific Taxonomy in the Seventeenth Century*. Cambridge: Cambridge University Press.

Spence, Jonathan (1984) *The Memory Palace of Matteo Ricci*. London: Faber and Faber.

Stagl, Justin (1995) *A History of Curiosity: The Theory of Travel, 1550–1800*. Chur Switzerland: Harwood Academic Publishers.

Stewart, Susan (1993) *On Longing: Narratives of the Miniature, the Gigantic, the Souvenir, the Collection*. Durham: Duke University Press.

Taussig, Michael (1980) *The Devil and Commodity Fetishism in South America*. Chapel Hill: The University of North Carolina Press.

Van Beek, Gosewijn (1996) "On Materiality," *Etnofoor* 9: 5–24.

Van Dijk, Rijk, and Peter Pels (1996) "Contested Authorities and the Politics of Perception: Deconstructing the Study of Religion in Africa," in: T.O. Ranger and R.P. Werbner (eds.), *Postcolonial Identities in Africa*. London: Zed Books, pp. 245–70.

Vickers, Brian (1984) "Analogy Versus Identity: The Rejection of Occult Symbolism, 1580–1680," in: B. Vickers (ed.), *Occult and Scientific Mentalities in the Renaissance*. Cambridge: Cambridge University Press.

Welch, Martin (1983) "The Ashmolean as Described by its Earliest Visitors," in A. MacGregor (ed.), *Tradescant's Rarities: Essays on the Foundation of the Ashmolean Museum.* Oxford: Clarendon Press, pp. 59–69.

Williamson, Lynne (1983) "Ethnological Specimens in the Pitt Rivers Museum Attributed to the Tradescant Collection," in A. MacGregor (ed.), *Tradescant's Rarities: Essays on the Foundation of the Ashmolean Museum.* Oxford: Clarendon Press, pp. 338–45.

Yates, Francis Amelia (1966) *The Art of Memory.* London: Routledge and Kegan Paul.

———. (1969) *Theatre of the World.* London: Routledge and Kegan Paul.

———. (1972) *The Rosicrucian Enlightenment.* London, Boston, and Henley: Routledge and Kegan Paul.

5

Stealing Happiness: Shoplifting in Early Nineteenth-Century England

Adela Pinch

Shoplifting is a fetishist's crime. When those who can afford to pay submit to the compulsion to steal from a store, they have fallen under the spell of the object, believing that it holds out the promise of a happiness that is both below and beyond price. Both fetishism and shoplifting are ways of casting value differently, as both the fetishist and the shoplifter proclaim that the object's value is a secret known only to themselves. Both involve a redetermination of the relations between subjects and objects, raising questions about how a thing comes to be legitimately one's own. Psychoanalysis conceives of kleptomania as a form of female fetishism: The kleptomaniac pockets fascinating objects to compensate for a gap within herself she both knows and doesn't know is there.[1] And, as cultural critics have come to rehabilitate "perversions" as symptoms of culture rather than of pathology, as ways of knowing rather than as mistakes, kleptomania has borrowed some of the glamour with which the concept of fetishism has recently been invested. For Leslie Camhi, for example, writing about the literature of the late nineteenth-century department store, female kleptomania is a critical activity, stealing the cover off the fraud of femininity itself:

> It is an entire social order that the female kleptomaniac calls into question by her actions. It is, perhaps, this very gamble with an entire social identity that compels her, the unconscious need to establish the fraudulence of inherited wealth and social position. . . . Thus the difference between buying and stealing, or between normal women and thieves, becomes increasingly attenuated, because the commodities that are bought or stolen are used to produce and maintain the permanent fraud of feminine sexuality, the deception of the feminine masquerade. . . . Femininity is always already stolen, a dissimulated mask, veil, or fiction of difference that functions, like fetishism, through the substitutional logic of the same. (1993: 38–39)

Just as some recent theorists of fetishism have revalorized practice of fetishism not as error but as a way of reevaluating the meaning of value, so Camhi—as well as other scholars of thieving—redefines theft not as a transgression against the world of consumption but as that which discloses its true meaning.[2] Shoplifting, in this view, is shopping's logical extension. By shopping the wrong way, the shoplifter gets it right.

This essay shares this view, and seeks to complicate further our sense of what the transgression of shoplifting might tell us about the happiness of things in a consumer culture. To do so, it focuses on an earlier conversation about the meaning of genteel theft in England from roughly 1800 to 1840. This conversation suggests that stories of shoplifting—stories of the luxury good's irregular crossing of the borders between shop and street and home—evokes other borders: not only the national borders that aided and impeded the luxury of late Georgian England, not only the borders between genders, but also borders between social classes. The essay will proceed by describing a context in which the stolen good—most prominently a piece of lace— attracted to itself and to the players in its drama a range of emotions: sympathy, anxiety, contempt, dread. It will involve going back and forth between things and persons, between shoplifters, shopkeepers, and the goods themselves, and between real and fictional people. I will begin with some information about the classification of genteel theft in early nineteenth-century England, and end with a story by Thomas de Quincey, romantic literature's patron saint of all forms of excessive consumption. His wild, gothic novella, "The Household Wreck," treats the story of a stolen piece of lace as a matter of life and death, and wonders how we make sense of the material thing.

I

Cultural historians have written about the emergence of the kleptomania diagnosis in the context of the rise of the *fin-de-siecle* department store (O'Brien 1983; Abelson 1989). However, the notion that a
propensity to shoplift amongst those who can legitimately afford to
pay might be a moral disorder rather than a crime, a compulsion
rather than a choice, goes back at least to the early nineteenth century. A stealing mania was codified by a Swiss doctor, André Matthey,
as *klopémanie* in 1816, and by 1830 the concept of kleptomania was
current enough that the British literary periodical the *New Monthly
Magazine* could note in passing that "instances of this cleptomania
are well known to have happened in this country, even among the
rich and noble" (1830: 15). (The term "shop-lift" itself appeared in
slang dictionaries as early as the 1670's). Early to mid-nineteenth-
century medical literature categorized such instances as species of
moral insanity—perplexing cases, in that they often seemed to occur
in persons who seemed otherwise neither mad nor criminal. The subjects of the medical narratives—often, though not always, women,
but always well-to-do—often lamented their unaccountable propensity: Things simply seemed to follow them home. For example,

> A gentleman, having an independent income of £2,000 a year, was at
> Scarborough. In passing through one of the streets, he saw a friend
> with his daughter, in a shop; he joined them. The party then left the
> shop together. In a short time the mercer waited on the father of the
> lady, and regretted much to state, that his daughter had, no doubt by
> mistake, taken a silk shawl from the counter of his shop. The father
> contradicted the charge, and inquired who was in the shop during
> the time when the shawls were exposed. The reply was "no one but
> himself, the lady, and gentleman." The shopkeeper accompanied the
> gentleman to his friend's residence, in the hall of which he found
> the great coat worn in the morning, and in one of the pockets was the
> lost shawl. . . . This theft could not have been committed for the pur-
> pose of gain, nor could he have stolen it for use. (Prichard 1847:
> 155–56; see also Prichard 1835: 28–53)

So common were tales of this kind that the *Times* asserted in 1855
that "everyone who is acquainted with London society could at once
furnish a dozen names of ladies who have been notorious for ab-
stracting articles of trifling value from the shops where they habitually dealt" (quoted in Bucknill, 1863: 264).

Such anecdotes were most often in the service of the growing field of forensic medicine, which was charged with helping justices determine whether these cases deserved criminal prosecution—a particularly vexing issue, because the penalties for conviction for shoplifting were severe. Until 1820, the punishment for stealing any goods valued at five shillings or more out of a shop was execution. The early nineteenth-century campaign to reform the Shop-lifting Act was waged against a bitter opposition that successfully blocked attempts to abolish capital punishment in shoplifting cases in the House of Lords in 1810, 1813, and 1816; and after 1820 (and after 1826, when further reforms were instituted), the penalty for shoplifting even goods of small value was still imprisonment or transportation. The enforcement of these draconian laws was highly variable, often tempered by the leniency or sympathy of the jury, who could, for example, render a defendant guilty of a lesser charge by simply declaring that the actual value of the goods stolen was in their view less than five shillings.[3]

It was, predictably, the cases of genteel thieves that were most likely to attract a diagnosis of moral mania rather than a criminal conviction. Contemporaries murmured that the rich and feminine got diagnosed while the poor hung. However, genteel shoplifters did get convicted, to the pained ambivalence of middle-class onlookers. Here is Harriet Martineau on a convict of the 1820's:

> It should appear to a stranger from another hemisphere a strange thing that we should boast of our Christian civilization, while we had such a spectacle as was seen even at a later time than this. —An elderly lady, of good station and fortune, might be seen on the treadwheel in Cold Bath Fields prison, in the jail-dress, and with her hair cut close—for the offense of shoplifting. It is difficult to write this fact; and it must be painful to read it; but the truths of the time must be told. (Martineau 1849–50, 2: 84)

"Justice," she moralizes, was sometimes "brought to persons of property and standing as well as the poor":

> A lady was convicted for shoplifting, who actually carried on her person, at the moment of the theft, the sum of £8,000 in bank-notes and India bonds. She underwent her punishment. In this case, if insanity had existed, it must have been proved. All parties would have been too happy to admit the plea. It was no doubt one of those cases of strong propensity for which neither our education, law, nor justice

makes provision. It is a case which makes the heart bleed . . . . the wretched woman of wealth suffered as if she had been a hungry mother, snatching a loaf for famishing children at home. (Martineau 1849–50, 3: 136)

In Martineau's accounts of the convictions of genteel shoplifters, we hear an uneasy assent. She is indignant when two respectable young ladies collude with the prosecution and are acquitted (see 3: 137); yet in the cases of successful prosecution she is mournfully at a loss: neither education, law, nor justice makes provisions for such cases. Genteel shoplifting posed an interpretive dilemma.

There are ways, of course, that we can interpret shoplifting in nineteenth-century England as occupying a space somewhere outside of crime and madness. We might begin by following the lead of physician John Bucknill, who started to describe that space in his own terms in an article on the abuse of the kleptomania defense. Surveying the literature on kleptomania, weighing it against the purported frequency of shoplifting-addiction amongst English ladies, Buchnill has difficulty consigning most cases either to crime or to insanity. "But there is another aspect to this matter," he argues:

> The struggle for existence in the middle, and even in the upper classes of our complex social system, combined with the prevailing fashion of an emulative and showy expenditure, make the sense of want felt keenly in many an English home, where no traces of vulgar poverty are discernable.

Shoplifting of this kind has nothing to do with vulgar poverty, but it speaks to other kinds of felt indigence, other needs. Pinpointing the pressures of "emulative . . . expenditure," Buchnill lays the blame at the doorstep of a society of conspicuous consumption: Veblen *avant la lettre*. He goes on with a series of rhetorical questions:

> And how are they tempted? How are women, whose education has been one system of skillful parade, who have been trained to derive a vast proportion of their daily happiness from that most personal of the aesthetic arts, the cultivation of dress, how are they tempted to possess themselves of its material? Are they not stimulated to covet its possession by every ingenious device which the mind of man or of woman can devise, by streets of gorgeous shops, touted in every possible manner by the most pertinacious inducements, and almost persecutions to buy, buy, buy; so that it has at last become the custom of the town-

bred Englishwoman of the present day to spend no inconsiderable portion of her time . . . in the new and peculiar duty of life called "shopping." Can we be surprised that when the means fail to gratify the desires thus stimulated . . . that in some instances the desire of the eye should prove too strong for the moral sense? It is painful and humiliating if these things are so, but it is not wonderful that they should be so; and on the whole we can find more pity for the poor woman who purloins a piece of lace, without which she thinks she will be absolutely not fit to be seen, than for the smirking fellow who has caught her in his haberdashery trap. (Bucknill 1863: 264)

The doctor's sympathy, his refusal to pathologize "the shop-lifting ladies" (263), his insistence on a social context that turns all women into thieves and fetishists are all striking; and all the more so for the ways he anticipates the agoraphobic explanations of feminist historians of shopping, who similarly point to the burdens and restrictions consumer culture places on women. But it is precisely such echoes that should make us pay attention to where Buchnill's sympathies do *not* lie: the "smirking" figure of the shopkeeper. For it is with this figure that some of the historical specificity of shoplifting in early nineteenth-century England can be found.

Shoplifting was—as we shall see in the following sections—a very intimate crime. The image of the department store shopper who can easily pass through the display shelves of merchandise that seductively calls out to her—as in Dreiser's *Sister Carrie*—is out of place in this period. Open shelves were unknown until the late nineteenth century; a customer's access to all goods, in shops large and small, was mediated by the shopkeeper behind his (and it often was, even in women's shops, his) counter. Thus shoplifting involved not a magical encounter between shopper and object of desire, but a triangle of desire between shopper, object, and shopkeeper. Professional thieves of Regency England such as James Hardy Vaux prided themselves on their ingenious tricks for outwitting the shopkeeper; female shoplifts often pretended to order goods, arranged for their delivery to a false address, and dexterously swiped stuff off the counter as the clerk busied himself or herself with the transaction. Shoplifting was an engagement with a shopkeeper.[4]

Another aspect of genteel shopping that made relations between shopkeeper and customer particularly intimate was the credit system. Cash rarely changed hands; the prestige of the haberdasher, draper, dry-goods purveyor to the well-to-do depended on his willingness to extend credit to customers. The wealthier or more prestigious the customer, the longer the leash of his or her credit. According to one historian, "a year was the normal time for high-class tradesmen or shopkeepers to be kept waiting for the settlement of accounts. Few indeed, if they wished to keep custom, would dare to send out their bills inside a year" (Fraser 1981: 92). One implication of the credit system was that in early nineteenth-century shops, walking out of stores with merchandise one hadn't actually payed for was the norm, rather than the exception. In this context, the difference between shoplifting and shopping indeed appears to be a difference of degree rather than of kind. Genteel shoppers constantly pushed at the boundaries of the credit system. Thomas de Quincey, who will soon become central to this paper, was caught up in a constant cycle of "buying and yet not paying for." A familiar figure of early nineteenth-century culture is that of the dandy who neglected to pay his bills, and in so doing, expressed a complex, intimate contempt for the shopkeeper who depended on the dandy for his status as a fashionable tradesman, and upon whom in turn the dandy himself depended for his own prestige. The genteel lady shoplifter may thus be seen as engaging in an odd combination of intimacy, privilege, and resentment similar to that of the Regency rakes and courtesans who refused to pay their bills.[5] The notorious, high-class whore Harriette Wilson recorded in her *Memoirs* her pleasure in deliberately withholding her debts owed to one "Smith, the haberdasher of Oxford Street":

> Not that I was in any sort of difficulty during the whole period I remained with Lord Ponsonby, who always took care of me, and for me, but Smith's scolding furnished me with so much entertainment, that I purposely neglected his bills, knowing his high charges, and how well he could afford to give long credit. (1909, 1: 142)

Why contempt for shopkeepers? While the answer to this question might seem obvious, we need to note that the shopkeeper was a crucial figure in early nineteenth-century political discourse. Napoleon's epithet for England—a "nation of shopkeepers"—resonated even with his worst enemies. (Another French observer of the period, social reformer Flora Tristan, thought the English were a nation of shop*lifters*—she was astonished by the existence of an entire branch of London commerce devoted to the sale of stolen silk handkerchiefs; Tristan [1840] 1982: 174–77). The same political party that fought successfully for years against Romilly's campaign to abolish capital punishment for shoplifting by championing the shopkeepers' right to protect their property, also demonized the shopkeeper as a figure for democracy and revolution. Foes of the Reform Bill of 1832, which enfranchised large and petty shopkeepers, feared that reform would give the "shopocracy" unprecedented political power. De Quincey's Tory diatribes in the pages of *Blackwood's Magazine* raged against their ascendancy. In an article on "The Progress of Social Disorganization," De Quincey sought to determine who was to blame for the social ills he itemized:

> We shall give the answer in the words of our bitterest enemy; of one who knows us in many respects better than we did ourselves. . . . "The English," says Napoleon, "are a nation of SHOPKEEPERS." In this single expression is to be found the true secret of the pecuniary difficulties in which all classes have been involved for the last fifteen years. (De Quincey 1834: 339)

For De Quincey, the battle against the shopocracy was the new domestic war that replaced the war against Napoleon. In "The Approaching Revolution in Great Britain," he positioned himself as spy on the trading classes, on their ways and their tendencies: "No symptom from which their predominant inclinations can be collected, has escaped me for the last sixteen years, —that is, since the general close of the European wars has left men entirely free and undisturbed for the consideration of domestic politics." The result of his observations is definitive proof that "this order of men is purely Jacobinical, and disposed to revolutionary courses, as any that existed in France at the period of their worst convulsions." Shopkeepers, for De Quincey and his *Blackwood's* colleagues, are driven by revenge, resentment, and desperation. Close to the bottom of the social scale, they have nothing to fear and will take any risks: "but their prospectus in the opposite direction, so naturally suggested by each man's ambition and vanity, seem altogether indefinite. The single step which they can lose, is soon reascended; and for the many which they can gain, new chances seem opened . . . by the confusions of revolution" (De Quincey 1831: 323).[6]

In this context we can make a little bit more sense of Buchnill's sympathy for the shoplifting ladies. The contempt for shopkeepers that De Quincey expresses indicates how resonant this particular class border was in early nineteenth-century England. The shopkeeper represented not only a particular political force, but also a new world in which at least the external markers of distinction were truly available to anyone who could pay. This is the context for the bizarre consumerist/anti-consumerist rituals of Regency Dandyism; and thus it is my hypothesis that genteel ladies walking out of shops with stolen goods might productively be seen as analogues to the dandies who did not pay their tradesmen. The perception of the shoplifting lady as victim masks and enables her privilege to imagine herself entitled to a luxury beyond price. Both the temptation to shoplift and the different languages addressing this temptation—debates about legal reform, about forensic diagnosis, both sympathy for and outrage at the genteel female shoplifters, confusion over victimage—can remind of us of the ways in which the moral disorder of Georgian and Regency culture had its uses as a method of maintaining social order.

II

In August of 1799 Mrs. Jane Leigh Perrot, a fifty-three-year-old gentlewoman, was arrested for stealing a card of lace from a shop in Bath. Her trial in March 1800, watched closely by her contemporaries, is best known to us today because Mrs. Perrot happens to have been Jane Austen's aunt.[7] Here is her account of what happened:

> It is now five Weeks since I went into *Smith's*, a Haberdasher in Bath St; to buy some black Lace to trim a Cloak; when I had bought it the Shopman took it into the further part of the shop to put it up—this might have struck me as something particular had I not given the man a 5-pound note to pay himself and bring me the difference— when he left me I turned from the Counter to the door to catch my Goodman [i.e. her husband, who was in Bath to drink its healing waters] who in going to drink his Water generally passed that way. When the Man brought me my Change and the Parcel I left the Shop carrying the Parcel in my hand. I went homewards the same way that Perrot usually came and had not gone far before I met him, we went together to the Cross Bath, stopt to pay a tradesman's bill, and as we had a letter to put into the Post Office were going through Bath St; where I had an hour before bought my Lace, and when we came opposite the Shop the Woman who had sold me the Lace came across the Street and accosted me with these words "I beg pardon, Madam, but was there by mistake a card of white lace put up with the black you bought?" I answered I could not tell as I had not been home but she might satisfye herself as the parcel had never been out of my hand—on saying which I gave it to her, She open'd it, and there was a Card of White Edging which She took out saying "Oh here it is" and returned to the Shop. This did not surprise me as I thought it might

have proceeded from Shop hurry or Negligence, but before we had gotten to the Abbey Church Yard the Man who had taken my Lace away to fold up, came after us to desire my Name and place of Abode as he never had put up that card of White Edging. This alarmed me a good deal because I had neither asked for White Lace nor had I seen any such thing in the Shop. . . . On Wednesday following (the 14th) I was sitting up in my dear Perrot's Bed Chamber when my Maid came up and said a Gentleman in the Parlour wanted to speak to me. Judge my horror upon going down to find he was a Constable with a Warrant from the Mayor for my immediate appearance. I went up to Perrot. . . who forgetting everything but my danger got up and attended me to the Mayor where we found these two Wretches had sworn solemnly the One to seeing me take the Lace, the Other to finding her Lace to the value of 20/- in my possession—this She certainly did, but how it came to be there they best can tell as the first I ever saw of it was on the Woman's unfolding the paper with my Black Lace. The Mayor and Magistrates, to whom we were well known, lamented their being obliged to commit me to prison on the oaths of these People— they could only act in the capacity of Magistrates whatever their own private opinions might be—to prison I was sent. . . .[8]

Mrs. Perrot endured over seven months in a jailor's house, was brought to trial, and acquitted: The jury, deliberating for only fifteen minutes, brought back a verdict of not guilty. In doing so they— along with the crowd of onlookers both male and female who wept openly at the spectacle of such innocence on trial—affirmed her version of the event. The Judge directed the jury to consider the character of a lady of Mrs. Perrot's social standing, and the characters of the genteel witnesses on her behalf, and the prosecution urged that they consider the likelihood that a weathly woman like Mrs. Perrot would stoop to steal such a trifle. The shopman, Mr. Filby, and the shopwoman, Mrs. Gregory, were painted by the prosecution as adulterous lovers with shady pasts, who hoped to shore up an insolvent shop by blackmailing the well-to-do Perrots.

Mrs. Perrot's letters are extraordinary. Those dating from her days in custody before her trial are ladylike and long-suffering; the letters written after her vindication bristle with an overwhelmingly unladylike rage at her accusers. She repeatedly stresses her regret that Filby and his associates cannot be persecuted within an inch of their lives; not enough can be said about their villainy to satisfy her. Once free she indulges in fantasies of Gregory and Filby's humiliation: "I own what partly consoled me for what I had undergone was the delightful

Idea of the *Pillory Exhibition* for my *pretty pair of Lovers*—but my Solicitor says," she laments, "that nothing can be done" (she was legally prohibited from prosecuting them). Through her account of her resentment of the judge—whom she felt hadn't said nearly enough about Filby's "vile" and "vicious" nature—one can hear the judge's protestations that indeed he had said enough to liberate her and thus his alarm at her excessiveness—and perhaps at least a doubt about her innocence. She crudely expresses her wish that her accusers should be hung: "The more I reflect on the diabolical Set that *swore* such abominable Falsehoods the less I wonder at the Numbers that *swing* every Year. . . . Query did he not richly deserve the Gallows?" And she desires to know "how can *we* blacken those People more than they have blacken'd themselves—*the Man is off* and the Shop I hear must be ruin'd" she reports with evident satisfaction.[9] That Mrs. Perrot's evident desire for Filby and Gregory's humiliation and extermination might indeed suggest her own guilt is for my purposes immaterial. If we wanted to indict her, we would have to look elsewhere, but a skepticism about the evidence of emotion should not prevent us from hypothesizing about the stability of the emotional ratio of aggression to aggrieved victimization that would seem to pertain either way. Innocent, that is, Mrs. Perrot mobilizes her arrest as an occasion for exploring the depths of contempt; if guilty, one suspects, the same balance of aggression and victimization that her letters express might have played some role in the deed itself.

But what about the piece of lace that sits at the center of this episode? That crosses the border—whether legitimately or illegitimately—between shop and street? For what is at issue in Perrot's trial is not her possession of the lace, but competing accounts of its travels: "how it came to be there they best can tell," as she insists. In this regard, the trial of Jane Leigh Perrot can be seen as the story of lace writ small, for the fetishism of lace in late eighteenth-early nineteenth-century England had everything to do with borders and border crossings. Borders between England and France, for example: The Napoleonic Wars suspended the importing of French lace—"real" lace—during much of the period 1799–1815, which, while aiding the domestic lace industry, made an attachment to good lace an invocation of the tensions among luxury, trade, and politics (Adburgham 1964: 1–11). Itself a border, moreover, lace is a classic fetish-object. Mrs. Perrot bought the black lace to "trim a cloak"; the white lace that attaches itself to her is "white edging." Diaphanous, barely there, both concealing and revealing what lies beneath, lace unavoidably has the erotic associations attendant upon fetish objects of all kinds.

The historical significance of Mrs. Perrot's adventure seems to have lodged itself not only in the De Quincey novella to which I will turn shortly, but also in another *Blackwood's* story, "The Lace Merchant of Namur" (1838). There, the erotic fascinations and cultural politics of lace come together in a silly historical romance about a desireable, seductive, French (of course) lace shop-man. On the eve of her trial, Mrs. Perrot lamented the expense of her case, and professed her innocence once more: "This ruinous Expense is what we shall long feel—but we are not expensive People, and believe me, *Lace* is not necessary to my happiness."[10] Her joking protestation—"believe me"—that she needs lace neither as something to steal nor as something to buy in her new, economically straighted circumstances after her expensive trial demonstrates the moral anxiety that causes us to banish the material good from the calculus of happiness. Rejecting lace's necessity to her happiness seems, for Perrot, to be incontrovertable evidence of her innocence of the crime. In her own defense, in other words, she places this piece of lace squarely in the context of Enlightenment rhetoric about luxury, value, necessity, and the pursuit of happiness. However, her declaration has the effect of both challenging and enforcing our ideas about what a lady's needs and desires are: Shouldn't what Mrs. Perrot says here go without saying? Shouldn't it be a truth universally acknowledged that a lady in possession of a good fortune, must not be in want of lace? Thus she expresses an uneasiness that dogs modern consumer society—an uneasiness that finds its home in the concept of fetishism—that happiness might in fact be found in the material thing.[11]

III

The narrator of Thomas De Quincey's extravagant and extravagantly titled novella, "The Household Wreck," worries that happiness can steal from itself. A suburban gentleman fondly anxious about his too perfect, too happy young wife, he finds his own happiness a self-consuming burden. "I lived," he confides,

> under the constant presence of a feeling which only that great observer of human nature [Shakespeare] . . . has ever noticed; viz, that merely the excess of my happiness made me jealous of its ability to last, and in that extent less capable of enjoying it; that, in fact, the prelibation of my tears, as a homage to its fragility, was drawn forth by my very sense that my felicity was too exquisite; or, in the words of the great master,—

"I wept to have (absolutely, by anticipation, shed tears in possessing) what I so feared to lose." (De Quincey [1838] 1890, 12: 176)[12]

The misquoted Shakespearean phrase, "weep to have," stresses the fragility of happiness conceived of as possession. It suggests that the objects of our affections cause us sorrow even in their presence; the mind's wayward motions lead us indiscriminately forward to their loss. Once you start "weeping to have," there's no end to weeping. Thus, while Jane Leigh Perrot's account of happiness could invoke the rationality of needs, in De Quincey's understanding, needs and desires eat away at themselves. The paradoxes of this kind of having which is also a not-having are revealed by the narrator's comparison of his "restless distrust" of happiness to that which

> in ancient times often led men to throw valuable gems into the sea, in the hope of thus propitiating the dire deity of misfortune by voluntarily breaking the fearful chain of prosperity, and led some of them to weep and groan when the gems thus sacrificed were afterwards brought back to their hand by simple fishermen, who had recovered them in the intestines of fishes. (HW 168)

The possession of goods is terrifying; it is a fearful chain one must break. One can see why this narrator turns out to be haunted by shoplifting: His fear is not simply that things may be lost; rather, it is that they may attach themselves to us in unfortunate ways. The things of this world have a deadly force to them: In their very innocence the gems seem worse not when they've been gotten in worldly ways, but when they return, purified by the sea, in the guts of fish. I should add here that De Quincey was a writer who was haunted by the possibility that, like the Shakespearean phrase he misquotes, many of his own writerly "gems" were derived from other authors. Highly self-conscious about literary possession and theft, De Quincey solved the matter by embracing—both in his literary and in his real life—a perpetual state of debt. At the time of the writing of "The Household Wreck," he was hiding from his creditors, living apart from his children, and concealing his lodgings. Happiness never got too close; it was always on borrowed time.[13]

The nameless narrator's fears are realized when his angelic wife, Agnes, is arrested for shoplifting. Agnes is falsely accused of stealing a piece of valuable French lace: The malevolent shopkeeper, Mr. Barratt, has slipped a piece of it into her muff, in hopes of blackmailing her into sex. The case in "The Household Wreck" thus resembles that of Jane

Leigh Perrot, and W.J.B. Owen has convincingly demonstrated that De Quincey would have known her story (1990). The narrator himself acknowledges that Agnes's story is not an unfamiliar one. At his long-delayed first meeting with Agnes in prison, his faith in her innocence wavers as he racks his brain with accounts of genteel shoplifting:

> A horrid thought came into my mind. Could it, might it, have been possible that my noble-minded wife . . . was open to temptations of this nature? Could it have been that in some moment of infirmity, when her better angel was away from her side, she had yielded to a sudden impulse of frailty . . . ? I had heard of such things. Cases there were in our own times . . . when irregular impulses of this sort were known to have haunted and besieged natures not otherwise ignoble and base. I ran over some of the names amongst those which were taxed with this propensity. More than one were the names of people in a technical sense held noble. (HW 210)

Shoplifting is a violation so troubling, for this narrator, that it can only be spoken of in the most euphemistic language: it is an "infirmity," a "frailty," an "irregular impulse." It is an alien thing that haunts and besieges its hapless victims. So awful is it that to have committed a bloody or murderous act would have been better, "because more compatible with elevation of mind" (HW 210). Though Agnes ultimately vindicates herself before her husband (who is stricken ill and unconscious throughout her trial, during which time their infant son also dies of the same infection), the incontrovertible evidence of the lace "secreted in her muff" convicts and sentences her to hard labor (HW 188). Her husband and friends liberate her from prison and take her into hiding, but just as the police come to take her back, she dies.

As this plot-summary, together with the overwrought, emotional rhetoric of the passages I've quoted might suggest, "The Household Wreck" is characterized by striking disproportions both stylistic and thematic: disproportions between the story's "source" in the real life of Jane Leigh Perrot and its fictionalized tragic weightiness; between the story's suburban, domestic theme and its doomed, gothic tone; between the slimness of its narrative incident—one shopping trip, one piece of lace—and its awkward length. Incurably digressive, it is too long to be called a short story, too thin to be a novella. The slimness of its incident seems barely able to bear the weight of its baroque prose, just as the narrator can scarcely bear his own happiness: It is, in one critic's words, an "elephantine dilation" (Sedgwick 1980: 78).[14] We

might see these disjunctions as De Quincey's way of articulating the relationship between modes of representation and the problem of the
meaning of the stolen luxury good. That is, "The Household Wreck"
testifies to the power of the "low plane reality" of things to disturb our
sense of time and proportion, and discloses a formal, narratological
analogue to modern commodity culture's crisis concerning the understanding of things, a crisis that speaks in the overlapping languages of
luxury, necessity, overproduction, impoverishment, and entitlement.[15]

This is a project that the narrator ponders at the beginning to the
novella when he muses on how one might fit ordinary, modern
crimes of property—such as an allegation of shop-theft—into a sense
of the tragic. His meditations on the fragility of human happiness re-
volve around this question. He notes that the "class of hasty tragedies
and sudden desolations" of a commercial society seem to fall with a
sudden, unprecedented speed ("often indeed it happens that the des-
olation is accomplished within the course of one revolving sun; often
the whole dire catastrophe . . . is accomplished and made known . . .
within one and the same hour"): If we don't slow things down, we
will miss them (HW 159). Contemplating the effects of this new kind
of calamity both requires and defies calculations of probability; requires a consideration of the stage on which we see them, for modern society in its enormity conceals the very tragedies it produces:

> The increasing grandeur and magnitude of the social system, the
> more it multiplies and extends its victims, the more it conceals them,
> and for the very same reason; just as in the Roman ampitheatres,
> when they grew to the magnitude of mighty cities (in some instances
> accomodating four hundred thousand spectators . . .), births and
> death became ordinary events, which in a small modern theatre are
> rare and memorable; and, exactly as these prodigious accidents multi-
> plied, *pari passu* they were disregarded and easily concealed; for cu-
> riosity was no longer excited; the sensation attached to them was little
> or none. (HW 160)

Like an optical effect, the lens of modernity exponentially multiplies
and diminishes its calamities. What the writer has to do, this passage
suggests, is focus an inverted lens on the incident, one that will
blow it up out of all proportion and make it stand alone. That is the
only way to reattach "sensation" to such tales. In order to become
visible and meaningful, what the story of the piece of lace requires
is neither the scale of a normative realism, nor Mrs. Perrot's normalizing invocations of necessity and non-necessity, nor Harriet Mar-

tineau's pained moralizings—but a mode of representation that defies all proportion.

It may seem perverse to insist on "The Household Wreck" as a story of a piece of lace. The incriminating frill barely appears; the encounter in the store, plus the trial itself, take place offstage. Though only minimally "represented" (in the sense of being named, described, kept before the reader's eyes), it is the center of the text, serving as the point from which it spins out centrifugally. In this respect "The Household Wreck" is typical of De Quincey's prose, which usually leaves hard facts behind. J. Hillis Miller's phenomenological descriptions of the disorienting, infinitely expanding inner space of De Quincey's sentences, his preference for a thickening spiral over a narrative line, stands up especially well with regard to "The Household Wreck." Speaking of De Quincey's aversion to discontinuity, Miller likens the imperative embodied in his prose to the making of lace:

> Each man must go, like the lace-maker, with the utmost care over every bit of the space between "here" and "there," connecting every point with every other point, and never for a moment allowing the thread to break. If necessary he must go over the same area repeatedly, recapitulating it, seeing it from slightly different angles, making sure he has not missed anything. He must be certain he is "filling up all those chasms which else are likely to remain as permanent disfigurations of [the] work." (Miller 1963: 38–39)

Describing an endless covering over and filling in of gaps, Miller's diagnosis of De Quincey's lace-like prose evokes the substitutive, apotropaic logic of fetishism. His assessment allows us to hypothesize that for De Quincey, the sheer verbal excessiveness of the novella is in a sense a substitute for the thing itself. Just as the wealth of the rich men is most reassuring when buried under the ocean—and most terrifying when it returns to the surface—the valuable piece of lace that sticks too close to Agnes makes its sense when sunk in an ocean of words. Wealth and representation do not only function as cognate terms; the latter can stand in for and stabilize anxieties attendant upon the former.[16]

Let me return from the style of "The Household Wreck" to its plot. Suffering perhaps from my own form of methodological fetishism, I have allowed myself to construe the piece of lace as the prime mover of the text. The lace is merely, one might object, a pawn in a human conspiracy: The evil shopkeeper plants the lace in Agnes's muff, and the muff is procured by a corrupt housemaid (HW 214). It goes without saying that in its human drama "The Household Wreck" exhibits some of the attitudes towards the players in the shoplifting scenario that have appeared in the writings examined earlier in this essay. De Quincey's treatment of Agnes embodies intense ambivalence about the shopping/shoplifting lady. She is a wavering figure: In spite of his great love for her, the narrator literally can't see her straight (see HW 165–67, 173–74, 176–78); and though the story insists on her innocence, everything about this creepy narration conspires to make her seem guilty. Agnes, the suburban shopping lady (the narrator dwells on her fashionable yet transcendent perfection as she sets off on the shopping trip to the metropolis where she meets her demise), is connected to at least one other lady in De Quincey's writings. She is a distant cousin of the title figure in his armchair-archaelogy piece, "The Toilette of the Hebrew Lady." There, the Hebrew lady, increasingly decked out with luxury ornaments, represents "ages of excessive luxury," both cultural advance and cultural decline (De Quincey [1828] 1890, 6: 164). And De Quincey's treatment of the lecherous shopkeeper, Barratt, violently dramatizes the venemous attacks of his political journalism. Discovered to be setting the same trap for another innocent woman, Barratt ultimately receives at the hands of a popular uprising what the law could not do. He is dragged into the street, and, as the police stand by, beaten to a pulp: "the mob had so used or so abused the opportunity they had long wished for that he remained the mere disfigured wreck of what had once been a man, rather than a creature with any resemblance to humanity" (HW 232). Barratt lives just long enough to confess his crime against Agnes. "My revenge was perfect," are the novella's last words (HW: 233).

But there is a sense in which Barratt's guilt seems strangely besides the point, and not simply because he is so obviously being scapegoated according to the political program described in the previous sections of this essay. Rather, his criminality is rendered a nonissue by the way in which De Quincey distributes guilt across all of the principle characters. As I've noted, the weirdly morphing Agnes (now she looks like a child, now like a woman; now she looks very tall, but really she's of average height; now she is utterly distinctive-looking, now she could be confused with anyone you see in the street) seems guilty of some complicity in her own demise. Her husband disingenuously refers to her as a "double character" (HW 173). And he is constantly indicting himself in our eyes, not only in his own self-incriminations and protestations (162), but more and more covertly. His relationship to Agnes comes to seem simultaneously sinisterly overprotective, domineering, and irresponsible, but it is largely in his absolute paralysis throughout most of the story that his moral turpitude seems to lie. He gets fixed to spots (185); frozen by icy terrors (179); struck speechless (179); blanks out (190). He shrinks from sight like a guilty man when the policeman first bearing news of Agnes's arrest comes to his door (185); immures himself in the house while a faithful servant looks into Agnes's case; decides both his and her life are over before he even knows what's happened, and of course becomes sick and unconscious throughout her trial. This is an unreliable narrator who is truly unreliable.

In making everyone guilty in "The Household Wreck," De Quincey has made everyone the same. The characters bleed into each other, and one slight hint of these floating identifications can be found in the way the word "wreck" circulates throughout. Does the title phrase "household wreck" refer to Agnes herself? Or does it come to attach itself to the narrator (HW 164, 200)? In the last pages, the shopkeeper Barratt becomes the wreck: "he remained the mere disfigured wreck of what had once been a man" (HW 232). At the end of her life, Agnes and her husband turn out to be actually having each other's dreams at night (HW 228). Elsewhere in this essay I've noted ways in which the stolen luxury good—the transgressive piece of lace—serves to police borders, enforcing the differences (of class, gender, privilege) among the several actors in the shoplifting drama. But in "The Household Wreck," it is as if the consumable, stealeable thing makes everyone the same. As its human partners become more and more corrupt in relation to it, the piece of lace at the center is rendered more and more innocent, like the gems washed up on the rich men's shores. Like those rich men who dread the very purity of the gems to which they're in thrall, it seems that literature's perception of things' social density, their ability to explain a social world, is inseparable from a perception of their asocial purity and deadliness. De Quincey's gothic shoplifting tale discovers the uncanniness of things in a society that is simultaneously consumerist and fundamentally antimaterialist, afraid of locating happiness in things: The more happiness one invests in them, the more they resist the human, sucking the life out of their human partners and enduring with an innocent, inhuman persistence.

IV

At the beginning of this essay I alluded to shoplifting's canonization as a form of fetishism in the psychoanalytic concept of kleptomania. I'd like at this point to cross out of the world of nineteenth-century shoplifting and back into the world of twentieth-century theory in order to conclude, briefly, with another perversion that can be seen as expressing a fear that the happiness of things can get too close: a pathological dread of shopping.

My text is a case study by the existential-phenomenological psychoanalyst Ludwig Binswanger, about a schizophrenic, Lola Voss. Among her many miseries and terrors, Lola has a phobia of clothes. She refuses to board a ship that is to take her from South America to Europe until a certain dress is removed; she frequently cuts up her own clothes; and, Binswanger continues, she "continuously wore the same old dress, hated her underwear, and used all possible means to resist the purchase and wearing of new clothes" (Binswanger [1949] 1968: 300).[17] A chief instance of the latter happens on a trip to Zurich that Lola is persuaded to go on, accompanied by a nurse from Binswanger's sanitorium, in order to replenish her wardrobe. Upon her arrival, "she felt happy and at ease as long as nobody spoke to her about shopping, or pointed out stores where she should shop tomorrow" (LV 275). She is finally persuaded to go into a cheap department store—and actualy purchases a dress—but only with her eyes closed, guided by the nurse.

In Binswanger's analysis, Lola's existence—her *Dasein*—is threatened by her having become overwhelmed by a particular, damaged, ideal: that of being perfectly alone. Under the sway of this ideal, Lola has rendered the world as something that is always threatening to take her over: " 'world' no longer means a totality of conditions that the existence has taken in its stride, but a condition definitely determined by the being as something frightful, a condition of hostility, of something that is, once and for all, hostile or threatening" (LV 337). She therefore must devote her life to fending off the incursions of this worldliness, and in her fear of being in the world in this particular way has opened herself up to a sense of the Dreadful—a fundamental, existential dread of being at all.[18]

Binswanger treats Lola's dread of shopping not from a psychopathological point of view which would seek to understand its biographical genesis, but rather from a phenomenological one. He seeks to describe the "world design" of such a phobia, asking not why garments play such a role in her phobias, but rather "how it is possible that garments *can* play so prominent a part" (LV 300, his emphasis).[19] Lola has ritualized all objects around her, turning them into potential embodiments of the world she fears, and this is especially true of clothes, because of their nearness. For Binswanger, a disordering of the *Dasein* has both spatial and temporal components; Lola seeks to keep the world at a distance, and what is closer to us than our clothes? Clothes are a worldly shell: They embody "the transformation of existential anxiety into the horrible fear of a 'worldly' shell" (LV 301). Clothing, the worldly things closest to her, becomes "actual carriers of the Dreadful" (LV 302).

There are two further points to add here that might make the distinctiveness of Binswanger's analysis clearer. First it is worth noting that in this analysis, clothing becomes terrifying not simply because—according to a more familiar associationist logic—it comes to bear memories, though in his analysis this is sometimes the case. It can be an old dress (such as the dress that has to be removed from the ship) or the prospect of getting a new dress that can seem too close: hence having to shop with one's eyes closed. Lola's way of going into stores declares not simply an agoraphobic asceticism, a refusal to know pleasure or to engage in the marketplace. Rather, eyes closed, she acknowledges things' power. A refusal of intimacy and of exposure, her way of shopping is the inverse of shoplifting: Closing her eyes, she suffers herself to assume the status of the object, blind and unknowing, not only so that she won't see the things for sale, but also so that they won't see her. She may not wish to take or buy them, but she knows they may be wishing to steal her.

Second, the specificity of the clothing phobia has not only to do with its spatial dimension—clothing's proximity—but like many of Lola's phobias it has a linguistic dimension as well. In German, Binswanger's translator points out, " 'unbearable' and 'unwearable' are the same word" (LV 312). The unwearable is exactly the name of the Dreadful in this case. Thus Lola tries to get rid of the unbearableness of the world by declaring clothes unwearable: cutting them up, refusing underwear, refusing to shop.

But if the unwearable, unshoppable clothes embody the unbearable Dreadful, Lola also weaves out of her clothing taboos a kind of defense against its incursions. Garments are a shell that both infects and protects: She "wears the same dress for a long time, enters the sanatorium without underwear, and surrounds the buying and wearing of a new dress with a network of safeguards against the breakthrough of the Dreadful." What all of her safeguards and rituals mean is that "she succeeds in wresting from the intangible, uncanny Dreadful a person-like character, a personification of a fate that proceeds according to predictable intentions, that warns or encourages her and thus saves her from being totally delivered to the Dreadful in its naked uncanniness" (LV 303, 302). Lola is able to transform an existential anxiety into a battle with clothes, making it more bearable, or wearable.

It might be difficult to bring some of the terms that surrounded the luxury good earlier in this paper—necessity, happiness, value—to bear on the case of Lola Voss: If it is clear that things could not have brought happiness to such a person, it's clear that they sometimes brought her terror, or respite. Further, it may seem completely strange to try to think together a historical person speaking for herself (Mrs. Jane Leigh Perrot), a figure in a gothic tale (Agnes from "The Household Wreck"), and a person described in a psychoanalytic case study. But "The Case of Lola Voss" could be seen as confirming the point De Quincey was in effect making about Mrs. Perrot: that in a modern, affluent society, the differences between luxury and necessity become blurry, and other senses of impoverishment or need besides that of real material want come to play in our relationships to things. It might suggest to us that when a Mrs. Perrot says that lace is not necessary to her happiness, her statement is, as I also tried to suggest earlier, neither mere antimaterialism, nor simple agoraphobia. Against the background of Binswanger's description of Lola Voss's existence, the thematics of things getting too close—lace that winds up, to ones horror, unaccountably on one's person, gems that return in the guts of fish—that we've seen in the shoplifting stories might appear as incursions of the Dreadful, of the worldliness of things taking over. While I wouldn't want to push these analogies very far at all, I do want to suggest that we need not banish from our efforts at a historical understanding of the emotions elicited by things, a phenomenological or psychoanalytic understanding of their powers. Refusing to do so might help us to explain the power of things without explaining it away.

NOTES

My thanks to Austin Booth for her assistance with the research for this paper; to the Program in Women's Studies, University of Michigan, for funding this research; and to William Galperin, Don Herzog, Deidre Lynch, and Patricia Spyer for their comments.

1. See Karl Abraham: "So-called kleptomania is often traceable to the fact that a child feels injured or neglected in respect to proofs of love. . . . It procures a substitute pleasure for the lost pleasure, and at the same time takes revenge on those who have caused the supposed injustice. Psycho-analysis shows that in the unconscious of our patients there exist the same impulses to take forcible possession of the 'gift' which has not been received" ([1920] 1949: 355). See also Zavitzianos 1971; Kohon 1987. Louise Kaplan revises the

kleptomania/penis envy thesis, arguing that kleptomania and fetishism in women can be responses to a whole variety of absences and losses (1991: 284–320).

2. On the revalorization of fetishism, see for example, Kofman 1981; Schor 1986; Apter 1991; Cvetkovich 1992; and Pinch 1998. Historical studies of theft as a means of exploring the culture of consumerism include O'Brien 1983; Abelson 1989; and Lemire 1990.

3. See, for example, the *Newgate Calendar's* account of the conviction in 1810 of Mary Jones and Elizabeth Paine, who appeared to be career shoplifters, of stealing twelve pairs of stockings worth four pounds, eight shillings, which concludes by reporting the officer's comment that "it was a great stretch of the jury's humanity that they were not capitally convicted." They were transported (1824–28: 5: 71–72). On shoplifting law, see Radzinowicz 1948; MacKinnon 1937: 32–50. The leading figure in the campaign to reform the Shop-Lifting Act was Sir Samuel Romilly (Romilly 1810; 1840).

4. On women shopkeepers in early nineteenth-century England, see Adburgham 1964: 25–32; for the tricks of the professional shoplifter, see Vaux 1819. The nature of shops and shopkeeping in England during the period covered by this paper is subject to some historical debate. While some historians of consumption have argued that modern innovations in retail—window display, advertising, fixed prices on merchandise tickets, a preference for "ready money" over credit—were not significantly put into place until the mid-nineteenth century (or at least after 1815), others have argued that many if not most of these changes had already begun in metropolitan, high-class shops in the eighteenth century. See, in addition to Adburgham, Davis 1966; McKendrick et al. 1982; Chung & Mui 1989; Alexander 1970; Winstanley 1983.

5. On the "system of credit" and its susceptibility to corruption, see Wade 1829: 125–27. On De Quincey and debt, see Lindop 1981: 380. On the cultural politics of Regency Dandyism, see Moers 1960; Low 1977. Running up debt could be a woman's weapon in her intimate war with a cheap husband, because until the Married Women's Property Act of 1870, married women could not be sued for delinquent debts.

6. On the political influence and interests of urban shopkeepers, Winstanley 1983. My argument about shopkeepers is indebted to Don Herzog's study of the politics of contempt in England, 1789–1832 (Herzog 1996; 1998).

7. An extensive modern account of Jane Leigh Perrot's trial can be found in MacKinnon 1937, which reprints one of several contemporary accounts, *The Trial of Jane Leigh Perrot . . . Charged With Stealing a Card of Lace* (Taunton, 1800). Copeland (1995) discusses the case briefly. Armed with the most revelatory investigation of the episode to date, Galperin (n.d.) uses Jane Austen's non-response to her aunt's trial as a starting point for an analysis of the politics of Austen's representational practices.

8. Jane Leigh Perrot to Montague Cholmeley, September 11, 1799, in Austen-Leigh 1942: 183–85.

9. Jane Leigh Perrot to Montague Cholmeley, April 1, 1800; April 8, 1800; April 14; 1800; in Austen-Leigh 1942: 207, 208, 214, 218–19. Mrs. Perrot's counsel, Joseph Jekyll, confided later that he suspected that she was like other genteel women "who frequent bazaars and mistake other people's property for their own." For this and other evidence that Perrot may have been guilty, see Galperin (n.d.).

10. Jane Leigh Perrot to Montague Cholmeley, September 11, 1799, in Austen-Leigh 1942: 183. Contemporary accounts of her trial, however, do suggest that she was a woman who cared about dress, describing in approving detail her elegant attire in the courtroom, including (of course) the "black lace veil, which was thrown up over her head" ("Account of the Trial of Mrs. Leigh Perrot": 171).

11. The literature on the politics of "luxury" in the eighteenth and nineteenth centuries is extensive; see Sekora 1977. The word "fetish" had come to be used to refer to ordinary household luxuries at least by the 1850's; see Hollingshead 1858.

12. In subsequent references, this text will be indicated by the abbreviation HW and page number.

13. The passage De Quincey quotes is from Shakespeare's Sonnet 64: "Ruin hath taught me thus to ruminate / That Time will come and take my love away. / This thought is as a death, which cannot choose / But weep to have that which it fears to lose." On De Quincey and debt, see Lindop 1981; Hubbard 1993; McDonagh 1994: 42–65. On De Quincey as a kind of literary pick-pocket, see Clej 1995: 233.

14. While "The Household Wreck" has received some passing attention from De Quincey's excellent recent critics, none have treated it as a story about what it is about: an accusation of shoplifting. Sedgwick (1980) treats the shopping episode merely as a way to get to the story's final scenes of imprisonment and violence. McDonagh (1995) focuses on the story's exposition of the structural vulnerability of the domestic sphere and the anxieties that attend woman's entry into the marketplace, as does Leighton (1992). Lindop (1981) attributes the affects of the story to De Quincey's feelings of guilt after the death of his wife, Margaret, in 1837. A number of readings, most brilliantly and complexly Barrell (1991), have linked some motifs from the story to the scene of De Quincey's sister Elizabeth's childhood death, which reverberates throughout his writing.

15. "Low plane reality": Bryson 1990: 14 and ff. I am indebted to Bryson's use of this phrase by which he designates the material, "authentically self-determining" (13) nature and slowness of the forms of everyday life and in particular the pressures these things put on modes of representation.

16. See Bryson (1990: 52). My point in this paragraph could be confirmed by studying the place of De Quincey's favorite object of luxury consumption: the supplemental relation, that is, between language and opium. On lace as a figure for language and on both as luxuries that can be hoarded or amassed, compare Samuel Johnson: "Greek, Sir . . . is like lace; every man gets as much of it as he can" (Boswell 1980: 1081).

17. In subsequent references this text will be indicated by the abbreviation LV and page number.

18. Binswanger tends to use "the Dreadful" and "the Uncanny" almost synonymously, but he distinguishes his use of "Uncanny" from that of Freud, for whom the uncanny came specifically to refer to feelings arising from repetition and the return of the repressed. Binswanger preferred to return to Schelling's definition—"anything which ought to remain in secrecy and obscurity and has become manifest is known as uncanny"—and believed that the uncanny pointed to an originary, existential dread (LV 306–7).

19. In contrast see Freud's approach, in his early *Project for a Scientific Psychology*, to a shopping phobia in his patient Emma Eckstein, for whom a fear of going into a shop alone is ultimately connected to an experience or fantasy of having been sexually molested by a shopkeeper as a child (Freud [1895] 1966: 353–56). Thanks to Professor H.U.E. Thoden van Velzen for bringing this case to my attention.

REFERENCES

Abelson, Elaine (1989) *When Ladies Go A-Thieving: Middle-Class Shoplifters in the Victorian Department Store*. New York: Oxford University Press.

Abraham, Karl [1920] (1949) "The Female Castration Complex." In *Selected Papers* London: Hogarth Press.

Adburgham, Alice (1964) *Shops and Shopping, 1800–1914*. London: Allen and Unwin.

Alexander, David (1970) *Retailing in England During the Industrial Revolution*. London: Athlone.

Anon. (1800) "Account of the Trial of Mrs. Leigh Perrot." *The Lady's Magazine* 31: 171–76.

———. (1824–28) *The Newgate Calendar, Comprising Interesting Memoirs of the Most Notorious Characters Who Have Been Convicted of Outrages on the Laws of England* . . . vol. 5. London: J. Robins.

———. (1830) "Recollections of a Gottingen Student, II." *The New Monthly Magazine* 28 (new ser.): 12–20.

————.(1836) "The Lace Merchant of Namur." *Blackwood's Edinburgh Magazine* 44: 245–67.

Apter, Emily (1991) *Feminizing the Fetish: Psychoanalysis and Narrative Obsession in Turn of the Century France*. Ithaca: Cornell University Press.

Austen-Leigh, R.A. (ed.) (1942) *Austen Papers 1704–1856*. London: Spottiswoode, Ballantyne.

Barrell, John (1991) T*he Infection of Thomas De Quincey: A Psychopathology of Imperialism*. New Haven: Yale University Press.

Binswanger, Ludwig [1949] (1968) "The Case of Lola Voss." Trans. Ernest Angel. In *Being-In-The-World: Selected Papers of Ludwig Binswanger*. Jacob Needleman, ed. New York: Harper and Row.

Boswell, James [1791] (1980) *Life of Johnson*. Oxford: Oxford University Press.

Bryson, Norman (1990) *Looking At The Overlooked: Four Essays on Still Life Painting*. Cambridge, Mass.: Harvard University Press.

Bucknill, John (1863) "Kleptomania." *Journal of Mental Science* 8, 24: 262–75.

Camhi, Leslie (1993) "Stealing Femininity: Department Store Kleptomania as Sexual Disorder." *differences* 5: 38–39.

Cheung, Hoh and Lorna H. Mui (1989) *Shops and Shopkeeping in Eighteenth-Century England*. London: Routledge.

Clej, Alina (1995) *A Genealogy of the Modern Self: Thomas de Quincey and the Intoxication of Writing*. Stanford: Stanford University Press.

Copeland, Edward (1995) W*omen Writing About Money: Women's Fiction in England, 1780–1820*. Cambridge: Cambridge University Press.

Cvetkovich, Ann (1992) "Marx's *Capital* and the Mystery of the Commodity." In *Mixed Feelings: Feminism, Mass Culture, and Sensationalism*. New Brunswick: Rutgers University Press.

Davis, Dorothy (1966) *A History of Shopping*. London: Routledge and Kegan Paul.

De Quincey, Thomas [1828] (1890) "Toilette of the Hebrew Lady." In *The Collected Writings of Thomas De Quincey* vol. 6. David Masson, ed. Edinburgh: A. and C. Black.

————. (1831) "On the Approaching Revolution in Great Britain, and its Proximate Causes." *Blackwood's Edinburgh Magazine* 30: 313–29.

————. (1834) "On the Progress of Social Disorganization." *Blackwood's Edinburgh Magazine* 35.

————. [1838] (1890) "The Household Wreck." In *The Collected Writings of Thomas De Quincey* vol. 12. David Masson, ed. Edinburgh: A. and C. Black.

Fraser, W. Hamish (1981) *The Coming of the Mass Market, 1850–1914*. Hamden, CT: Archon.

Freud, Sigmund [1895] (1966) "Project for a Scientific Psychology." *The Standard Edition of the Complete Psychological Works of Sigmund Freud* vol. 1. Trans. and ed. James Strachey. London: Hogarth Press.

Galperin, William (n.d.) *The Historical Austen*. Manuscript.

Herzog, Don (1996) "The Trouble With Hairdressers." *Representations* 53: 21–43.

———. (1998) *Poisoning the Minds of the Lower Orders*. Princeton: Princeton University Press.

Hollingshead, John (1858) "Fetishism at Home." In *Household Words* 17: 445–47.

Hubbard, Stacy Carson (1993) "Telling Accounts: De Quincey at the Bookseller's." In *Postmodernism Across the Ages*. Bill Readings and Bennet Schaber, eds. Syracuse: Syracuse University Press.

McDonagh, Josephine (1994) *De Quincey's Disciplines*. New York: Oxford University Press.

Kaplan, Louise (1991) *Female Perversions*. New York: Doubleday.

Kofman, Sarah (1981) "Ca Cloche." In *Les Fins de l'homme: a partir du travail de Jacques Derrida*. Philippe Lacoue-Labarthe and Jean-Luc Nancy, eds. Paris: Galilee.

Kohon, Gregorio (1987) "Fetishism Revisited." *International Journal of Psychoanalysis* 68: 213–28.

Leighton, Angela (1992) "De Quincey and Women." *In Beyond Romanticism*. Stephen Copley and John Whale, eds. London: Routledge.

Lemire, Beverly (1990) "The Theft of Clothes and Popular Consumerism in Early Modern England." *Journal of Social History* 24: 255–76.

Lindop, Grevel (1981) *The Opium Eater: A Life of Thomas De Quincey*. New York: Taplinger.

Low, Donald A. (1977) *That Sunny Dome: A Portrait of Regency Britain*. London: Dent.

MacKinnon, Frank Douglas (1937) *Grand Larceny, Being the Trial of Jane Leigh Perrot, Aunt of Jane Austen*. Oxford: Oxford University Press.

Martineau, Harriet [1849–50] (1877–78) *A History of the Thirty Years' Peace* vols. 2 and 3. London: G. Bell and Sons.

McKendrick, Neil, John Brewer, and J.H. Plumb (1982) *The Birth of a Consumer Society: The Commercialization of Eighteenth-Century England*. Bloomington: Indiana University Press.

Miller, J. Hillis (1963) *The Disappearance of God: Five Nineteenth-Century Writers*. Cambridge, Mass.: Harvard University Press.

Moers, Ellen (1960) *The Dandy: Brummell to Beerbohm*. New York: Viking.

O'Brien, Patricia (1983) "The Kleptomania Diagnosis: Bourgeois Women and Theft in Late Nineteenth-Century France." *Journal of Social History* 17: 65–77.

Owen, W.J.B. (1990) "De Quincey and Shoplifting." *The Wordsworth Circle* 21: 72–76.

Pinch, Adela (1998) "Rubber Bands and Old Ladies." In *In Near Ruins: Essays in Cultural Theory*. Nicholas B. Dirks, ed. Minneapolis: University of Minnesota Press.

Prichard, James Cowles (1835) *Treatise on Insanity and of the Disorders Affecting the Mind*. London: Sherwood, Gilbert, and Piper.

———. [1842] (1847) *On The Different Froms of Insanity, in Relation to Jurisprudence*. London: Balliere.

Radzinowicz, Leon (1948) *A History of English Criminal Law and Its Administration from 1750* vol. 1. New York: MacMillan.

Romilly, Samuel (1810) *Observations on the Criminal Laws of England*. London: Cadell and Davies.

———. (1840) *Memoirs of the Life of Sir Samuel Romilly* 3 vols. London: J. Murray.

Schor, Naomi (1986) "Female Fetishism: The Case of George Sand." In *The Female Body in Western Culture*. Susan Rubin Suleiman, ed. Cambridge: Harvard University Press.

Sedgwick, Eve (1980) *The Coherence of Gothic Fiction*. New York: Arno Press.

Sekora, John (1977) *Luxury: The Concept in Western Thought, Eden to Smollet*. Baltimore: Johns Hopkins University Press.

Tristan, Flora [1840] (1982) *The London Journal of Flora Tristan*. Trans. Jean Hawkes. London: Virago Press.

Vaux, James Hardy (1819) *The Memoirs of James Hardy Vaux Written By Himself*. London: W. Clowes.

Wade, John (1829) *Treatise on the Police and Crimes of the Metropolis*. London: Longman, Rees, Orme, Brown, and Green.

Wilson, Harriette [1825] (1909) *The Memoirs of Harriette Wilson, Written By Herself*. vol. 1. London: Eveleigh Nash.

Winstanley, Michael J. (1983) *The Shopkeeper's World 1830–1914*. Manchester: Manchester University Press.

Zavitzianos, George (1971) "Fetishism and Exhibitionism in the Female and their Relationship to Psychopathy and Kleptomania." *International Journal of Psycho-Analysis* 52: 297–305.

6

The Tooth of Time, or Taking a Look at the "Look" of Clothing in Late Nineteenth-Century Aru

Patricia Spyer

At the height of its power and imperial glory[1]—a moment that some in Holland still like to recall as a time in which "something great was done" (*er wérd wat groots vericht*)[2]—the former Netherlands East Indies came to be refered to with increasing familiarity by the Dutch as an "emerald girdle" (*gordel van smaragd*). Although the immediate referent of this precious chain was the glittering band of glassy green islands that trace out an arch(ipelago) across the great Malay Sea, a more fitting description could hardly have been found for the close link between conquest, clothing, and booty, or between the fashioning of gendered subjects and imperial design. In studies of colonialism, sexuality, and subject formation, much has been made of the capacity of cloth to embrace, shape, and subjugate persons and populations—with special attention usually paid to the so-called "civilizing" import of European forms of dress and comportment (Cohn 1989; Murra 1989).

If cloth had a particular role to fulfill abroad in the elevation of colonial subjects to the heights of European civilization, at home and especially as the nineteenth century progressed, it had also come into its own. Draperies, carpets, and fabrics with heavy folds and multiple accoutrements wrapped and sheltered an increasingly private and prosperous bourgeois world. In France, as most elsewhere, this was "the age of the *tapissier*," "the heyday of trimming," and the day that the tassel can be said to have "arrived" (Corbin 1990: 369). In the Aru Islands on the fringes of the fashionable world in what is today eastern Indonesia, this was also the time when feathers of the famed and Greater Bird of Paradise were exported—especially to France—in unprecedented numbers. It was simultaneously the highpoint of European travel to these far-flung parts. What such meant in Aru was that in addition to the regular coterie of colonial officials—including what the Dutch in their usual no-nonsense manner termed "controlers" (*controleur*)—especially naturalists of different breeds and persuasions flocked to the islands to take in and as often as not take out Aru's unusual, hybrid fauna and, to a much lesser extent, flora.

Reigning supreme among Aru's natural attractions was that Greater Bird—once known simply among Malays as God's Bird (*manuk dewata*) and subsequently among Europeans as the Legless Paradise (*Paradisaea apoda*)—which increasingly was relinquishing its feathers to fashion and whose very habits and habitat already seemed to prefigure such a fate (cf. Savage 1984: 35–38). It is, importantly, as I will argue, the *male* bird that is by far the most splendid. He lives permanently in towering "display" trees[3] where—when the season for such shows comes around—he puts on a magnificent production for the females of his species displaying thereby what is only one of many strategies through which a bird can market his reproductive charms (Purcell & Gould 1992: 76). In the late nineteenth-century sources on Aru, descriptions in naturalists' accounts of Aruese in various modes of dress are almost on a par with those of birds and their plummage, in terms of the regularity with which they appear and the extraordinary detail of their documentation. More than a curious parallelism, this twofold preoccupation with the appearance of Aru's birds and that of its human inhabitants points, I argue, to a conundrum whereby colonial authority was caught in a double bind: On the one hand, its reproduction demanded the preservation of a strict demarcation between colonizers and colonized; on the other, the very dynamics of colonial rule constantly threatened to blur such divide as it also presumed the fabrication of colonized others in its own imperial image. Although, of course, such a conundrum was intractable in actuality, it nonetheless offered many possibilities to the imagination. I suggest here that while testifying in its very instability to the power of the dilemma, the alternation in colonial accounts between Paradise's birds and its all too human inhabitants was also one way of playing out this problem in the imaginary register with results that, if nothing else, were both emotionally and aesthetically satisfying. Rather than a focus here on any single fetish, the shifting zone described in the gap that opens up between birds and men is a space of border fetishisms where the fetishization of nature enables the naturalization of colonial authority while hinting along the way at some high imperial imaginings of class, gender, and race.

Especially the 1870s, 1880s, and 1890s witnessed the elaboration by the different European powers of a " 'theology' of an omniscient, omnipotent, and omnipresent [Imperial] monarchy" (Ranger 1983: 212) for their colonial possessions, which went together with a hypertrophy of the aristocratic and seignorial trappings of command and rule. This was a time when antique conceptions of patrimony and privilege were resurrected in remote corners of the European empires, when the full-blown capitalism of the metropole flaunted itself abroad (but not at home) in "feudal-aristocratic drag" (Anderson 1991: 150)," when following a code of courtliness and glory, colonial officers "dressed [themselves] to kill in bed- or ballroom" and "armed [themselves] with swords and obselete industrial weapons" (Anderson: 151), and when the dominant authorial position of European travel writing was the decisively gendered "monarch-of-all-I-survey" mode (Pratt 1992: 213). Beyond the golden feathers of the Greater Bird of Paradise or the birds that between the 1880s and 1920s nested in their entirety on European women's hats[4]—either in themselves sufficient to tickle the stereotypical fetishist's fancy[5]—it is especially the fetishism on the part of the colonizers of their own imperial forms of power and privilege that emerges out of the juxtaposition of the late nineteenth-century descriptions of Aru's birds and those of its human inhabitants.

There are a number of good historical reasons having to do, among other things, with the fault lines of class, race, and gender as these both conjoined and divided European metropoles and their colonies, that help to explain what Anderson has aptly termed this "Tropical Gothic" *imaginaire* at the apex of European imperialism (Anderson: 151). One such reason was already implied above, namely, the enormous power that high capitalism had given the metropole and the concomitant surplus of neo-traditional capital that became available for investment in the colonies. Another reason is the rising numbers of bourgeois and petty-bourgeois men in the colonial service who were encouraged to "lord" it over the subjugated peoples, following a principle of colonial racism according to which class difference at home became subsumed—though by no means effaced—within the idea of an all-around European racial superiority; "the idea that if, say, English lords were naturally superior to other Englishmen, no matter: these other Englishmen were no less superior to the subjected natives" (Anderson: 150).[6] At the same time, the last decades of the nineteenth-century were also the moment when many European powers were pressed to make their colonies look more legitimate, respectable, and even benevolent. In so doing, they often bolstered their claims with quasi-aristocratic, regal expressions of patrimony, according to the same kind of attitude that the imagining of the Indies as an emerald girdle so thoroughly captures. In the Netherlands East Indies, 1900, the same year that saw Princess Wilhelmina's coronation as Queen celebrated amidst much feudal fanfare in the colonies, also witnessed the enunciation of the so-called Ethical Policy (*Ethische Politiek*); while the following year the Queen herself in her annual oration before the Dutch parliament spoke of the "debt of honor" that the Netherlands in something quite like a gesture of *noblesse oblige* wished to repay for what by then amounted to three hundred years of colonial exploitation.

In the Netherlands East Indies, as elsewhere, this was then the moment when the objects, rituals, and routines that articulated, legitimated, and produced the colonizer's position vis-à-vis their colonized subjects became matters of a heightened and even "Tropical Gothic" obsession.[7] By the second half of the nineteenth century in Aru, along with all the attention bestowed on the archipelago's birds, lengthy descriptions of Aruese in "native," "national" or "European" styles of dress are a regular feature of both travelers and official accounts of the islands. For the most part, the kinds of clothing encountered in Aru could be cast comfortably within the increasingly standardized genres of customary and folkloric Otherness available at the time. Yet what seems to have made for a somewhat distinct and at times unsettling experience for visiting Europeans were those moments when they felt their own gaze turned back upon themselves, when the gaze, as it were, became a "look" as Aruese appeared before them in European guise.

Clothing in Paradise

As in other colonial places, the *mission civilisatrice* involving in Aru especially naturalists, colonial administrators, members of the Indische (Protestant and State) church, and self-styled "wanderers," always entailed gestures of a practical and more often than not godly kind. Nomination was, of course, the christening act par excellence (Greenblatt 1991: 52–85; Pratt 1992). If it was especially in naming that the religious and territorial projects of Europe initially tended to come together, it was from the eighteenth century on nature itself—as revealing through study and knowledge the handiwork of God—that increasingly became the object of attention. A century later, following the publication of Darwin's *The Origin of Species* (1859) and—more relevant here—Wallace's *The Malay Archipelago* (1869),[8] evolutionists and creationists would wage battle over the source of the excessive beauty of creatures like Aru's Paradise Birds—how could such extravagance be earthly was the challenge posed by the latter, how could their showy garishness or that of say peacocks, hummingbirds, or orchids exist in the world other than as part of a divine plan to edify humanity (Quammen 1996: 610)?

Another prevalent gesture with which divinity had long been—though much less contestedly—interwoven was the colonial practice of giving cloth or clothes to local rulers and the more extended, openended effort to encloth persons and even entire populations. More explicitly borne out in the association between the robe and the priesthood, between "men of the cloth" and the service of God,[9] the primacy of clothing in the often godlike authorizing actions of Europeans was rooted not simply or always in moral or chaste ideas about personhood and propriety but, equally importantly, in the fact that "God Himself 'clothed' the earth in the process of Creation and that He manifests Himself 'clothed' with honor and majesty, who coverest thyself with light as with a garment" (Psalm 104.1–2 in Perniola 1989: 238). More than the familiar story of Creation and its aftermath in which the substitution of clothing for nudity discloses the original sin, at issue here is the important relationship between Christian thought and certain notions of European statecraft and political theory which from the Late Middle Ages on posited a close connection between divine or divinized kingship and the mantles of authority and rule (Kantorowicz 1957; Marin 1988; Wilentz 1985). It is especially this genealogy that accounts for the long tradition in the Indies of handing out cloth or clothing to subjugated peoples in order to consecrate and give substance to the officializing gestures of colonial politics.

One of the most common acts of rule in the former Netherlands East Indies upon the installment of a headman was the bestowal of cloth (sometimes but not always in the form of a flag) and/or clothing, which commonly accompanied an act of appointment, and often a silver or gold-knobbed staff of office. As a practice dating from the time of the VOC (Vereenigde Oostindischen Compagnie) or Dutch East India Company and continued throughout the colonial period, such ceremonies of investiture displayed not only a remarkable persistence over time but also a certain uniformity across the archipelago. To give an example, the objects presented by colonial administrators in the 1890s to Aru chiefs upon their official installments were virtually the same as those given in 1623 by Jan Carstensz., the commander of the Pera, when he was dispatched from the Moluccan capital Ambon to Aru with the mission of establishing ties of "friendship" with "all kings" (*alle connighen*) (F.W. Stapel 1943: 32–40; Corpus Diplomaticum III, 1943, v. 91: 180). Nor were such gestures limited to the Dutch alone. A good century later, de Bougainville interrupted his circumnavigation with a stopover on the island of Buton just south of Celebes where he left some gifts of cloth (and accepted a deer), made certain that another cut of cloth—the flag of the French nation—was displayed and made "known," and commented as well on local attire (de Bougainville 1982 [1771]: 377). Such scenes of encounter and exchange were often the stuff of serious competition between European nations, although there was, not surprisingly, considerable divergence both among individuals and at different historical junctures in the scrupulousness with which these ceremonies were carried out.

Figure 8.   Regent in Official Costume (1919)

Besides the trail of cloth left behind after such official moments
in the Moluccas where—as in other parts of the Indies—the costumes, flags, and gifts of fabric tended to be "preserved with the
greatest of care as heirlooms, and used only on official occasions"
(Kolff 1840: 229–39; cf. Merton 1910: 119), a formal decision to import cloth into Aru was taken in 1761 for reasons that do not concern
us here. By the mid-nineteenth century cloth and clothing were
being imported to the islands in impressive number and variety.

In an article on the "State of Imports and Exports to the Aru Islands, during the Year 1849," cloth heads a double list of imports that
was compiled by the commissioned official for the archipelago and
that is subdivided into "Goods of European Origin" and "Goods of
Asian Origin" (Bosscher 1853: 327–31). Some ten years later cloth
continues to prevail in a detailed list drawn up by another colonial
official and, again subdivided into "European cloth" comprising:
"unbleached cotton—Madapolam, the brand NHM [Nederlandsche
Handels Maatschappij] is carefully watched out for, the Belgian and
English Madapolams have less value—, chintzes of various sorts, blue
cotton of various sorts, red Adrianopol cotton, slendangs, abdominal
belts and the like, headcloths of various sorts, sarongs of English and
Dutch imitation, kodie, thread and unspun cotton" (van der Crab
1862: 87–88). Under the heading "Cloth from elsewhere, outside of
Europe" we find "sarongs: Java, Buginese [South Celebes], Gorontalo
[North Celebes], and Bengal, kodies, Tjindees, gingans, and other fabrics" (van der Crab 1862: 88). During the latter half of the nineteenth-century, only alcohol occasionally rivaled cloth's precedence
on the list of imports to Aru.

Notwithstanding the insistence on keeping goods of European
versus those of Asian or "Elsewhere" provenance apart, the above testifies not only to the complex circuits traveled by cloth as it made its
way from diverse sites of "origin" to Aru, but even more to the prolific hybridizations that characterized colonial cloth production itself.
"Chintz," from the Hindi *chint* is, of course, a famous example. Looking over the lists, however, others appear. What is one to make, for
instance, of European *batiks*, or NHM, Belgian, or English Madapol-
lams, sarongs of English and Dutch imitation, or gingans "from elsewhere, outside of Europe?" Such examples underscore the import of
attending to the complicated criss-crossings and crossovers characteristic of cloth production within the larger colonial situation that
comprised not only "Elsewhere" or Europeans in "Elsewhere" but always and inevitably Europe or the metropole itself. It is important to
recall, for instance, that the intensive dissemination of cloth in a

place like Aru was only possible as a consequence of the revolution in cloth production that was occasioned as much by the colonial enterprise itself as it was by an "industrial revolution" that traditional historiography records as exclusively European in origin (McKendrick 1982; Mukerji 1983). Along these same lines, it is probably not for nothing that Adam Smith's famous example of the division of labor was none other than a pin factory (Smith 1976 [1776]: 8–9), or that a coat makes such an early appearance in Marx's *Capital* (in addition to the other reasons that Peter Stallybrass gives in his contribution to this volume) (Marx 1967 [1867]: 41). Likewise, it is crucial to recognize that at the same time that Aruese ornamented and outfitted themselves in the garb of European and Eurasian civilization, their own islands were being stripped of the luxury articles of fleeting European and Asian fashions.

One account has it that during the fin de siècle feather craze that overtook Europe, 3000 Bird of Paradise skins were being exported from Aru's capital Dobo annually (Quammen 1993: 38). In the 1880s a self-styled "naturalist's wife" writes of her distress upon seeing in the port of Makassar a cargo from these same parts comprising "2000 skins of the orange-feathered bird of paradise, 800 of the kingbird, and a various lot of others" (Forbes 1987 [1887]: 36). In New Guinea, no less than three European nations—the Netherlands, England, and Germany—vied for the privilege and profit that would come from the plumes destined for European women's hats. At the height of this trade, between the 1880s and World War I, up to 80,000 birds were killed and exported per year from Dutch New Guinea alone, while the ban on hunting in 1924 together with the change in fashion left behind a ghostly landscape of abandoned settlements that had arisen or boomed during the great feather hunt (Purcell & Gould 1992: 76).[10] Nor, incidentally, were the naturalists themselves always circumspect in their own collecting, and for some like Alfred Russel Wallace this was a primary source of income. Thus, Wallace financed his expedition to the Malay archipelago with collecting for museums and private individuals with a passion for natural history. Seen in this light, Aru was not only a crucial case for the formulation of his theory of nature but also the place where he accumulated the most lucrative collections of his eight-year travels (Quammen 1993: 38).

Rather than insisting on what risks becoming a fairly seamless story of imports and exports, or of commodities and their conspicuous collection, I focus in what follows on one of this story's most striking denouements: the dressed aspect of Aruese as such appeared to visiting Europeans. A look at some of the descriptions left by nineteenth-century travelers to Aru of "native," "national," and "European" attire suggests that appearance was, indeed, all important. In focusing on this dressed aspect of Aruese, the accent here is on the embodiment and fit of costume understood as embracing not only cloth but anything else that either accompanied its transmission or became part of its trappings in Aru.

Following the contours of cloth on Aruese bodies compels at the same time several critical moves. It means, first, leaving behind the museumizing that all too long has hung up the history of cloth, making of it an endless train of death-dealing descriptions of disembodied dress and technologies of production. For if, following Barthes, "it is impossible to conceive of a dress without a body . . . the empty garment, without head and limbs . . . is death, not the neutral absence of the body, but the body mutilated, decapitated" (Barthes in Gaines 1990: 3), it is also true that after a death, cloth—having once received a body—can never be neutral again (Stallybrass 1993). Indeed, it may be more saturated with life than ever before. The point being that, as the next best thing to bodies, cloth tends to commingle in itself life and death in an often uncanny fashion. One guiding assumption here is that this uncanniness is itself a product of modernity insofar as the latter introduces a novel sense of timing in which "old" and "new," "traditional" and "modern," and perhaps even the living and the dead become clearcut alternatives as they are made to jostle for places in the positioning of things. Another assumption is that historically the perceived relations between human bodies and clothing has been highly variable. The fact that in the language of nineteenth-century English tailors clothing retained the "memories" of the bodies it had once contained—most obviously in the creases left behind by them in sleeves (Stallybrass in this volume)—suggests a deeper connection or more intimate embeddedness of human bodies in the clothes they wore than is possible in our own fast-paced times. Today, perhaps more than at any other moment, only death seems to stay the frenetic donning and discarding of clothing that both materially and socially registers fashion's compulsive swings. Another example of a marked difference in the historic relations between bodies and clothes would be the moment when modern medicine begins to emerge and some of the first anatomical drawings depict human skin as itself a kind of bloodless, luxurious fabric that can be folded back to reveal the wondrous secrets lying within (Perniola 1989: 250; 258–59). It follows from the above that the approach taken here also departs from the kind of perspective that sees cloth as always already more than skin-deep, embedded as it is held to be in underlying meanings that model and color the more superficial phenomena of the sloppy and slipshod everyday. Let us turn then now to engage the "look" of Aru as it was received and recorded by nineteenth-century visitors to the islands.

THE STANDARD ADULT MALE SPECIMEN

Not unlike the pursuit of Birds of Paradise in their customary habitat, Wallace opined—expressing a view that was increasingly shared by others in an age that witnessed the beginnings of ethnologizing if not anthropology proper—that "one must see the savage at home to know what he really is" (Wallace 1962 [1869]: 332). If the two forms of description privileged in late nineteenth-century writings on Aru—namely, those of birds and their plumage, especially Birds of Paradise, and those of Aruese in different kinds of dress—are set side by side, then a funny thing happens. What this juxtaposition makes clear is that the "savage at home" in his natural setting, as it were, bears a marked resemblance to the Bird of Paradise as he is also captured in his characteristic surroundings. This striking overlap becomes even more blatant when we consider the gendered dimension of these descriptions. Thus, writers often insisted on the dramatic difference in appearance between men and women or, likewise, between the male and the female of a given bird species. In what was presumably a more widely reiterated theme, the former's flamboyance, exuberance, and bejeweled beauty contrasted sharply with the aspect of the latter—inevitably drab, less decorated, and easily overlooked. This was almost a golden rule in the creation of natural collections where the unmarked and prize specimen was always the adult male while the female sometimes did not even warrant a description (Pratt 1992: 64).[11]

After a lavish passage devoted to the "King Bird of Paradise" Wallace begins his short aside on what I would call the Queen by observing that, "the female of this little gem is such a plainly coloured bird, that it can at first sight hardly be believed to belong to the same species" (Wallace 1962 [1869]: 427). Regarding another "rare and elegant little bird" found in neighboring New Guinea, Wallace writes that the female of this variety much resembles that of the King and "we may therefore conclude that its near ally, the 'Magnificent,' is *at least* equally plain in this sex" (ibid: 428; emphasis added.).

A similar sexual dimorphism in decoration was extended to so-called savages as these were observed "at home."[12] Again Wallace, with characteristic confidence notes that "the men, as usual among savages, adorn themselves more than the women" (ibid: 355) while another visitor frequenting Aru at the absolute fin de siècle notes that "the Aru women wear a considerable number of ornaments, but the men, like all true Papuans, wear by far the greater number" (Cayley-Webster 1898: 207). Likewise in Tanimbar southwest of Aru, the aforementioned "naturalist's wife" noted that if the women "do not dye their hair as the men do, and give little time to its arrangement" (Forbes 1987 [1887]: 169),

> the gay young beaux [in these islands] spend much time in arranging the hair; those to whom nature has given only straight locks use a crimping instrument. Just behind the postholder's house stood a long unused prahu, in which rain-water collected, and this was the village mirror. It was an unfailing amusement to me to watch the row of youths standing there in the morning, tying with utmost nicety, and apparently with great vanity, the different coloured bandages, one just edging over the other to see that the well-combed locks were properly confined (ibid: 160).[13]

At a time when in Europe men, at least of the "better classes," went about only in black and gray, thereby displaying "a drabness that caused Baudelaire to exclaim that the male sex looked as if it were always in mourning"[14] and women, as we have already seen, bedecked themselves with plumes and could also claim "perfume, makeup, coloring, silk and lace" as their "exclusive province," at such a time Nature as Aru and Culture as—of course—France seemed to stand each other off in customary fashion (Corbin 1990: 488).

But unlike the changing fashions of the metropole, whatever the peoples of Aru or their neighbors chose to wear is either inscribed in essentialized gendered differences analogous to those that in nature distinguish male and female bird species, in the unchanging rules of custom, or in another timeless primordialism—the nation. As so often in colonial and subsequently some anthropological accounts, native custom appears carved in stone, as a kind of idol that the savages bow before in fear and unwavering submission. One Dutch official writes, for instance, that some traders claimed that they had suggested to the men of Aru's Backshore or eastern side of the islands that these should make their women wear sarongs. The men, however, had rejected this proposal on the grounds that their mothers had not worn sarongs either and furthermore that they feared a divergence from custom would elicit punishment and cause their villages to die out (Brumond 1853: 291).

The following suggests, however, that the stubbornness with which Backshore Aruese allegedly held to their own ways was probably at least as much a pervasive reluctance to accept those of the Europeans and the traders as their own.

> Although the inhabitants of the backshore possess enough means in their pearl banks to supply themselves with better clothing, they remain stubbornly attached to their national costume. They seem to have a distinct prejudice against clothing, and only the heads dress themselves, for better or for worse, upon visits of officials (Baron van Hoëvell 1890: 22–23).

Whatever their own reasons might have been, it is clear that the inhabitants of Aru's Backshore, at least in part and at certain historical moments, resisted some of the things that the colonials would put upon them. At the same time it is also clear that they busied themselves refashioning cloth into those cuts that most pleased themselves. A brand consciousness of sorts was already in place such that, as we have already seen, NHM Madapollam was prefered over Belgian and English variants. Predilections for particular colors or cloth patterns observed among the Frontshore Aruese were duly noted while more dramatic alterations documented in descriptions of what in the late nineteenth century came to be called "the national costume" (*nationale kleederdracht*) testify as well to the creativity on which cloth could count in Aru (Baron van Hoëvell 1890: 22–23).

Reading through the nineteenth-century sources on Aru it is often hard to be certain what "nation" was in fact conveyed by the local costume. If Backshore Aruese were at times not overly eager to accept the staffs of office offered to them by the colonial government and persisted as well in adhering to their own styles of dress, the Dutch flag nonetheless provided the design for men's loincloths—and one, I was told, that remained popular until the Japanese occupation of the islands during World War II. Then, for obvious reasons, the so-called "flag loincloth" boasting the red, white, and blue stripes of the Dutch national banner was rapidly abandoned. Striped tails, however, continue to decorate the loincloths worn by men during *adat* or customary feasts.[15] Nor should it surprise us that in a place soon to be designated the "Tropical Netherlands,"—reiterating the Dutch Islamicist Snouk Hurgronje's famous vision that foresaw "only Oriental and Occidental Netherlanders,"—the colonizer nation increasingly if not consistently assumed the place of an original, with the colony defined as its copy (Snouck Hurgronje in van Doorn 1994: 60).

This kind of imaginary goes at least some way toward explaining the workings of a prevalent process of recall in which, for instance, a colonial visitor was struck by the "costume of a Dutch fisherman" (*het costuum eenen Hollandschen visscher*) unwittingly reproduced, as it were, in the clothing worn by an Aru chief (Brumond 1853: 252–53). Similarly, a fleeting sense of a familiar fashion might also be felt in the "look" left by an Aruese. Anna Forbes, the naturalist's wife, mistook at one point a group of Aruese pearldivers for women—a mistake, she explained, "due to the arrangement of the hair; for their immense mops of frizzy locks were gathered behind in a large chignon or knot, while the short escaped hair formed a fringe, the whole coiffure being an untidy copy of the fashionable style I had left behind in England" (Forbes 1987 [1887]: 129). In the latter half of the nineteenth century fashion reigned supreme in metropolitan capitals while the rural countrysides of European nations became the site for a nostalgic folklorization of, among other things, costume.[16] Abroad, however, identifications of fashion and folklore remained limited to such ephemeral feelings of *déja-vu*, both generally giving way in the colonies to more timeless readings of local custom or of native life lived out in more positively or negatively valued states of nature.[17]

IMAGINARY HEADS AND MOCK CHIEFS

Like some other colonials, the Dutch made much of mimicry. At the same time they also often feared it as something that could easily get out of hand and, drifting from the original, take on, as it were, a life of its own. A clear instance of this can be traced in the concerns and correspondence about the circulation of the staffs of office topped by the silver or golden "apples" already admired by de Bougainville at the end of the eighteenth century. Tokens like these together with acts of appointment and flags assumed an almost talismanic importance for the Dutch around the turn of the century or that time that, across the Malay archipelago, witnessed the transformation of a colonial project into a properly imperial one. In Aru, the location of staffs of office within different settlements pinpointed for the Dutch their influence in the islands and formed part of a wider process through which different "landscapes" (*landschappen*) were mapped together as a whole.[18] The importance of disseminating such tokens of Dutch rule in marginal places was repeatedly reiterated by the colonial authorities (Mailrapport 1885: 6448, #342+, Afschrift #1002, ARA). By the same token, the Netherlands East Indies government confiscated all flags, acts of appointment, and staffs of office when it chastised a rebellious village (Mailrapport 1887: 6460, #342+, Afschrift #1002, ARA).

As in the capital Ambon where the staff of office was always returned to the colonial government upon the death of the office holder thereby assuring the authorities the opportunity to give it out again, so too should have been the arrangement in Aru. Here, however, the staff together with the office it embodied, appears to have been passed on from father to son, causing the Dutch to bemoan their inability to control the excessive circulation of the staffs. Through a kind of crazy mathematics, the prolific passings-on had—for them at least—the unfortunate consequence of multiplying the number of native chiefs (Mailrapport 1880: 6392, ARA). One might suggest, drawing on Marc Shell's insights regarding tromp-l'oeil and fake money, that the counterfeit, having an inflationary value, always robs its subjects of their originality (Shell 1992: 23)[19] Indeed, from the perspective of colonial bureaucrats, the unauthorized multiplication of chiefs produced an untidy and troubling situation in which, "one finds in addition to the true heads, a multitude of imaginary heads, still armed with the staffs of office of their forefathers, even though [their] family has not exercised authority for a long time" (Mailrapport 1876: 6042, Afschrift #486+, ARA). Presumably this depends on whose authority one is talking about. In New Guinea as well the presence of "mock chiefs" was reported, and described by one Dutchman as "founded on the idea that any foreign strand dweller would think himself the lord and master of every living thing in the interior"—unlike, of course, the Europeans.[20] Although the latter represents a different possibility built around the coastal/hinterland or, if you like, Frontshore/Backshore distinction that was prevalent throughout the Malay world, the lingering sense left by the specter of a multitude of imaginary heads and mock chiefs is that of a landscape drifting from the intended Dutch one, an alternative administrative vision disruptive of their own mappings, and, importantly, something much closer to a mockery than a mimicry of themselves.

Indeed, the fine line between mimicry and mockery runs like a red thread through the descriptions of Aruese as they appeared before nineteenth-century visitors in quasi-European dress.[21] One of the problems must have been that the islanders—made over in something akin to metropole mode—seemed to stand before the Europeans as an unsettling, slightly skewed copy of themselves as well as of the "civilization" they had come to convey through clothes.[22] I suspect that the sheer materiality of this "meeting ground"—the mere physical fact of being confronted with native bodies contained in one's own colonizer clothes—is one aspect of the discomfort that seems to filter through the writings of these Europeans. Given that their visits coincided with the high point of colonial racism when the divide between the colonizers and the colonized became increasingly construed as founded in the physiognomic, material differences between the races, this particular form of "contact" may have had profound unsettling effects.[23] Following this line of argument, savage bodies in civilized clothes would defy the distinction that, in part, determined the double list of European cloth and clothing versus the same kind of thing imported from "Elsewhere," that underwrote the constant concern on the part of colonials with categories like *métis, indo,* "Brown Gentlemen" (Stoler 1992) and so on, and that caused, more diffusely, an "invisible line" to be obsessively imagined as cropping up wherever and whenever the twain would meet (Pemberton 1994: 96–101). A major conundrum faced by colonials in the Indies lay, for instance, in what the authorities called "artificially fabricated Europeans" (*kunstmatig gefabriceerde Europeanen*) or persons who condensed the fear that a copy could be taken for the Real Thing, that more concretely "children were being raised in cultural fashions that blurred the distinction between ruler and ruled" (Stoler 1992: 531). Clothing was, indeed, as Stoler suggests, critical in all of this as borne out by the notion in French Indochina, for example, of "an *indigene* in disguise," or the accusations of Annamite women who had lived in concubinage of clothing their métisse daughters in European attire, "while ensuring them that their souls and sentiments remained deeply native" (Stoler ibid). Such, indeed, are some of the colonial contradictions that help to reveal the cracks in modernity's mirror (Dirks 1990: 29). Was it then not only in the moves of mimicry but perhaps even more in the close physical containment of native bodies by European clothing that the contamination of the colonizer by the colonized could most concretely be felt? Taussig's insistence on the necessary collaboration between copy and contact, on "the magical power of replication" whereby the image affects—or even contaminates—what it is an image of, is, I believe, also relevant here (Taussig 1993: 2). Let us consider then some of these contaminations and the ways in which Europeans, in turn, attempted to contain them.

THE TOOTH OF TIME

Like Macaulay's translator and other mimic-men, Aru chiefs—and more those of the Frontshore than the Back—could in Homi Bhabha's words be called "the appropriate objects of a colonialist chain of command, authorized versions of otherness. But they are also . . . the figures of a doubling, the part-objects of a metonymy of colonial desire which alienates the modality and normality of those dominant discourses in which they emerge as " 'inappropriate' subjects" (Bhabha 1994: 88). This kind of doubleness can be discerned in the colonial attitude toward Aru chiefs in quasi-European clothes as perhaps the privileged site where copy and contact, containment and contamination accompany each other and ambivalently collide. In ceremonies of investiture, Aru "savages" were turned into "true heads" as the appropriate objects of a colonial chain—or even girdle—as well as the concrete investments of a "civilization" that was held to emanate outwards from Europe to the farthest corners of the globe. By extension, the chiefs were also those persons who most often faced the Europeans in their old hand-me-down clothes, motivating thereby and once again, colonial gestures of containment.

In their writings, European visitors to Aru deployed a number of strategies that were aimed, I suggest, at displacing and disarming the apparition of Aruese as quasi-metropolitans, an apparition that proved disorienting to their own imperial pretensions—if perhaps only in passing. Thus, one move made repeatedly by the colonizers when describing Aruese in European-style clothes was to highlight the discomfort with which such dress was worn, in an effort, I suspect, to disguise from themselves their own sense of being unsettled by the clothing's off-centered "look." As Freud would long have us know, what we tend to see as other and outside of ourselves more often than not dwells within, while what appears most uncanny or *unheimlich* is commonly quite familiar and close to home (Freud 1955 [1919]). It follows from this that some of the late nineteenth-century writings deploying strategies of displacement and containment probably say more about a sense of out-of-placeness experienced by visiting Europeans than about the islanders themselves. Beyond the colonial racism that underwrote the rift running between native bodies and civilized clothes, what I believe the Europeans may also have faced in the distorted "look" reflected back to them by Aruese was, among other things, their own "off-center" subject positions—as colonials far removed in every possible respect from the fashionable, tone-setting, and policy-making metropolitan centers of Europe, as persons who could pretend to aristocratic privilege when abroad but could never escape from their class origins at home, and perhaps as other things as well. All this and more may have been brought home to them—if only fleetingly—in the *unheimlich* apparition of Aruese in cast-off, quasi-metropolitan clothes.

Especially shoes, as perhaps the quintessential marker of the shod and unsavage Western world were often marshalled forth in colonial writings to make a comforting point (cf. Schulte Nordholt 1997). "The Orang Kaya [or headman]," writes one European visitor, "paid me a visit directly I let go the anchor. He was dressed in a black coat and hat with white trousers and boots, which kept him in a constant state of unrest the whole time he was on board" (Cayley-Webster 1898: 203). At other times, a rejection or absence of shoes was simply noted (Brumond 1853: 252–53; Riedel 1886: 258).

Another sort of strategy that seems to have been prevalent among Europeans when sizing up Aruese outfitted as their quasi-metropolitan selves was to stress that the "savages," in multiple ways, fell short—or big or loose or long or simply silly—of that which they were (allegedly) trying to imitate.

> Already from afar, several cannon shots rang out toward us; when we arrived, the Orang kaya awaited us with his following on the bank. . . . A small, puny little man with a dried out and sallow face, he was decked out in a red general's uniform. The tails of the much too wide frock coat hung to his heels, while the broad golden collar enclosed his head far above the ears, leaving scarcely an opening through which one could discover his insignificant little face. The with braid richly decorated pants hung with many pleats on his boots, which surely each could have accommodated two of his feet . . . in one hand his staff of rank with the golden knob held by its middle stiffly against his nose, in the other a red handkerchief [this] completed the highly remarkable portrait of the great man. Immobile, he awaited us in this pose and received all greetings: his face remained entirely unaltered; a hand and stiff bow, worthy of the greatest monarch, was his response to all (Brumond 1853: 81).

Described in the fullest of detail, every aspect of the "great man's" attire as well as the stiff embodiment with which he wore it is, to paraphrase Bhabha, "not quite, not right."[24]

Ever both amused and scrupulously observant, Anna Forbes, the naturalist's wife, writes of her encounter with some Aruese who stopped by her ship to report the murder of the son of "the Rajah of some place in the neighborhood."

> I could not refrain from laughing aloud at the ludicrous appearance of the group before us, but was soon checked when I saw their really sorrowful countenances. . . . The old chief wore bright green trousers, a

long black coat, and *over* this a *kabia* [her emphasis, this was obviously not done] or native jacket of bright purple satin with inch-wide gold-thread stripes, and a very dirty and starchless collar lay untidily on his neck. Another had trousers of bright scarlet, with large butterfly pattern, a faded green silk coat brocaded with large gold flowers, and a shabby grey felt hat; and another a long surtout coat, with a much worn black satin vest, wrong side out, over it. Two others were not so abundantly clothed, for one suit served them both. It had evidently descended to the present wearers from some passing vessel where the theatrical entertainments had been whiling the tedium of a voyage, for the coat had a blue tail and a red, and the trousers one leg of green and the other of yellow. Somehow the man with the trousers looked much better clad than the man with the coat. These garments formed doubtless the entire wardrobe of the village, accumulated during who knows how many generations (Forbes 1987 [1887]: 134–35).

More than the fit or the embodiment of the clothing, Forbes focuses repeatedly in on the real wrongness with which the tenue is put together—a vest worn "the wrong side out," a *kabia* (sic) pulled on— oh my goodness!—*over* a long black coat, or a costume, already theatrical in design, harlequin-like, and split, *again* split to be shared between two "savages"— just as, she speculates, the entire wardrobe seems itself to have been pieced together from the scraps of clothing accumulated through the ages in one Aru village.

One of the concrete effects of the writing strategies that I have so far considered—the lack of a "fit" between Aruese and European clothing or the real wrongness with which it was worn—was to impose a distance between "savage" bodies and "civilized" clothes. Or, put otherwise, everything in these late nineteenth-century descriptions happens as if a very visible line had been drawn between Aruese and the kinds of figures they cut in European clothes. The distance thus effected highlights the difference between Europeans who wore their clothes—and especially when abroad—not simply as a sort of social skin but even more as a "civilized" one (Turner 1980), and Aruese concerning whom and quite concretely, a slippage served to separate them almost physically from the costumes that they created with the colonizer's clothes—at least that is if one takes the Europeans at their word.

Nor is it surprising that in the context of the thoroughly "modern" endeavor constituting late nineteenth-century colonialism, fashion figured as another prevalent mode invoked by the Europeans to make more or less the same important statement. Following this fashion statement, time served as the raw material with which distinctions of dress were marked and made, and thereby, as a way of denying the coevalness between colonizers and colonized through the medium of their very clothes (Fabian 1983). Note, however, that if the Europeans always ascribed one or another "traditional" outfit to the natives, the move that would deny coevalness through contrasts in European costume was maybe even more effective or, at any rate, differently so than when the natives appeared in their own alleged timeless attire. The crucial difference between customary native garb and a costume configured after the colonizer is that the latter—whatever else one might say—was always anachronistically at a once or twice remove from the latest colonial, not to mention metropolitan look. And this, of course, was not that different from the colonizer's own sartorial position vis-à-vis the European metropole.

A particularly telling passage from one Dutchman's piece on the "Religious Practices in the Residence of Amboina" provides the title of this essay and informs us that:

> The Christian natives in Ambon are now wild about these high silk hats. They show off with them on Sundays, when they go to Church, to funerals and on festive occasions. They are usually overly old examples that have suffered from the tooth of time, so that like shoes they are sometimes shined with polish, but it does look distinguished, and the man who can get hold of such a gem is more than a little proud of it! (de Vries 1921–22: 112).[25]

Sometimes insisting on a separation between colonized bodies and civilized clothes gets the better of European writers, as here where the Sunday bests worn by Ambonese Christians truly separate from their bodies in a fetishistic turn in which clothing and church-going come entirely apart thereby allowing a hat to wander off by itself. Following a slippage that betrays how the author may himself have lost a stable position from which to speak—and which ensues from the recollection of the *shining* sometimes given to high silk hats—the hat takes on a life of its own—"but it *does* [apart from Ambonese bodies] look distinguished." Not unlike Paradise's birds, the antique silk hat, transfigured into a precious "gem," becomes both elusive and something to be eagerly pursued and taken hold of.

Taking a look now at the time that the Europeans threaded through clothes it is important to realize that Aruese like the Ambonese Christians captured in the above quote, were regarded as always already out of date and—what is more—doubly so. Both overly old and out of fashion, their costumes were literally *and* metaphorically gnawed by the aforementioned "tooth of time." Besides the issue of time itself, one crucial, material consequence of the quick turnover characteristic of what Barthes called "the fashion system" (1967) is that "a disproportionate volume of cloth ends up in the ragbag or as hand-me-downs"—or, indeed, I would add, as something to be given away in the colonies (Schneider & Weiner 1989: 11). Even in this century and culminating in the conversion offensive launched in Aru by Dutch missionaries in the 1960s and especially mid-1970s (Spyer 1996), boxes of clothing containing the cast-offs of Catholic families in the southern Netherlands were shipped in to be distributed in the islands. Another consequence of "the cult of the transitory"—the essence of fashion and, more generally, "[capitalist] modernity"—is that its built-in momentum for making things obsolete simultaneously promotes both desire and a disdain for material goods (Lefebvre in Lears 1994: 385). And if the fluctuations of desire that make up fashion were felt over and over again in Aru, fashion's flipside—disdain, derision, or a more mild ironic amusement—tends to describe the tone of the Europeans as they took in the look of the Aruese. The thing about fashion, as we all know, is that once passé, it very rapidly looks ridiculous. In colonial accounts therefore, fashion could readily be called upon to make precisely those kinds of statements that many scholars of colonialism today regard as typifying the colonial attitude towards colonized peoples. For like history and like time, fashion belonged to the colonizers and never the colonized, and, consequently, just as Aruese and other others were by definition always out of history and out of time, so too, and even more concretely, were they always out of fashion (cf. Dirks 1990: 28). At the same time, of course, it is possible to suggest that through their own creative configurations of costume and their refashionings of a retro colonial or even company "look," Aruese and others in confronting the Europeans with their own cast-off and hand-me-down clothes turned, in a fashion, the clock back at them.

THE LEGLESS PARADISE

The overinvestment in vestment characteristic of these late nineteenth-century colonial accounts—again, and crucially, only rivaled by the drawn-out descriptions of the splendid, bejeweled birds that made of this place a kind of Paradise—and the compulsion on the part of visiting Europeans to embellish their writings continually with descriptions of dress describes the kind of obsessive desire that both makes for and repeatedly motivates the fetishistic focus on a given thing. But only rarely in the colonizers' accounts did clothing truly take on a life of its own to become a full-fledged fetish on a par with Paradise's birds. Thus, whether for Europeans Paradise was linked to cloth or, inversely, lay in the romantic desire of keeping such "civilization" afar, in the various colonial readings of the relation between "civilization" and cloth, cloth repeatedly served as a kind of border, a "civilizing" skin which, depending upon one's inclinations, could be filled in favorably or not. In clothing Paradise, and in playing God going about the important business of Creation, the Europeans also created a conundrum for themselves. The act of clothing their colonized subjects in the garb of quasi-metropolitan "civilization" somehow seemed to imply for the colonials that they themselves might not be fully installed in their own clothes. Yet not doing so seemed to suggest much the same thing. In other words, given the close creative fit between colonial authority and "civilized" clothes, there was simply no way for the Europeans to retain full authority over their colonized subjects *and* simultaneously carry out their "civilizing" mission to its logical implications—that is, the making over of these same subjects into a mirror, albeit tropical reflection of themselves. Although offering in its materiality the promise of fulfillment, clothing always pointed beyond itself to a "civilization" that could never be fully attained.

Yet if Aruese in quasi-metropolitan clothes might be seen in some sense as a concretization of the colonizers' "civilization" as well as—in being unfinished and fragmentary—its negation, so, too, though somewhat differently, might those birds who from the beginning provoked the association between this place and Paradise. If, we consider, for instance, the names that the Europeans bestowed on the most flamboyant of Aru's birds then the utopics of an imperial design begins to emerge. Because the first of such birds arrived in Spain from the Moluccas legless—as purely a splendid and preserved skin—the belief spread that lacking apparently any means to alight on earth such beings could only originate in Paradise. Hence also Linnaeus's commemoration of this old legend in the name the "Legless Paradise." Later nomenclature continued the paradise theme while at the same time providing it with somewhat more earthly dimensions. Following this vision, paradise was a place presided over by kings wielding an authority that was immediately manifest and provided with substance in the resplendant showiness, Gothic theatricality, and glittering presence of their royal highness. As Purcell and Gould write about the birds named for kings: "The names chosen for Birds of Paradise reinforce their gaudy majesty. Most were given monikers to honor various European monarchs" (Purcell & Gould 1992: 69). In addition to the lofty leglessness of "Paradise" himself, we find the somewhat Lesser though equally regal King Bird of Paradise, the King-of-Saxony Bird of Paradise, and the Blue Bird of Paradise or *Paradisaea rudolphi*, named after the only son of Emperor Franz Joseph, the Archduke Rudolph of Austria (ibid.) as well as others whose names reflect a more generic royal splendor like the "Magnificent." Some names simply invoke the patrimony of kings. Thus, if the descriptions of Birds of Paradise left by nineteenth-century travelers to Aru and neighboring New Guinea commonly rely on a language of opulence and treasure to convey the breathtaking beauty of these creatures, at least one species was actually named after a jewel: Among French authors, the so called Lesser Bird of Paradise is known as "Le petit Emeraude" (Wallace 1962 [1869]: 423). As the classic exception that proves the rule, perhaps the best example of the kind of royalty repeatedly assigned to Paradise's birds is the *Diphyllodes respublica*, named by the French ornithologist Charles Louis Bonaparte who also happened to have been a nephew of the lesser, more farcical emperor, Napoleon III. In his own words, the French ornithologist chose this name because, "I have not the slightest regard for the sovereignty of all the princes in the world." As Purcell and Gould explain, however, "he also thumbed his nose at earthly governments, selecting his label in mock honor of 'that Republic which might have been a Paradise had not the ambitions of Republicans, unworthy of the name they were using, made it by their evil actions more like a Hell'" (Purcell & Gould 1992: 69–70).

On either side of the turning of the present century, and at the height of its power and glory, a certain telos underwrote the imagining of the Netherlands East Indies as an archipelago of imperial proportions and design. Traced out in the glassy brilliance of the Indies as an "emerald girdle"—as simultaneously a possession and a prize—this kind of imaginary had its refractions even in Aru, located, as it were, at one far end of the imperial chain. If, for Europeans, the Legless Paradise embodied in its disembodied skin the ethereal heights of a fully dressed beyond, the men and, even less, the women of Aru, could never approximate the exalted "civilization" that the Europeans hid in their clothes. Indeed, one might say that the repeated distancing of natives from their "civilized" clothes had as its counterpart a colonial reverie of a legless Paradise from which all Aruese had been excluded. More specifically, a fetishized and thoroughly "Tropical Gothic" vision of civilization in which obsessions about endlessly proliferating heads thought to make a mockery of colonial rule, could be momentarily displaced by those splendid birds that as surrogates for European monarchs displayed civilization in its most exuberant, exalted, and authoritative excess. It is through this particular fetishization of nature as a displaced thoroughly "Tropical Gothic" civilization that colonial authority came to be naturalized in many of the late nineteenth-century writings on Aru. This naturalization of the guise and trappings of rule took place, moreover, with reference to monarchy or that form of government which by drawing all power to a single center and demanding the abdication of all self-dependant power before itself, has been characterized as the most fetishistic form of government (Godwin in Simpson 1982: 24). Monarchy, following Godwin, was also one big fakery with therefore "the most fatal opinion that could lay hold upon the minds" of a king's subjects being that "kings are but men" (ibid.). Much the same could I think be said regarding the Dutch colonizers at that high Imperial moment immediately preceding the onset of the nationalist movement, at least regarding the fatal consequences for them that this kind of revelation on the part of their colonized subjects would eventually lead to.

In the gap, then, between birds and men lies a certain nostalgia, and one that like the emerald girdle itself is best imagined as an impossible conjunction between the pure nature of glassy-green islands and the authority of kings as concretely reflected in the unchallenged possession of their patrimonial treasures. As a constitutive moment of the modern, this nostalgia motivated not only the museumizing and racist insistence on separating over and over again and in differing fashions, "savage" bodies from "civilized" clothes, but that also harkened back to an imagined time when kings were true kings and every emperor was well-installed in his own clothes. In short, as with other jewels and other crowns, there was to the Dutch emerald girdle[26] considerably more than met the eye.

NOTES

1. Twenty-four months of fieldwork in Aru, Southeast Moluccas (1984, 1986–88, 1994) were funded by a Department of Education Fulbright-Hays Dissertation Fellowship, the Wenner-Gren Foundation for Anthropological Research, the Institute for Intercultural Studies, the Southeast Asian Council for the Association for Asian Studies with funds from the Luce Foundation, the Netherlands Foundation for the Advancement of Tropical Research (WOTRO),

and was conducted under the sponsorship of the Lembaga Ilmu Pengetahuan Indonesia and Universitas Pattimura. I am grateful to these institutions for their generous support of my work. Versions of this article were presented at an informal seminar at the University of Amsterdam Research Centre Religion & Society and at the "Border Fetishisms" conference organized by the same, at the Amsterdam School for Cultural Analysis (ASCA), the Center for Literary and Cultural Studies at Harvard University (CLCS), and the 1996 Association for Asian Studies meetings. I have been helped by the discussions on those occasions especially by Inge Boer, Johannes Fabian, John Pemberton, Adela Pinch, Peter Stallybrass, Mary Steedly, and Hent de Vries. I would also like to thank my colleagues Gerd Baumann, Birgit Meyer, Prahbu Mohapatra, Peter Pels, and Peter van Rooden for their comments on an early draft of the paper, James Scott for his on a somewhat later version, and Rafael Sánchez for his incisive reading of the penultimate version. I am especially grateful to the many Aruese women and men who talked to me about their clothes and inadvertedly encouraged me to investigate their history.

2. This expression, especially prevalent in the 1930s and 40s in the debates between Dutch conservatives and progressives concerning the significance of three hundred years of Dutch rule in the Indies, was also the title of a 1941 volume edited by W.H. van Helsdingen en H. Hoogenberk. Today in the Netherlands, a similar celebratory tone pervades the nostalgia-industry oriented advertising of such former colonial products as tobacco.

3. Ornithologists refer to such trees as "leks," while the dancing back and forth by males on a lek's branches is termed "lekking behavior." A tree with the right shape—a sparse crown and horizontal limbs that can easily accommodate the displays—might serve many consecutive generations of *P. apoda* (Quammen 1996: 620).

4. The book *Women's Hats* contains many pictures of hats adorned with feathers from different bird species as well as several topped by a whole bird. Page 111 shows a "pagoda of black draped silk velvet" crowned by a bird of paradise "complete with its two lateral tufts of magnificent feathers" (Campione 1989). The same book points out that the nineteenth-century craze for birds and feathers on European womens' hats went together with the perfection of taxidermy (ibid. 26–27). From the metropole the feathers and birds from the Indies sometimes made their way—refashioned—back to the colony. See Nieuwenhuys (1988: 44) for a photo from the early 1880s of the favorite concubine of the Javanese ruler Mangkunegoro V in full riding gear and sporting an "amazon" hat decorated with a paradise bird.

5. For the same reasons as velvet or fur which, following Freud, "reproduce [for a fetishist] the sight of the pubic hair which ought to have revealed the longed-for penis"(Freud 1950 [1927]: 201). This is presumably why the position of the decorative feather(s) in relation to the wearer is so crucial and why the further down the body it gravitates, the more erotically charged and socially suspect it becomes (like the cotton-"tails" on Playboy bunnies).

6. The role played by European women in this colonial racism was both crucial and highly complex. See Stoler 1992; 1995.

7. There were, of course, considerable differences among the European colonial powers regarding the kinds of relations they constructed with their various colonies, as, indeed, there were often important differences in the relations that any single colonizing nation might maintain with its different colonies. Furthermore, although usually in many respects differently than at home in the metropole, differences of class, gender, race, occupation, the moment of arrival to the colony, and so on distinguished the various sectors making up the colonizing population itself at any given historical moment. Nonetheless, for this article I have chosen to largely gloss over these differences in order to focus on the "tropical gothic" imagination that in certain important respects seems to have been shared by the major European colonial powers at this time. I believe that this approach is not entirely unjustified given that the various colonizing powers carefully watched and learned from each other—the 1857 Mutiny in India contained, for instance, a lesson that none could ignore. Furthermore, the texts I draw upon here are not exclusively those written by Dutch colonial officials, but also include the writings of French and especially English travelers to Aru.

8. There is considerable scholarly debate about how much influence Wallace's own ideas may have had on Darwin especially regarding the theory of natural selection. For a recent evaluation, see Quammen 1996: 102–14.

9. For a detailed discussion of such "religious habits," see Garber 1992: 210–33.

10. And they left behind more than that. Besides the "considerable supply" of dead birds left in the traders' hands and the scores of dry-docked motorboats that had once served the feather-hunters, the Dutch colonial officer who in 1937 encountered all of this in New Guinea writes that the hunters also spread venereal disease to the island's interior (van Baal 1985: 101). I would like to thank Bonno Thoden van Velzen for bringing this source to my attention.

11. In the case of cultural "specimens" this worked somewhat differently. For sure, as Pratt observes, it was often and indeed until quite recently the case that "the initial ethnographic gesture" was one of total homogenization, "a collective *they*, which distills down further into an iconic *he*" or, again, "the standard adult male specimen" (Pratt 1992: 64). At the same time it should not be forgotten that descriptions of native women in the downtrodden and exploitative conditions in which they were allegedly found by Europeans and kept by their own men also became an elaborated genre of colonial literature. Whether one wants to call this kind of description ethnographic or not, it meant that women could not always be so easily overlooked as the "female of the species." Importantly, the genre also served the purpose of setting up European men as the liberators of local women while

simultaneously displacing along with the agency of colonized women and men, their own exploitative interventions (Mani 1992).

12. Sometimes the fusion between man and bird has been even more complete as, for instance, in those cases when an Aruese dons a headdress fashioned out of Bird of Paradise plumes (Brumond 1853: 273). Today the so-called Bird of Paradise dance in which Aruese sport such headdresses is this archipelago's contribution to the regional dance competitions held annually in the south Moluccas. For an extended reflection on similar headdresses in neighboring West Irian, see Rutherford 1996.

13. Aesthetic-psychological notions of caprice, foolish vanity, and of being swayed by the superficial appearance of things as opposed to their real value has long been a part of fetish discourse (Pietz 1988: 111).

14. This kind of sobriety in male dress was in fact quite recent and ensued from what one historian describes as "a shift in style from peacock male to sombre man of action." She explains: "every European élite had taken note of the sartorial and political disaster represented by the first procession of the Estates General in Paris in 1789, the prelude to the French Revolution. On that occasion, the representatives of the Third Estate, dressed in sombre black, had been cheered; but the traditionally lavish costumes of the nobility and clergy had met with jeers or silent disgust. 'The magic of ostentation,' as Jean Starobinski puts it, had 'stopped having an effect on spectators who had learned to add up the cost.' From now on, the *habit à la francaise*, the wigs, powdered hair, brocades, silks, lace, and parrot colours, which had been fashionable from Boston to Berlin, and Moscow to Manchester, was increasingly abandoned in favour of far more subdued and functional male dress" (Colley 1992: 187).

15. A remarkable black rock with bold white stripes located in one of the broad channels that cuts across Aru and known locally as "Flag Rock" is said to have been formed from the loincloth of the mythical ancestor Urlima. For a photo, see Merton 1910: 151. Baron van Hoëvell mentions men's striped loincloths but fails to note whether they were fabricated from Dutch flags (Baron van Hoëvell 1890: 29). I believe it is safe to assume that had Aruese at the time been wearing Dutch flags this would have been deemed worth noting (at the very least). I conclude therefore that the loincloths seen by Baron van Hoëvell were not made from Dutch flags and, that probably this fashion is of a later, albeit pre-World War II, date.

16. According to Corbin, the period between 1840 and 1860 in France, a kind of golden age for traditional regional costume, was followed by "a period of mimicry" in which "peasant traditions were lost, and regional costumes, no longer worn, were piously collected by folklorists." Even though such a trajectory may seem to record a dislocation of the "past" by the "present," the emergence of "fashion"—in the form of prints and plates that circulate even in rural areas, mail order purchases, provincial branches of the

Printemps department store and so on—as a "modern" phenomenon went, of course, hand in hand with the finding of folklore as an item that became defined as a collectible (Corbin 1990: 490).

17. This is, of course, not an absolute contrast. An overlap in this respect between colony and metropole can, for instance, be found in the idea of a "national costume." In late nineteenth-century writings about Aru, however, this category fulfills the role of yet another reading of allegedly timeless native dress with the "national costume" none other than "the well-known Tjidako" or man's loincloth familiar to Europeans as standard male "savage" garb throughout the Moluccas and different from the "aprons" worn by women (van Doren 1854: 396). Notwithstanding the replacement of the prior bark and "leaf" loincloths with ones made of cloth for men, or the hybrid cloth and mat coverings worn by women, the "national costume" of Aru in the eyes of Europeans remained, it appeared, unchanged (Baron van Hoëvell 1890: 22–23; de Hollander 1898: 522).

18. This meaning of the Dutch word *landschap* refers to a portion of land or a region that may or may not have clearly defined borders. The term was common throughout the Netherlands East Indies where it came to designate administrative territories, a usage that historically predates the more familiar meaning the term "landscape" enjoys in art history. It is from the latter that the English word "landscape" derives.

19. On Africa's Gold Coast in the early eighteenth century, the so-called "Fetiche Gold" designating the religious objects made by Africans out of an admixture of gold and other substances captured for Europeans the fear of betrayal and counterfeit accompanying cross-cultural trade. As Pietz observes; "the falsity of 'sophisticated' gold in economic transactions inevitably echoed the religious falsity embodied by the gold fetish figures" (Pietz 1988: 110).

20. In actuality, Europeans themselves often had a hand in the production of "mock chiefs," as when "the wife of a celebrated trader"—who seems to have been quite a tradeswomen herself—raised several persons in New Guinea to the rank of Majoor and Kapitein (Ellen 1986: 60).

21. Bhabha in his "Of Mimicry and Man" hones in on "the area between mimicry and mockery" as that space "where the reforming, civilizing mission is threatened by the displacing gaze of its disciplinary double . . . so that mimicry is at once resemblance and menace" (Bhabha 1994: 86).

22. Of course, the colonizers were out of step with metropolitan mode as well. One colonial author writes that the fashions worn by the colonizer women in the Netherlands East Indies were "a full year" behind those of Europe (Victor Ido in Bronkhorst & Wils 1996: 50). This statement presumably applies to the colonial capital of Batavia where women would have more easily been able to keep abreast of the fashions in Europe and would have had

more means available to them to do so—either ordering the popular styles from the metropole directly or having local dressmakers imitate and adapt them to life in the Indies—than in the more remote outposts of the empire. Beyond the time lag, there were other important differences between what a recent book on Indies dress refers to as the "Tropical Authentic" (*tropen echt*) style of the colonies and those at home, although the gap between the two narrowed with time (Bronkhorst & Wils 1996).

23. This proposition is supported by the evidence of similar reactions on the part of colonials elsewhere. "Writing about British attitudes toward Indians wearing European clothes, N.C. Chaudhuri trenchantly sums up the situation: 'They, the British, were violently repelled by English in our mouths and even more violently by English clothes on our backs.' " (Chaudhuri in Cohn 1989). It is my belief that generally the British were even more stringent in the policing of difference between colonizers and colonized—especially after 1857—than the Dutch. This view resonates with Jean Gelman Taylor's claim that the brief British interregnum of the Dutch East Indies between 1815 and 1819 was an important factor that led the Dutch to draw harder boundaries between themselves and those over whom they ruled in the latter half of the nineteenth century (Taylor 1983).

24. This is, of course, a take-off of Bhabha's "not quite, not white" (Bhabha 1994: 89).

25. In a similar fashion, Cohn notes the impression made on Europeans upon the occasion of a visit to India of the Prince of Wales in 1876 of the "military fossils" that were paraded out before them. Due to the ancient (and heterogeneous) style of the uniforms and arms of the troops, an artist who recorded the scene remarked that the twelfth and the nineteenth centuries (the latter being, of course, the British) stood face to face (Cohn 1989: 326–27).

26. The expression "the emerald girdle" derives from the concluding paragraph of Multatuli's *Max Havelaar* (1860). After detailing the abuses of the Dutch colonial regime in Java, Multatuli dedicates his book to William III: "for I dedicate my book to you, William the third, King, Grand Duke, Prince . . . EMPEROR of this splendid realm of INSULINDE, which garlands itself around the equator, like an emerald girdle! . . . And I ask you in confidence if it is your Imperial will that: . . . that over yonder your more than *Thirty million* subjects are *mistreated and exploited in your name?*" (Multatuli 1860: 185).

REFERENCES

Anderson, Benedict (1991) *Imagined Communities*, London: Verso.

van Baal, J. (1985) *Ontglipt Verleden; Tot 1947; Indisch bestuursambtenaar in vrede en oorlog*, Franeker: T. Wever.

Baron van Hoëvell, G.W.W.C. (1890) "De Aroe-Eilanden, Geographisch, Ethnographisch en Commercieel," in *Tijdschrift van Taal-, Land-, en Volkenkunde*, 32: 1–45.

Barthes, Roland (1967) *Système de la Mode*, Paris: Seuil.

Bhabha, Homi K. (1994) "Of Mimicry and Man: The Ambivalence of Colonial Discourse," in *The Location of Culture*, London: Routledge.

Bosscher (1853) "Staat van den in-en uitvoer op de Aroe-eilanden, gedurende het jaar 1849," in *Tijdschrift van Indische Taal-, Land- en Volkenkunde* I: 327–331.

Bougainville, Louis-Antoine de (1982 [1771]) *Voyage autour du monde par la frégate La Boudeuse et la flûte L'étoile*, Paris: Gallimard.

Bronkhorst, Dorine and Wils, Esther (1996) *Tropen Echt: Indische en Europese kleding in Nederlands-Indië*, Den Haag: Stichting Tong Tong.

Brumond, J.F.G. (1853) "Aanteekeningen gehouden op eene reis in het oosterlijk gedeelte van den Indischen Archipel." *Tijdschrift voor Nederlandsch-Indië*, 7, 2: 69–89; 251–99.

Campione, Adele (1989) *Women's Hats*, Milan: Be-ma Editrice.

Cayley-Webster (1898) *Through New Guinea and the Cannibal Countries*, London: T. Fisher Unwin.

Cohn, Bernard S. (1989) "Cloth, Clothes, and Colonialism: India in the Nineteenth Century," in Annette B. Weiner and Jane Schneider (eds.) *Cloth and Human Experience*, Washington: Smithsonian Institution Press.

Colley, Linda (1992) *Britons: Forging the Nation 1707–1837*, New Haven, CT: Yale University Press.

Corbin, Alain (1990) "Backstage," in Phillipe Ariès and George Duby (eds.) *A History of Private Life IV: From the Fires of Revolution to the Great War*, Cambridge: The Belknap Press of Harvard University Press.

Corpus-diplomaticum Neerlando-Indicum, 1596–1799. 6 vols. The Hague: Martinus Nijhoff.

Crab, P. van der (1862) *De Moluksche Eilanden: reis van Z.E. den Gouverneur-Generaal Charles Ferdinand Pahud, door den Molukschen Archipel*, Batavia: Lange & Co.

Dirks, Nicholas B. (1990) "History as a Sign of the Modern," *Public Culture* 2, 2: 25–32.

Doorn, J.A.A. van (1994) *De laatste eeuw van Indië*, Amsterdam: Bert Bakker.

Doren, J.B.J. van (1854) *Fragmenten uit de Reizen in den Indischen Archipel, enz*, Part I, Amsterdam: J.D. Sybrandi.

Ellen, Roy (1986) "Conundrums about Panjandrums: On the Use of Titles in the Relations of Political Subordination in the Moluccas and Along the Papuan Coast," *Indonesia* 41: 47–62.

Fabian, Johannes (1983) *Time and the Other: How Anthropology Makes its Object*, New York: Columbia University Press.

Forbes, Anna (1987 [1887]) *Unbeaten Tracks in Islands of the Far East: Experiences of a Naturalist's Wife in the 1880s*, Singapore: Oxford University Press.

Freud, Sigmund (1955 [1919]) "The 'Uncanny,' " in James Strachey (ed.) *The Standard Edition of the Complete Psychological Works*, London: Hogarth Press.

Freud, Sigmund (1950 [1927]) "Fetishism" in James Strachey (ed.) *Collected Papers*, Vol. V, London: Hogarth Press.

Gaines, Jane (1990) "Introduction: Fabricating the Female Body," in Jane Gaines and Charlotte Herzog (eds.) *Fabrications: Costume and the Female Body*, New York: Routledge.

Garber, Marjorie (1992) *Vested Interests: Cross-Dressing & Cultural Anxiety*, New York: Routledge.

Greenblatt, Stephen (1991) *Marvelous Possessions: The Wonder of the New World*, Chicago: University of Chicago Press.

Hollander, J.J. de (1895) *Handleiding bij de beoefening der land- en volkenkunde van Nederlandsch Oost-Indië*, 2 vols., Breda: van Broese & Co.

Kantorowicz, Ernst H. (1957) *The King's Two Bodies: A Study in Medieval Political Theology*, Princeton, NJ: Princeton University Press.

Kolff, D.H. (1840) *Voyages . . . through the Southern and Little Known Parts of the Moluccan Archipelago, and along the Previously Unknown Southern Coast of New Guinea . . . 1825–1826*, London: James Maddon & Co.

Lears, Jackson (1994) *Fables of Abundance: A Cultural History of Advertising in America*, New York: Basic Books.

Mailrapporten (1876, 1880, 1885, 1887) Unpublished reports in a series filed under the Ministerie van Koloniën (Ministry of Colonies) and housed in the Algemeen Rijksarchiet (ARA or General State Archives), the Hague.

Mani, Lata (1992) "Cultural Theory, Colonial Texts: Reading Eyewitness Accounts of Widow Burning," in Lawrence Grossberg, Cary Nelson, and Paula Treichler (eds.) *Cultural Studies*, London: Routledge.

Marin, Louis (1988) *Portrait of the King*, Minneapolis: University of Minnesota Press.

Marx, Karl (1967 [1867]) *Capital*, Vol. I, New York: International Publishers.

McKendrick, Neil (1982) "Introduction. The Birth of a Consumer Society: The Commercialization of Eighteenth-century England" and "Part I: Commercialization and the Economy," in Neil McKendrick, John Brewer and J.H. Plumb (eds.) *The Birth of a Consumer Society: The Commercialization of Eighteenth-century England*, London: Europa Publications Limited.

Merton, Hugo (1910) *Forschungsreise in den Sudostlichen Molukken (Aru- und Kei-Inseln)*, Frankfurt A.M.: Senckenbergischen Naturforschenden Gesellschaft.

Mukerji, Chandra (1983) *From Graven Images: Patterns of Modern Materialism*, New York: Columbia University Press.

Multatuli (1860) *Max Havelaar of de Koffij-Veilingen der Nederlandsche Handel-Maatschappij*, Amsterdam: J. de Ruyter.

Murra, John (1989) "Cloth and Its Function in the Inka State," in Annette B. Weiner and Jane Schneider (eds.) *Cloth and Human Experience*, Washington: Smithsonian Institution Press.

Nieuwenhuys, Rob (1988) *Met vreemde ogen*, Amsterdam: E.M. Querido.

Pemberton, John (1994) *On the Subject of "Java"*, Ithaca, NY: Cornell University Press.

Perniola, Mario (1989) "Between Clothing and Nudity," in Michel Feher (ed.) with Ramona Naddaff and Nadia Tazi, *Fragments for a History of the Human Body*, Part 2, New York: Urzone Inc.

Pietz, William (1988) "The Problem of the Fetish, IIIa," *Res* 16: 105–23.

Pratt, Mary Louise (1992) *Imperial Eyes: Travel Writing and Transculturation*, London: Routledge.

Purcell, Rosamund Wolff and Stephen Jay Gould (1992) *Finders, Keepers: Eight Collectors*, London: Hutchinson Radius.

Quammen, David (1996) *The Song of the Dodo: Island Biogeography in an Age of Extinction*, New York: Scribner.

Quammen, David (1993) "Trinket from Aru: Window-Shopping in the Markets of Paradise," *Outside* (September): 35–40.

Ranger, Terence (1983) "The Invention of Tradition in Colonial Africa," in Eric Hobsbawn and Terence Ranger (eds.) *The Invention of Tradition*, Cambridge: Cambridge University Press.

Riedel, J.G.F. (1886) *De Sluik- en Kroesharige Rassen tusschen Selebes en Papua*, 's-Gravenhage: Martinus Nijhoff.

Rutherford, Danilyn (1996) "Of Gifts and Birds: The Revival of Tradition on an Indonesian Frontier," *Cultural Anthropology*. 11, 4: 577–616.

Savage, V.R. (1984) *Western Impressions of Nature and Landscape in Southeast Asia*, Singapore: Singapore University Press.

Schneider, Jane and Annette B. Weiner (1989) "Introduction" in Annette B. Weiner and Jane Schneider (eds.) *Cloth and Human Experience*, Washington: Smithsonian Institution Press.

Schulte Nordholt, Henk (1997) "Introduction" in Henk Schulte Nordholt (ed.) *Outward Appearances: Dressing State and Society in Indonesia*. Leiden: KITLV Press.

Shell, Marc (1992) "Money and Art: The Issue of Representation in Commerce and Culture," *Regional Review* 2, 4: 20–24.

Simpson, David (1982) *Fetishism and Imagination*, Baltimore: Johns Hopkins University Press.

Smith, Adam (1976 [1776]) *An Inquiry into the Nature and Causes of the Wealth of Nations*, Chicago: University of Chicago Press.

Spyer, Patricia (1996) "Serial Conversion/Conversion to Seriality: Religion, State, and Number in Aru, Eastern Indonesia" in Peter van der Veer (ed.) *Conversion to Modernities: The Globalization of Christianities*, New York: Routledge.

———. (forthcoming) *The Memory of Trade*, Durham, NC: Duke University Press.

Stallybrass, Peter (1993) "Worn Worlds: Clothes, Mourning, and the Life of Things," *The Yale Review* 81, 2: 35–50.

Stapel, Dr. F.W. (1943) *De Oostindische Compagnie en Australie*. Amsterdam: P.N. van Kampen en Zoon.

Stoler, Ann Laura (1995) *Race and the Education of Desire*, Durham, NC: Duke University Press.

Stoler, Ann (1992) "Sexual Affronts and Racial Frontiers: European Identities and the Cultural Politics of Exclusion in Colonial Southeast Asia," *Comparative Studies in Society and History* 34, 3: 514–51.

Taussig, Michael (1993) *Mimesis and Alterity: A Particular History of the Senses*, New York: Routledge.

Taylor, Jean Gelman (1983) *The Social World of Batavia: European and Eurasian in Dutch Asia*, Madison: University of Wisconsin Press.

Turner, Terence S. (1980) "The Social Skin," in J. Cherfas and R. Lewin (eds.) *Not Work Alone*, London: Temple Smith.

Vries, J.H. de (1921–22) "Godsdienstige Gebruiken en Christelijke Overblijf-selen in de Residentie Amboina," *Nederlandsch-Indië Oud en Nieuw* 6: 111–23.

Wallace, Alfred Russell (1962 [1869]) *The Malay Archipelago*, New York: Dover Publications, Inc.

Wilentz, Sean (ed.) (1985) *Rites of Power*, Philadelphia: University of Pennsylvania Press.

7

Marx's Coat

Peter Stallybrass

1. FETISHIZING COMMODITIES, FETISHIZING THINGS

Marx defines capitalism as the *universalizing* of the production of commodities. He writes in the Preface to the first edition of *Capital* that "the commodity-form of the product of labour, or the value-form of the commodity" is "the economic cell-form" (Marx 1976 [1867]: 90).[1] The "economic cell-form" that occupies the first chapter of *Capital* takes the form of a *coat*. The coat makes its appearance not as the object that is made and worn but as the commodity that is exchanged. And what defines the coat as a commodity, for Marx, is that you cannot wear it and it cannot keep you warm. But while the commodity is a cold abstraction, it feeds, vampire-like, on human labour. The contradictory moods of Marx's *Capital* are an attempt to capture the contradictoriness of capitalism itself: the most abstract society that has ever existed; a society that consumes ever more concrete human bodies. The abstraction of this society is represented by the commodity-form itself. For the commodity becomes a commodity not as a thing but as an exchange value. It achieves its purest form, in fact, when most emptied out of particularity and thingliness. As a *commodity*, the coat achieves its destiny as an *equivalence*: as 20 yards of linen, 10 lb.

of tea, 40 lb. of coffee, 1 quarter of wheat, 2 ounces of gold, half a ton of iron (Marx 1976 [1867]: 157). To fetishize the commodity is to fetishize abstract exchange-value—to worship, that is, at the altar of the *Financial Times* or *The Wall Street Journal* which trace the number of paper cups that will buy you an academic book, the number of academic books that will buy you a Cuisinart, the number of Cuisinarts that will buy you a snowmobile. In *Capital*, Marx's coat appears only immediately to disappear again, because the nature of capitalism is to produce a coat not as a material particularity but as a "supra-sensible" value (Marx 1976 [1867]: 165). The work of Marx's *Capital* is to trace that value back through all its detours to the human labor whose appropriation produces capital (see Scarry 1985). This leads Marx theoretically to the labor theory of value and to an analysis of surplus-value. It leads him politically to the factories, the working conditions, the living spaces, the food, and the clothing of those who produce a wealth that is expropriated from them.

The coat—the commodity with which Marx begins *Capital*—has only the most tenuous relation to the coat that Marx himself wore on his way to the British Museum to research *Capital*. The coat that Marx wore went in and out of the pawnshop. It had very specific uses: to keep Marx warm in winter; to situate him as a suitable citizen to be admitted to the Reading Room. But the coat, *any* coat, as an exchange-value is emptied out of any useful function. Its physical existence is, as Marx puts it, "phantom-like":

> If we make abstraction from [the commodity's] use-value, we abstract also from the material constituents and forms which make it a use-value. . . . All its sensuous characteristics are extinguished (Marx 1976 [1867]: 128).

Although the commodity takes the shape of a physical thing, the "commodity-form" has "absolutely no connection with the physical nature of the commodity and the material [*dinglich*] relations arising out of this" (Marx 1976 [1867]: 165). To fetishize commodities is, in one of Marx's least-understood jokes, to reverse the whole history of fetishism.[2] For it is to fetishize the invisible, the immaterial, the supra-sensible. The fetishism of the commodity inscribes *im*materiality as the defining feature of capitalism.

Thus, for Marx, *fetishism* is not the problem; the problem is the fetishism of *commodities*. So what does it mean that the concept of "fetishism" continues to be used primarily in a *negative* way, often with the explicit invocation of Marx's use of the term? This is the gesture of exploitation that established the term in the first place. As William Pietz has brilliantly argued, the "fetish" emerges through the trading relations of the Portuguese in West Africa in the sixteenth and seventeenth centuries (Pitez 1985, 1987). Pietz shows that the fetish as a concept was elaborated to demonize the supposedly arbitrary attachment of West Africans to material objects. The European subject was constituted in opposition to a demonized fetishism, through the *disavowal* of the object. It is profoundly paradoxical that widely antagonistic ideological critiques of European modernity share the assumption that that modernity is characterized by a thoroughgoing materialism. The force of that denunciation depends upon the assumption of a place before the fall into materialism, a society where people are spiritually pure, uncontaminated by the objects around them.[3] But to oppose the materialism of modern life to a nonmaterialist past is not just wrong; it actually *inverts* the relation of capitalism to prior and alternative modes of production. As Marcel Mauss puts it in *The Gift*, his founding book on precapitalist exchange, objects in such exchanges can be "personified beings that talk and take part in the contract. They state their desire to be given away." Things-as-gifts are not "indifferent things"; they have "a name, a personality, a past" (Mauss 1967 [1925]: 55).[4] The radically dematerialized opposition between the "individual" and his or her "possessions" (between subject and object) is one of the central ideological oppostions of capitalist societies. As Igor Kopytoff notes, "this conceptual polarity of individualized persons and commoditized things is recent and, culturally speaking, exceptional" (Kopytoff 1986: 64).

One aspect of this dematerializing polarity was the development of the concept of the "fetish." The *fetisso* marks, as Pietz shows, less the ancient distrust of false manufactures (as opposed to the "true" manufactured wafers and images of the Catholic Church) than a suspicion both of material embodiment itself and of "the subjection of the human body . . . to the influence of certain significant material objects that, although cut off from the body, function as its controlling organs at certain moments" (Pietz 1985: 10). The *fetisso* thus represents "a subversion of the ideal of the autonomously determined self" (Pietz 1987: 23). Moreover, the fetish (in contrast to the free-standing idol) was from the first associated with objects *worn on the body*—leather pouches, for instance, worn round the neck containing passages from the *Koran* (Pietz 1987: 37). The concept of the "fetish" was developed literally to *demonize* the power of "alien" worn objects (through the association of *feitiço* with witchcraft). And it emerged as the European subject simultaneously subjugated and enslaved other subjects and proclaimed its own freedom from material objects.

This disavowal of the object has often been read as merely a ruse. In this view, European entrepreneurs proclaimed their detachment from objects, while "fetishistically" collecting them. But this constant repetition of "fetishism" as a category of abuse repeats rather than illuminates the problem. For European entrepreneurs did not, at least after the early trading stages, fetishize objects; on the contrary, they were interested in objects only to the extent that they could be transformed into commodities and exchanged for profit on the market. As a term of economic abuse, the concept of the fetish defined those with whom the Europeans traded in Africa and in the Americas as people who worshipped "trifles" ("mere" fetishes) and "valuable" things (i.e. gold and silver) alike. This meant that they could be "duped" (i.e. what the Europeans considered valueless—beads, for instance—could be exchanged for "valuable" goods). But it also implied a new definition of what it meant to be European: that is, a subject unhampered by fixation upon objects, a subject who, having recognized the true (i.e. market) value of the object-as-commodity, fixated instead upon the transcendental values that transformed gold into ships, ships into guns, guns into tobacco, tobacco into sugar, sugar into gold, and all into an accountable profit. What was demonized in the concept of the fetish was the possibility that history, memory, and desire might be materialized in objects that are touched and loved and worn.

A by-product of this demonization was the impossible project of the transcendental subject, a subject constituted by no place, no object—by nothing worn. "The Word *Fetish*," John Atkins wrote in 1737, "is used in a double signification among the *Negroes*: It is applied to dress and ornament, and to something reverenced as a Deity" (quoted in Pietz 1988: 110). The European subject, on the other hand, "knew the value of things"—that is, disavowed any but a financial investment in objects. Clothes could be "fashion"—detachable and discardable goods—but they were less and less likely to be fashionings, the materializations of memory, objects that worked upon and transformed the body of the wearer. In attributing the notion of the fetish to the commodity, Marx ridiculed a society that thought it had surpassed the "mere" worship of objects supposedly characteristic of "primitive religions." For Marx, the fetishism of the commodity was a regression from the materialism (however distorted) that fetishized the object. The problem for Marx was thus not with fetishism as such but rather with a specific *form* of fetishism that took as its object not the animized object of human labor and love but the evacuated nonobject that was the site of exchange. In the place of a coat, there was a transcendental value that erased both the making and the wearing of the coat. *Capital* was Marx's attempt to give back the coat to its owner.

2. MARX'S COAT

1852 was another catastrophic year for the Marx household.[5] In the early months of the year, Marx was writing *The Eighteenth Brumaire*, itself an attempt to come to terms with the failures of the 1848 revolutions and the triumph of reaction. From January 2nd to the 24th, he was ill in bed, writing with the greatest difficulty. But he had to write, since that, along with gifts from Engels and what they could pawn, was the source of the household's income, a household consisting of four children and three adults. In fact, not only did Marx have to write; he had to write *journalism*. In June 1850, Marx had obtained a ticket to the Reading Room of the British Museum, and he had begun to do the research that would be the basis for *Capital*. But to finance that research, he needed to write for money.[6] Moreover, during his illness, he couldn't get to the Museum anyway. But when he recovered, he wanted to put in at least some time at the library. He couldn't do it. So desperate had the financial situation become that not only had his credit with the butcher and the greengrocer dried up, but he had been forced to pawn his overcoat.[7] On the 27th February, he wrote to Engels: "A week ago I reached the pleasant point where I was unable to go out for want of the coats I have in pawn" (Marx 1983a [1852–55]: 50). Without his overcoat, he could not go to the British Museum (see Draper 1985: 61). I do not think there is a simple answer to why he could not go. No doubt, it was not advisable for a sick man to face an English winter without an overcoat. But social and ideological factors were probably equally significant. The Reading Room did not accept just *anyone* from off the streets, and a man without an overcoat, even if he had a ticket, *was* just anyone. Without his overcoat, Marx was, in an expression whose force it is hard to recapture, "not fit to be seen."

Marx's overcoat was to go in and out of the pawnshop throughout the 1850s and early 1860s. And his overcoat directly determined what work he could or could not do. If his overcoat was at the pawnshop during the winter, he could not go to the British Museum. If he could not go to the British Museum, he could not undertake the research for *Capital*. What clothes Marx wore thus shaped what he wrote. There is a level of vulgar material determination here that is hard even to contemplate. And yet vulgar material determinations were precisely what Marx contemplated, and the whole first chapter of *Capital* traces the migrations of a coat as a commodity within the capitalist marketplace. Of course, if he had pawned his coat, there was a simple sense in which Marx needed to stop his researches and get back to journalism. His researches brought in no money; his journalism brought in a little. Only through his journalism (and through the support of Engels and of relations) could he raise the money not only to eat and pay the rent but also to get his overcoat out of pawn, and only with his overcoat was he fit to return to the British Museum. But there was a further direct connection between the pawnshop and the materials of Marx's writing. Even journalism, and particularly the journalism which Marx undertook, required materials: newspapers, books, pen and ink, paper. In September of the same year, he was unable to write his articles for the *New York Daily Times* because he couldn't afford the newspapers that he needed to read for his articles. In October, Marx had to pawn "a coat dating back to my Liverpool days in order to buy writing paper" (Marx 1983a [1852–55]: 21; see Draper 1985: 64–65).

A sense of just how precarious the Marxes' economic life was during this period is captured by the report of a Prussian spy, probably from the fall of 1852:

> Marx lives in one of the worst—therefore, one of the cheapest—quarters of London. He occupies two rooms. The one looking out on the street is the living room, and the bedroom is at the back. In the whole apartment there is not one clean and solid piece of furniture. Everything is broken down, tattered and torn, with a half inch of dust over everything and there is a large old-fashioned table covered with an oilcloth, and on it there lie his manuscripts, books and newspapers, as well as the children's toys, and rags and tatters of his wife's sewing basket, several cups with broken rims, knives, forks, lamps, an inkpot, tumblers, Dutch clay pipes, tobacco ash—in a word, everything topsy-turvy, and all on the same table. A seller of second-hand goods would be ashamed to give away such a remarkable collection of odds and ends (McLellan 1981: 35).

A second-hand dealer might have been ashamed but the Marxes could not afford to be. Their broken-down furniture, their pots and pans, their cutlery, their own clothes had exchange value. And they knew just what that value was, since item after item of their belongings travelled to and from the pawnbroker.

What the family had acquired from the von Westphalens, Jenny's aristocratic family, was turned into liquid assets. In 1850, Jenny pawned the family silver. According to the recollections of Henry Hyndman, Marx's own attempts to pawn more silver had met with disaster:

> On one occasion Marx himself being in great need went out to pawn some household silver. He was not particularly well dressed and his knowledge of English was not so good as it became later. The silver, unfortunately, as it turned out, bore the crest of the Duke of Argyll's family, the Campbells, with which house Mrs. Marx was directly connected. Marx arrived at the Bank of the Three Balls and produced his spoons and forks. Saturday night, foreign Jew, dress untidy, hair and beard roughly combed, handsome silver, noble crest—evidently a very suspicious transaction indeed. So thought the pawnbroker to whom Marx applied. He therefore detained Marx, on some pretext, while he sent for the police. The policeman took the same view as the pawnbroker and also took poor Marx to the police station. There again appearances were strongly against him. . . . So Marx received the unpleasant hospitality of a police cell, while his anxious family mourned his disappearance . . . (McLellan 1981: 149).

This was a story that Mrs. Marx told late in her life, and it may be that she condensed many tribulations into one vivid story. But whatever the literal truth of the account, it captures the contradictory life of the Marxes in the 1850s, defined now not by their aristocratic and middle-class connections in Germany but by their poor clothes, their foreignness, and, in Marx's case, by his being Jewish.

In *The Eighteenth Brumaire*, Marx analysed the power and instability of clothes. The text is actually suspended between two different accounts of the appropriation of clothes. The first account is an almost exact inversion of Marx's own situation. That is, his own project was constantly threatened by the dispersal of his clothes and the pawning of his overcoat, with the constant diminishment of his authority even to enter the British Museum. But *The Eighteenth Brumaire* begins with the attempts of others to assume the authoritative clothes of the past so as to create authority in the present. If "the tradition of all the dead generations weighs like a nightmare on the brain of the living," it is only by the reawakening of the dead that previous revolutions have legitimated themselves. Revolution has previously appeared in borrowed "names" and borrowed "costumes": Luther put on the "mask" of St. Paul; the Revolution of 1789 to 1814 "draped" itself successively as the Roman republic and the Roman empire; Danton, Robespierre, Napoleon "performed the task of their time in Roman costume" (Marx 1963 [1852]: 16). These are, of course, metaphors. But they are metaphors that have been historically literalized. That is, the dress codes and the iconography of both the French revolution and the French empire drew upon the dress codes and iconography of the Roman republic and the Roman empire. "Unheroic as bourgeois society is," Marx writes, in its first revolutionary moments it clothes itself in the past so as to imagine itself in terms of "the great historical tragedy" (Marx 1963 [1852]: 16).

Ironically, Marx finds his own historical purpose in the grotesque image of Louis Bonaparte's reclothing of the present in the splendid robes of the past, a reclothing that discredits past and present alike. Although Marx begins his polemic against Louis Bonaparte's rise by representing it as a grotesque farce (or "second edition" [Marx 1963 (1852): 15]) of the "tragedy" of the eighteenth Brumaire, when Napoleon I came to power, Marx concludes by asserting that Louis's parody strips bare the past. The present is less a story of decline (the decline from tragedy to farce) than an unmasking of the past as itself farce. At the very conclusion of *The Eighteenth Brumaire*, Marx writes that Louis has revived "the cult of the Napoleonic mantle." "But when the imperial mantle finally falls on the shoulders of Louis Bonaparte, the bronze statue of Napoleon will crash from the top of the Vendome Column" (Marx 1963 [1852]: 135). Louis Bonaparte thus achieves by accident precisely what Marx himself tries to achieve: the dismantling of the triumphalist forms of the State.

Yet the concept of ideological or political dismantling was, as Marx's work increasingly argued, inadequate to address the economic forces which quite literally dismantled the proletariat and the lumpenproletariat while dressing the bourgeoisie in the borrowed robes of emergent capitalism—the robes that the bourgeoisie acquired through the appropriated labor of those who worked above all in the textile industries. England, where Marx now lived, was the heartland of capitalism *because* it was the heartland of the textile industries. Its wealth had been founded first on wool and then on cotton. Engels was himself sent to England to work in and then manage a Manchester cotton mill in which his family held a partnership. To the extent that the Marxes survived on Engels's generosity, they lived on the profits of the cotton industry. But they survived through the 1850s and early 60s only marginally. Engels's father insisted that he learn the industry from the bottom up, and, particularly in the early part of this period, he did not have much money to spare. Even to earn the little he did, he had to sacrifice his own ambitions as a journalist in London and follow a trade that repelled him (see McLellan 1978: 21–29). We confront here a curious paradox in Marx's life. That is, while he undertook in a way that had never been done before an analysis of the systematic workings of capitalism, he himself depended mainly upon precapitalist or marginally capitalist practices: small inheritances; gifts; the writing of tracts that often had to be subsidized. But while he worked mainly outside the capitalist marketplace, he still lived during the period of which I write what can only be called a proletarian and at times subproletarian life.

Marx learned about the workings of capitalism mainly from political work and conversation and from his massive reading in the British Museum, but he learned about the kind of domestic life that the working classes lived first-hand. It was a life lived in crowded rooms (for the Marxes between six and eight people in two and then three rooms in the 1850s) (see Padover 1978: 23); a life in debt to bakers and grocers and butchers[8]; a life in which a purchase often had to be balanced out by the selling or pawning of some previous purchase. Like any working class household, the hopes and despairs of the Marxes could be traced by their journeys to the pawnbrokers. Let me give just a very selective account of the Marx household's dealings with the pawnbrokers. In 1850, Jenny Marx pawned silver in Frankfurt and sold furniture in Cologne (Marx 1982 [1844–51]: 38). In 1852, Marx pawned his overcoat to buy paper on which to continue to write (Draper 1985: 65). In 1853, "so many of our absolute essentials ha[ve] found their way to the pawnbroker's and the family ha[s] grown so shabby, that for the past ten days there hasn't been a sou in the house" (Marx 1983a [1852–55]: 385). In 1856, to finance the move to a new house, they needed not only all of Engels's help but also to pawn household possessions (Marx 1983b [1856–59: 70). In 1858, at another time of drastic financial crisis, Jenny Marx pawned her shawl, and, at the end of the year, she was beset with dunning letters from her creditors and was forced "to run errands to the pawnshops in town" (Marx 1983b [1856–59]: 255, 360). In April 1862, they owed £20 for the rent and had pawned their own, their children's, and Helene Demuth's clothes (Marx 1985 [1860–64]: 380). They redeemed them later in the spring but had to put them back in pawn in June. In January of the next year, not only were they in need of food and coal, but the children's clothes were again pawned and they couldn't go to school. In 1866, the household was again in distress, everything possible was pawned, and Marx could not afford to buy writing paper (Draper 1985: 133).

The most complete account of their accounts during this period are in a letter from Marx to Engels in July 1858 (Marx 1983b [1856–59]: 329–30). He writes that the situation is "absolutely untenable" and that he is *"completely disabled* [in English] from doing any work" because of his domestic miseries. On top of debts to the baker, the butcher, the cheesemonger, the greengrocer, and £3 10s. for chemises, dresses, shoes, and hats for the children, he payed £3 in interest to the pawnshop, and another £3 10s. for redeeming linen and other things from the pawnshop. On top of that, he was paying weekly money to the tallyman for a coat and trousers for himself. A tallyman was someone who supplied goods on credit, to be payed for by installments. They were, as a dictionary of canting terms put it in 1700, "Brokers that let out Clothes at moderate Rates to wear per Week, Month, or Year." An earlier pamphlet more harshly asserted that "The unconscionable Tally-man . . . lets them have ten-shillings-worth of sorry commodities, . . . on security given to pay him twenty shillings by twelve-pence a week."[9] In other words, the poorer you were, the more expensive it was to live. Pawn-tickets had to be regularly payed, if the pledge was not to be lost. And if you couldn't afford to buy clothes outright, you had to pay much more to buy them over an extended period.

Marx's domestic life, then, depended upon the "petty calculations" that characterized working class life. Any pleasure or luxury had to be priced in relation to the sacrifice of another pleasure or even necessity. "Respectability," that central nineteenth-century virtue, was something to be bought and, in times of need, pawned. In *The Condition of the Working Class in England*, written in 1844, Engels had described both the materiality and the fragility of that respectability. He recorded a thousand small stories, as of the woman prosecuted for her children's thefts. She had sold her bedstead and pawned the bedding to buy food (Engels 1987 [1845]: 74). Respectability was a bed, bedding, kitchenware, but, above all, suitable clothes. Clothes, Engels wrote, were the visible markers of class:

> The clothing of the working people, in the majority of cases, is in a very bad condition. The material used for it is not of the best adapted. Wool and linen have almost vanished from the wardrobe of both sexes, and cotton has taken their place. Shirts are made of bleached or coloured cotton goods; the dresses of the women are chiefly of cotton print goods, and woollen petticoats are rarely seen on the wash-

line. The men wear chiefly trousers of fustian or other heavy cotton goods, and jackets or coats of the same. Fustian has become the proverbial costume of the working men, who are called "fustian jackets," and call themselves so in contrast to the gentlemen who wear broad cloth. When Fergus O'Connor, the Chartist leader, came to Manchester during the insurrection of 1842, he appeared, amidst the deafening applause of the working men, in a fustian suit of clothing (Engels 1987 [1845]: 102–3).

If the clothes of the poor were haunted by the spectre of dispossession (their transformation into cash at the pawnbrokers), they could also become the materialization of class resistance. Engels' account of Fergus O'Connor's fustian points to the construction of a symbolic discourse of class through the very materials of class oppression.

"Fustian" was a coarse cloth made of thick, twilled cotton with a short pile or nap. It was usually dyed an olive, leaden, or other dark color. By the nineteenth century, fustian had become exclusively associated with the working classes. In 1861, Digby wrote of "the fustian rascal and his lack-linen mate" and Hardy wrote in 1883 of the "hob-nailed and fustianed peasantry."[10] What is striking about Fergus O'Connor's performance as a Chartist is that, despite his pretensions to Irish royal ancestry and his financial independence, he self-consciously adopted the dress of his followers. When he was released from prison in 1841, he was, the *Northern Star* records,

habited, as he had promised, in fustian. He wore a full suit made out of one piece which had been manufactured expressly for the occasion, and was presented by those who had not only his welfare at heart but were imbued with his principles and with his spirit—the blistered hands and fustian jackets of Manchester (quoted in Pickering 1986: 157).

On his release, O'Connor explicated the class significance of the clothes he was wearing: "I have appeared Brother Chartists and working men amongst you in fustian, the emblem of your order, in order to convince you, at a single glance, that what I was when I left you, the same I do return to you." In fact, O'Connor's identification with fustian preceded his release; his contributions to the *Northern Star* had been consistently addressed to the "fustian jackets" and "blistered hands." And O'Connor's assumption of fustian transformed a cheap material into the badge of radical class consciousness. In August 1841, a Preston Chartist wrote to O'Connor:

> the greatest object of my writing to you [is] to know what colour of
> fustian or moleskin you would come out of prison in . . . [I]f we poor
> devils are ever permitted to have another new jacket, we would like
> the same colour (quoted in Pickering 1986: 161).

Fustian thus became a material memorial, an embodiment of a class
politics that preceded a political language of class.

But the day to day experience of working people reveals that
even the poorest of clothes—including fustian—were not the stable
markers of social identity. The clothes constantly migrated. Working
men might buy a woollen coat for Sunday, but it would be made of
the cheapest wool, so-called "Devil's dust" cloth that tore easily and
was soon threadbare, or it would come from a second-hand dealer.
Engels wrote that "the working man's clothing is, in most cases, in
bad condition, and there is the oft-recurring necessity for placing the
best pieces in the pawnbroker's shop" (Engels 1987 [1845]: 103).
"Furniture, Sunday clothes where such exist, kitchen utensils in
masses are fetched from the pawnbrokers on Saturday night only to
wander back, almost without fail, before the next Wednesday . . ."
(Engels 1987 [1845]: 152). Clothes, in fact, rather than kitchen utensils, were the usual pledge. In a survey of pawnbrokers in 1836, clothing accounted for more than 75 percent of the total, with metal
goods (including watches, rings, and medals) a mere 7.4 percent, and
Bibles accounting for 1.6 percent (Tebbutt 1983: 33).

The usual pattern of pawnshop trade, as Melanie Tebbutt has
finely shown, was for wages received on Friday or Saturday to be used
to get one's best clothes out of pawn. The clothes were worn on Sunday and then pawned again on Monday (a day in which one pawnshop received three times as many pledges as on any other day)
(Tebbutt 1983: 6). And the cycle was a rapid one, the majority of
items being pawned and redeemed again on a weekly or monthly
basis. The rate of pawning and redemption was itself an indicator of
wealth and poverty. At two pawnbrokers in Liverpool in the 1860s, at
the poorest 66 percent of the pledges were redeemed within the week
and 82 percent within the month, while at the more upscale pawnbroker there was a slower turnover, 33 percent of the pledges being
redeemed weekly and 62 percent monthly (Tebbutt 1983: 9). A carpenter who had pawned his tools for 15 shillings during a strike
pawned his best clothes to redeem them when the strike ended.
When he returned to work, he took his tools back to the pawnshop
every Saturday to redeem his best clothes, which he repawned every
Monday in exchange for his tools. For the 15 shillings he got in ex-

change for his pledges, he had to pay 8d. a week (an interest rate of about 4.5 percent weekly, 19 percent monthly, and 235 percent yearly) (Tebbutt 1983: 32–33). The extent to which many families' best clothes inhabited the pawnshop for the majority of the year is suggested by the sudden increases in their redemption at major festivals, such as Whit Week, when people dressed up as best they could for the celebration of Spring (Tebbutt 1983: 33)

For the Marxes, the pawning of their clothes sharply delimited their social possibilities. In the winter of 1866, Jenny Marx could not go out because all her respectable clothes were pawned (Marx 1987 [1864–68]: 331). The following year, their three daughters were invited for a holiday in Bordeaux: not only did they have to calculate all the expenses of the journey but they also had to redeem their children's clothes from the pawnshop to make them presentable (Marx 1987 [1864-68]: 397). Happiness was often measured in the buying of new clothes or the redemption of things from the pawnshop. When Wilhelm Wolff died in 1864, leaving Marx a sizeable legacy, Marx wrote: "I should very much like to buy Manchester silk for the *whole* family" (Marx 1985 [1860–64]: 527). Death, in fact, produced the most contradictory of emotions. If it was one of the family, a coffin had to be bought, funeral expenses to be met, and the Marxes frequently did not have the money to meet those expenses (see McLellan 1981: 25). But if a relative with money died, it was a cause for celebration.[11] Naked commercial transactions and the most intimate of family ties are framed in the same language: "uncle" or "pop" are the names for both relatives and pawnbrokers. Both "uncle" and "pop" suggest not only the familiarity of the repeatedly visited pawnbroker but also the conception of a relative as someone one hopes to get some cash out of, as from a pawnbroker. For the Marxes, uncles and "uncles" were often equivalent and alternative sources for their financial survival.

But relations with the pawnbroker were structurally antagonistic.[12] For it was at the pawnshop that the double life of things appeared in its most contradictory form. Things to be pawned might be household necessities and markers of achievement and success, but they were also often the repositories of memory. But to pawn an object is to denude it of memory. For only if an object is stripped of its particularity and history can it again become a commodity and an exchange value. From the perspective of the pawnshop, any value other than exchange-value is *sentimental* value, a value of which the object must be stripped if it is to be "freely" exchanged on the market. It was thus in the pawnshop, not in the factories that were increasingly the motor of capitalist production, that the opposition between the particularity of a thing and the abstract exchange-value of a commodity was most visible. If you had as privileged a past as Jenny Marx, you might take to "uncle" table napkins of old Scottish descent (Marx 1985 [1860–64]: 570–71). But that family history, which was of undoubted significance to Jenny Marx, would be of no significance to the pawnbroker unless it added to the objects' exchange value. The pawnbroker did not pay for personal or family memories. To the contrary. In the language of nineteenth century clothes-makers and repairers, the wrinkles in the elbows of a jacket or a sleeve were called "memories." Those wrinkles recorded the body that had inhabited the garment. They memorized the interaction, the mutual constitution, of person and thing.[13] But from the perspective of commercial exchange, every wrinkle or "memory" was a devaluation of the commodity.

Memories were thus inscribed for the poor within objects that were haunted by loss. For the objects were in a constant state of being-about-to-disappear. The calculation of the likely future journeys of clothes and other objects to the pawnshop was inscribed within their purchase.[14] As Ellen Ross notes, "the 'bank' of ornaments" on a working class mantle was indeed a bank, since it represented the scarce resources which could nevertheless be pawned and turned into cash in times of need (Ross 1993: 46). Objects, and the memories attached to them, did not stay in place for the poor. They could rarely become heirlooms. And the objects used as pledges could be anything that still had exchange value. In the 1820s, Charles Dickens while still a boy went to the pawnshop with the family's valued books: *Peregrine Pickle, Roderick Random, Tom Jones, Humphrey Clinker* (Johnson 1952: I, 31). Worse was to come. After his father's release after being imprisoned for a debt of £40, insolvency proceedings were brought against him. "The law provided that the clothing and personal effects of the debtor and his dependents must not exceed £20 in value" (Johnson 1952: I, 37). Charles was consequently sent to an official appraiser to have his clothes valued. He was wearing a boy's white hat, a jacket, and corduroy trousers, nothing of much value, but he was painfully aware of his grandfather's silver watch ticking away in his pocket.

Dickens's painful awareness of the relations between memory, exchange-value, and the pawnshop shape his later account of "The Pawnbroker's Shop" in *Sketches by Boz*. A young woman and her mother bring in "a small gold chain and a 'Forget-me-not' ring," given "in better times" and "prized, perhaps, once, for the giver's sake" (Dickens 1994 [1833–39]: 192). Now, the two women argue with the broker over how much the objects are worth. This account of the pawnshop, though, not only establishes a distance from Dickens's own experiences but also violently regenders it so as to associate commodity exchange with being female. For the women are depicted as on their ways to becoming commodities. This is already figured in the fact that they part with their memorials "without a struggle" (Dickens 1994 [1833–39]: 192). In fact, Dickens's account simultaneously sentimentalizes and demonizes the transaction. As he himself noted, costermongers and fishwomen showed what he elsewhere called "strange forethought," buying "great squab brooches" and "massive silver rings" as "convenient pledges" (quoted in Tebbutt 1983: 17). In contrast, memorial jewelry tended to be pawned in exceptional circumstances. In 1884, it was a sign of how bad the depression was that a single Sunderland pawnbroker received 1,500 wedding rings as pledges and 3,000 watches (Tebbutt 1983: 26). One woman recollected women crying as they looked at "the wedding rings in the window, their own wedding rings," which "they'd no way of redeeming at all" (Tebbutt 1983: 26). Nevertheless, the future possibility of pawning could enter into the buying of a memorial ring:

> A young war bride who grew up in Jarrow during the 1930s and had stark memories of how her mother had pledged her own ring during the depression made her fiancé buy the most expensive one he could afford as similar insurance against the future (Tebbutt 1983: 26).[15]

This endemic tension between forms of memorialization and self-constitution and forms of commodity exchange is treated by Dickens in "The Pawnbroker's Shop" only in terms of female corruption. Cruikshank's accompanying illustration shows the mother and her daughter framed by, on one side, a "young female, whose attire, miserably poor but extremely gaudy, wretchedly cold but extravagantly fine, too plainly bespeaks her station" and, on the other, a woman who is "the lowest of the low; dirty, unbonneted, flaunting, and slovenly" (Dickens 1994 [1833–39]: 192). Dickens displaces onto women the relation between the particularity of the object-as-memory and the generality of the object-as-commodity, the former figured as "true love," the latter as prostitution.

Dickens and Cruikshank represent in demonized form the actual gendering of the pawnshop, where, as Ellen Ross has shown, the transactions were largely conducted by women.[16] Ross writes:

> That pawning was so heavily a female domain in Victorian and Edwar-
> dian London tells us something about the sorts of things commonly
> pawned—clothing and household goods—and also that pawning was
> often a stage of meal preparation (Ross 1993: 47).

The pawnings of Marx's household were no different in this respect.
If Marx wrote about the workings of money, it was his wife, Jenny,
and their servant, Helene Demuth, who organized the household's finances and made the trips to the pawnbroker. Wihelm Liebknecht, a
German exile who visited the Marxes almost daily in the 1850s,
noted "all the work" that Helene Demuth did: "I will only remind
you of the many trips to that mysterious, deeply hated and still assid-
uously courted, all-benevolent relative: the 'uncle' with the three
globes" (McLellan 1981: 59). And Jenny Marx was also back and forth
to the pawnshop throughout the 1850s. Looking back at this period,
she wrote in a letter to Liebknecht that

> In all these struggles, the harder because the pettier part falls to us
> women. While the men are invigorated by the fight in the world out-
> side, strengthened by coming face to face with the enemy, be its
> number legion, we sit at home darning stockings (Padover 1978: 42).

She might have added, providing the material forms of survival from
the pawnshop.

Yet Marx himself was never isolated from the crisis of the household's finances, as his endless begging letters to Engels witness. And
even his stories to his children are shadowed by the migration of objects under the pressure of debt. When, in 1895, Eleanor Marx recalled her life with her father, she wrote:

> of the many wonderful tales Moor told me, the most wonderful, the
> most delightful one, was "Hans Röckle." It went on for months; it was
> a whole series of stories. . . . Hans Röckle himself was a Hoffmann-like
> magician, who kept a toyshop, and who was always "hard up." His
> shop was full of the most wonderful things—of wooden men and
> women, giants and dwarfs, kings and queens, workmen and masters,
> animals and birds as numerous as Noah got into the Ark, tables and
> chairs, carriages, boxes of all sorts and sizes. And though he was a ma-
> gician, Hans could never meet his obligations either to the devil or to
> the butcher, and was therefore—much against the grain—constantly
> obliged to sell his toys to the devil. These then went through wonder-
> ful adventures—always ending in a return to Hans Röckle's shop
> (McLellan 1981: 100–101).

Hans Röckle's toyshop seems to incorporate the plenitude of the world of made things. And those things, like their owner, have magical powers. But, because Röckle is constantly in debt, he is forever obliged to sell his toys to the devil. The moment of sale is the moment of alienation, of the stripping of the magic of the toys as they are transformed into exchange-values. But Marx's story refuses the transformation of the toys into commodities. Although they are sold to the devil, he never becomes their possessor, for they have a life of their own, a life which finally leads them back to their point of origin, Hans Röckle. The stories that Marx told to his young daughter surely allegorize both the moments of absolute dispossession and the trips to the pawnbroker's shop. Before Eleanor was born, her parents had watched the bailiffs enter their lodgings and take away everything, including "the best of the toys belonging to the girls"; they had watched Jenny and Laura weeping for the loss. But in the stories, as in the trips to the pawnbroker's shop when they were in cash, the moment of loss is undone: the toys come back.

It was to the systematic undoing of loss that Marx dedicated his entire life. The loss, of course, was not his own; it was the loss of the entire working class, alienated from the means of production. That alienation meant that they, the producers of the greatest multiplicity of things that the world had ever known, were forever on the outside of that material plenitude, their faces peering in through the toyshop window at the toys that they had made but that now had been possessed as "private property." The private property of the bourgeoisie was bought at the price of the dispossession of the working classes from the things of this world. In so far as they had possessions, they held them precariously. If their things were sometimes animated by their loves, their histories, their handlings, they were often animated by the workings of a marketplace that took back those things and stripped them of their loves and their histories, devalued them because they had been handled. But, for Marx, the pawnshop could not be the starting point for an analysis of the relation between object and commodity. There are, I think, two reasons for this. The first is that the pawnbroker is, from Marx's perspective, an agent in the consumption and recirculation of goods rather than in their production. The second is that, although at the pawnshop one sees the transformation of object into commodity, this particular transformation is as much a feature of precapitalist as of capitalist formations. There is nothing specifically new about exchange value or, for that matter, about pawnbrokers. And to figure the pawnbroker as the capitalist leads into all the most predictable forms of reactionary ideology: the middle man as exploiter; the Jew or Korean as the origin of oppression.[17] The pawnbroker both precedes capitalism and is marginal to it, at least in its later manifestations.

There was, as Marx knew, a form of magic in the material transformations that capitalism performed. It is a magic that Hans Christian Andersen captures in his story, "The Shirt Collar." The collar wants to get married, and proposes in the wash to a garter. But she won't tell him her name, so he proposes to the iron, who burns a hole in him, and addresses him disdainfully as "You rag." Finally, at the papermill, the collar says

> it's high time I changed into white paper. And that's what happened. All the rags were turned into white paper; but the collar became this very bit of paper we have before us, on which the story has been printed (Andersen 1982 [1849]: 231).

Andersen restores to the notion of the book, which had become increasingly the "invisible" medium joining the immaterial ideas of the writer to the immaterial mind of the reader, the literal matter of the book and the participation of "literature" in the life-cycle of cloth. What Marx restores to the notion of the book, as to every other commodity, is the human labors that have been appropriated in the making of it, the work that produced the linen of shirts and petticoats and bedsheets, the work that transformed bedsheets into sheets of paper.

Marx, in fact, wrote at the moment of crisis in that very process. The massive developments of the paper industry (for the production of newspapers, bureaucratic paperwork, novels, wrapping-paper and so on) had led to an ever greater demand for rags, a demand that could no longer be met. In 1851, the year in which Marx began writing *The Eighteenth Brumaire*, Hugh Burgess and Charles Watt made the first commercially useful paper from ground-wood pulp (Hunter 1978: 555). From 1857–60, in the desperate search for replacements for rags, esparto grass was imported from Algeria and it was upon paper made from this grass that the *Illustrated London News*, the *Graphic*, and the *Sphere* were printed. The first newspaper printed entirely on paper from wood pulp was probably the *Boston Weekly Journal*, and that was not until 1863 (Hunter 1978: 565). As late as 1860, rags still formed 88 percent of the total papermaking material (Hunter 1978: 564). Yet by 1868, a year after the publication of the first volume of *Capital*, paper was being used for almost every conceivable use: for boxes, cups, plates, wash-bowls, barrels, table tops, window blinds, roofing, towels, napkins, curtains, carpets, machine belts. And in 1869, paper coffins began to be manufactured in the

United States (Hunter 1978: 568). But nowhere were the revolution-ary inversions of capitalism more apparent than in the fact that paper, previously made out of the residue of cloth and clothing, now became the material out of which collars, vests, cuffs, aprons, but-tons, hats, handkerchiefs, raincoats, corsets, slippers, and petticoats were made. Men's paper collars were given such resounding names as "Lord Byron," "Longfellow," "Shakespeare," and "Dante." In 1869, a paper collar was named after Harriet Beecher Stowe's brother, Henry Ward Beecher, who promoted anti-slavery and women's suffrage. The collar was popularly known as the "Beecher garotte" (Hunter 1978: 385). In 1860, a song called "The Age of Paper" was popular in Lon-don music halls; it was sung by Howard Paul "attired in a suit of paper" (Hunter 1978: 386, 388).

But if there was, indeed, a magic to these transformations, there was also a devastating appropriation of the bodies of the living and even of the clothing of the dead. In 1855, Dr. Isaiah Deck, a New York scientist, suggested that paper could be made out of the wrappings of Egyptian mummies. "At this period of sepulture," he wrote, "it is by no means rare to find above 30 pounds weight of linen wrappings in individual mummies." He continued:

> The supply of linen rags would not be limited to the mummies of the human species alone; independent of that obtainable from this source, a more than equal amount of cloth could be depended on from the mummies of the sacred bulls, crocodiles, ibides, and cats as all of these animals were embalmed and swathed in a superior quality of linen. . . . [S]ome bandages, from 5 inches to 5 feet wide and 9 yards long, have been stripped from mummies their entire length without tearing. . . .

> The question, Will it pay? may be readily answered by assuming the value of rags to be from 4 to 6 cents per pound; in the United States this is considered to be under the market estimate of fine linen rags . . . (Hunter 1978: 384).

A Dr. Waite recalled that when he was a young man, he had indeed made paper out of mummies: he noted that "the rolled-up vestments retained the shape of the mummy, so that when the workmen tried to straighten or unroll the 'cocoon,' as it might be called, it sprang back at once into the shape of the mummy it had encased so long" (Hunter 1978: 383). It is in such surreally grotesque transformations that one can trace the emergence of the commodity from the death of a material memory. In *Capital*, Marx tried to restore that material memory, a memory literally embodied in the commodity although suppressed *as* memory.

In *Capital*, Marx wrote about a coat as a commodity—as the abstract "cell-form" of capitalism. He traced the value of that cell-form to the appropriated body of alienated labor. In the process of production, he argued, the commodity takes on an exotic life, even as the body of the worker is reduced to an abstraction. But the actual coats of workers, as of Marx himself, were anything but abstractions. What little wealth they had was stored not as *money* in *banks* but as *things* in the *house*. Well-being could be measured by the coming and going of those things. To be out of pocket was to be forced to strip the body. To be in pocket was to reclothe the body. The extraordinary *intimacy* of the pawnbroker's stock, and the massive preponderance of clothes, can be guaged from the accounts of a large Glasgow pawnbroker in 1836. He had taken as pledges:

> 539 men's coats; 355 vests; 288 pairs of trousers; 84 pairs of stockings; 1980 women's gowns; 540 petticoats; 132 wrappers [women's loose outer garment]; 123 duffles [thick flannel shawl or coat]; 90 pelisses [women's long coat]; 240 silk handkerchiefs; 294 shirts and shifts; 60 hats; 84 bed ticks; 108 pillows; 206 pairs of blankets; 300 pairs of sheets; 162 bedcovers; 36 tablecloths; 48 umbrellas; 102 Bibles; 204 watches; 216 rings; 48 Waterloo medals (Hudson 1982: 44).

To keep a roof over one's head and food on the table, the intimate materials of the body had to be pawned. And sometimes, one had to choose between house and body. In July 1867, Marx decided to use the £45 set aside for the rent to get back the clothes and watches of his three daughters, so that they could go to stay with Paul Lafargue in France (Marx 1987 [1864–68]: 397). To take one's clothes to the pawnbroker meant to teeter on the edge of social survival. Without "suitable" clothes, Jenny Marx wouldn't go out on the street; without "suitable" clothes, Marx would not work at the British Museum; without "suitable" clothes, the unemployed worker was in no state to look for new employment. To have one's own coat, to wear it on one's back, was to hold on to oneself, even as one held on to one's past and one's future. But it was also to hold onto a memory system that at a moment of crisis could be transformed back into money:

> Yesterday I pawned a coat dating back to my Liverpool days in order to buy writing paper (Marx 1983a [1852–55]: 221).

For Marx, as for the workers of whom he wrote, there were no "mere" things. Things were the materials—the clothes, the bedding, the furniture—from which one constructed a life; they were the supplements the undoing of which was the annihilation of the self.

It has become a cliché to say that we should not treat people like things. But it is a cliché that misses the point. What have we done to things to have such contempt for them? And who can afford to have such contempt? Why are prisoners stripped of their clothes, if not to strip them of themselves? Marx, having a precarious hold upon the materials of self-construction, knew the value of his own coat.

NOTES

1. I am indebted to the Society for the Humanities at Cornell University for a fellowship that allowed me to begin work on this project, and for the support and criticisms of the fellows at the Society. Since then, I have benefited from criticisms and suggestions from Crystal Bartolovich, Robert Foster, Webb Keane, Ann Rosalind Jones, Annelies Moors, Adela Pinch, Marc Shell, and Patricia Spyer. Above all, I am indebted to the work of Bill Pietz (cited below) and to conversations with Margreta de Grazia and Matthew Rowlinson. See also Matthew Rowlinson's fine meditation on the relation between money, commodities, and things in "Reading Capital with Little Nell."

2. For Marx and commodity fetishism, see Marx 1976 [1867], pp. 163–77. For Marx's assertion of the *necessity* of "alienation" in the positive form of the imbuing of objects with subjectivity through our work upon them and of the imbuing of the subject with objectivity through our materializations, see his "On James Mill," in Marx 1977, pp. 114–23.

3. For an analysis of the history of the changing relations between subject and object in early modern Europe, see de Grazia, Quilligan, and Stallybrass (1995).

4. For development and critiques of Mauss's theory, see Gregory 1983; Weiner 1985 and 1992; Appadurai 1986; Strathern 1988; Thomas 1991; Derrida 1992.

5. My account of the day to day life of the Marx household draws above all on Marx's constant stream of letters to Engels, published in Karl Marx and Frederick Engels, *Collected Works* (1975–). I have also found particularly useful Draper 1985; McLellan 1981; Marx 1973; Seigel 1978; Padover 1978; Kapp 1972.

6. On the 20th February, Marx wrote to Joseph Weydemeyer: "I have been so beset by money troubles that I have not been able to pursue my studies at the Library" (Marx and Engels 1983a [1852–55[: 40).

7. On the Marxes, their debts, and their visits to the pawnshop during the 1850s and 1860s, see, for instance, Marx 1982 [1844–51], pp. 224, 402, 556–57; Marx 1983a [1852–55], pp. 181–82, 216, 385; Marx 1983b [1856–59], pp. 70, 255, 328–30, 360; Marx 1985 [1860–64[, pp. 380, 399, 433, 442, 445, 570–71, 577; McLellan (1981), pp. 22–29, 35–36, 149.

8. For Marx's own detailed account of his debts in 1858, see Marx (1983b [1856–59]), pp. 329–30.

9. Both quotes are taken from the OED under "tallyman."

10. Both quotations are taken from the OED under "fustian."

11. See, for example, Marx's description of the death of his wife's uncle as "*a very happy event* [in English]," Marx 1983a [1852–55]: 526.

12. I would emphasize that I am analysing here the structural relation between the object and the commodity. The actual relations between pawnbrokers and their customers were highly variable. As Tebbutt notes, "the pledge shop was firmly rooted in the community and trusted in a way which external organizations [like banks] were not" (Tebbutt 1983: 17). And there was sometimes an air of carnival at the Saturday gatherings at the pawnshop (see Ross 1993: 47).

13. On clothes and memory, see Stallybrass 1993: 35–50.

14. The inscription of loss within the act of purchase was a feature of everyday life for those who regularly used the pawnbroker. Melanie Tebbutt notes that the poor "had, in fact, a qualitatively different view of material resources, which they regarded as a tangible asset to be drawn on in periods of financial difficulty. When buying sales goods the poor habitually asked what they would fetch if offered in pawn, and frequently confessed they were influenced in their choice by the articles' potential pledge value" (Tebbutt 1983: 16). See also Annelies Moors's essay in this collection. She notes that richer Palestinian women tend to buy jewelry made of gold of relatively low value but that has been highly worked. Poorer women, on the other hand, tend to buy jewelry made of unworked gold of higher value, since they need to get the highest possible value for it if and when they pawn it.

15. For a fascinating analogy, see again Annelies Moors's essay.

16. Not only did women do most of the pawning; it was their own clothes that they most commonly pawned to raise money for the household. In a breakdown of the clothes pawned in 1836, 58 percent of garments clearly gender-identified were women's, while a significant percentage of the rest could have been either men's or women's. See Tebbutt 1983: 33.

17. In fact, despite the ideological association of Jews and pawnbroking, pawnbrokers were not mainly Jewish in nineteenth-century England (see Hudson 1982: 39).

REFERENCES

Andersen, Hans Christian (1982 [1849]) *Eighty Fairy Tales*, trans. R. P. Keigwin, New York: Pantheon.

Appadurai, Arjun (1986) "Introduction: Commodities and the Politics of Value" in Arjun Appadurai (ed.) *The Social Life of Things: Commodities in Cultural Perspective*, Cambridge: Cambridge University Press, pp. 3–63.

Derrida, Jacques (1992) *Given Time: 1. Counterfeit Money*, trans. Peggy Kamuf, Chicago: the University of Chicago Press, pp. 34–70.

Dickens, Charles (1994 [1833–39]) *Sketches by Boz and Other Early Papers, 1833–39*, ed. Michael Slater, Columbus: Ohio State University Press.

Draper, Hal (1985) *The Marx-Engels Chronicle*, vol. 1 of the Marx-Engels Cyclopedia, New York: Schocken.

Engels, Friedrich (1987 [1845]) *The Condition of the Working Class in England*, Harmondsworth: Penguin.

Grazia, Margreta de, Maureen Quilligan, and Peter Stallybrass (1995) "Introduction," *Subject and Object in Renaissance Culture*, Cambridge: Cambridge University Press, pp. 1–13.

Gregory, Chris (1983) "Kula Gift Exchange and Capitalist Commodity Exchange: A Comparison," in *The Kula: New Perspectives on Massim Exchange*, Cambridge: Cambridge University Press, pp. 103–17.

Hudson, Kenneth (1982) *Pawnbroking: An Aspect of British Social History*, London: The Bodley Head.

Hunter, Dard (1978) *Papermaking: The History and Technique of an Ancient Craft*, New York: Dover.

Johnson, Edgar (1952) *Charles Dickens: His Tragedy and Triumph*, vol. 1, New York: Simon and Schuster.

Kapp, Yvonne (1972) *Eleanor Marx*, New York: Pantheon.

Kopytoff, Igor (1986) "The Cultural Biography of Things," in Arjun Appadurai (ed.) *The Social Life of Things: Commodities in Cultural Perspective*, Cambridge: Cambridge University Press, pp. 64–91.

Marx, Karl (1963 [1852]) *The Eighteenth Brumaire of Louis Bonaparte* New York: International Publishers.

Marx, Karl (1976 [1867]) *Capital: A Critique of Political Economy*, vol. 1, trans. Ben Fowkes, New York: Vintage.

Marx, Karl (1977) *Karl Marx: Selected Writings*, ed. David McLellan, Oxford: Oxford University Press.

Marx, Karl and Frederick Engels (1982 [1844–51]) *Collected Works*, vol. 38, New York: International Publishers.

Marx, Karl and Frederick Engels (1983a [1852–55]) *Collected Works*, vol. 39, New York: International Publishers.

Marx, Karl and Frederick Engels (1983b [1856–59]) *Collected Works*, vol. 40, New York: International Publishers.

Marx, Karl and Frederick Engels (1985 [1860–64]) *Collected Works*, vol. 41, New York: International Publishers.

Marx, Karl and Frederick Engels (1987 [1864–68]) *Collected Works*, vol. 42, New York: International Publishers.

Mauss, Marcel (1967 [1925]) *The Gift: Forms and Functions of Exchange in Archaic Societies*, trans. Ian Cunnison, New York: Norton.

McLellan, David (1973) *Karl Marx: His Life and Thought*, New York: Harper and Row.

McLellan, David (1978) *Friedrich Engels*, Harmondsworth: Penguin.

McLellan, David (ed.) (1981) *Karl Marx: Interviews and Recollections*, London: Macmillan.

Padover, Saul K. (1978) *Karl Marx: An Intimate Biography*, New York: McGraw-Hill.

Pickering, Paul A. (1986) "Class without Words: Symbolic Communication in the Chartist Movement," *Past and Present* 112: 144–62

Pietz, William (1985) "The Problem of the Fetish, I," *Res* 9: 5–17.

Pietz, William (1987) "The Problem of the Fetish, II," *Res* 13: 23–45.

Pietz, William (1988) "The Problem of the Fetish, IIIa," *Res* 16: 105–23.

Pietz, William (1993) "Fetishism and Materialism: The Limits of Theory in Marx," in Emily Apter and William Pietz (eds.) *Fetishism as Cultural Discourse*, Ithaca: Cornell University Press, pp. 119–51.

Ross, Ellen (1993) *Love and Toil: Motherhood in Outcast London, 1870–1918*, New York: Oxford University Press.

Scarry, Elaine (1985) *The Body in Pain: The Making and Unmaking of the World*, New York: Oxford University Press.

Stallybrass, Peter (1993) "Worn Worlds: Clothes, Mourning, and the Life of Things," *Yale Review* 81: 35–50.

Strathern, Marilyn (1988) *The Gender of the Gift: Problems with Women and Problems with Society in Melanesia*, Berkeley: University of California Press.

Tebbutt, Melanie (1983) *Making Ends Meet: Pawnbroking and Working-Class Credit*, Leicester: Leicester University Press.

Thomas, Nicholas (1991) *Entangled Objects: Exchange, Material Culture, and Colonialism in the Pacific*, Cambridge, Mass.: Harvard University Press.

Weiner, Annette (1985) "Inalienable Wealth," *American Ethnologist* 12: 52–65.

Weiner, Annette (1992) *Inalienable Possessions: The Paradox of Keeping-While-Giving*, Berkeley: University of California Press.

8

Wearing Gold

Annelies Moors

INTRODUCTION

Palestinian women in various positions hold divergent views on wearing gold. When I did fieldwork in Jabal Nablus (West Bank, Palestine) in the 1980s, older rural women showed me with pride the gold coins sewn on pieces of cloth that they wore as necklaces inside their dresses. Younger rural women pointed to the heavy gold bracelets they were wearing, the necklaces with large pendants, their earrings and so on. Most of this jewelry was at least 21-carat gold. Higher class urban women, on the other hand, especially the well-educated and professionally employed, would wear different types of gold, usually finer-worked, smaller items of a much greater variety. This was 18-carat gold, often imported from Italy. These women considered the heavier bracelets, which were also commonly worn by the less well-off urbanites, and may well have been part of their own mothers' gold assets, as traditional and old-fashioned, and therefore as not suitable for modern women to wear. Younger rural women, on the other hand, and the poorer urbanites liked to have some small items of Italian gold, yet would still hold most of their gold in the form of 21-carat bracelets. In their eyes, 18-carat gold is not really gold.

"Wearing gold" is the literal translation of the Arabic *lâbsa dha-hab*, a standard expression used to inquire or make a statement about the jewelry a woman is wearing. It brings together two different, yet connected aspects of gold jewelry: on the one hand, holding gold as an economic resource, and on the other, displaying it as jewelry. Ownership of gold as a material asset invites a discussion about the place gold occupies in the world economy (its status as a "supercurrency"), as well as about local manifestations of the property-power nexus. Wearing jewelry brings to the fore how bodily adornments are employed in processes of identity formation and in negotiations of status. Gold jewelry then connects what is otherwise often seen as separate: the monetary system and notions of personhood, economy and emotions, investments and adornments.

In Jabal Nablus women received and continue to receive most of their gold jewelry as gifts at marriage. Gold, however, is not only part and parcel of a "gift economy," expressing elements of the "fetishism of the gift," that is the lack of separation between persons and things. It is also a commodity (or rather, with its specific money-gold nexus, a supercommodity), created by people, yet holding a certain power over them. Valuations of (different types of) gold jewelry depend in part on the ways in which the "gift" and "commodity" elements are brought together, and the various ways in which processes of person-ification (gold acquiring attributes of persons) and objectification (with its owners being defined as thing-like) are intertwined.[1]

In this paper I focus on the distinct valuations of "wearing gold," or rather, of wearing specific (carat) types of gold, and the ways in which these tie in with, produce, and subvert differences and hierarchies. Before addressing the various positions Palestinian women have taken up with regard to gold, I turn first to another way in which "wearing gold" can be seen as a "border fetish," that is with respect to the very different economies of value Western observers and Palestinians attach to "wearing gold."

WEARING THE VEIL VERSUS WEARING GOLD

The preoccupation of Westerners with "the veil" has a long history. As Ahmed (1992) has convincingly argued for Egypt, Western authors and policy makers, at least from the late nineteenth century on, have paid excessive attention to women wearing veils. Within the context of colonial politics, women's veiling practices were seen as the most visible sign of the backwardness of Muslim societies, and, as such, became a convenient legitimization of the Western civilizing mission. Westerners (and in their wake sections of the local elite) came to consider the veil as instrumental to women's objectification in a double and connected sense. Wearing a veil was taken as the material expression of the particular subordination Muslim women had to suffer at the hands of their own men, and veiled women were seen as bereft of any trace of individuality, as exchangeable one for the other. This focus on veiling also set the stage for those expressing their resistance against the European colonial presence. In an inversion of the colonial discourse, they considered veiling as central to Muslim women's cultural authenticity; as such, they reproduced the fixation on the veil. Up till the present, debates on veiling continue to be framed by different evaluations of processes of modernization and westernization, and quests for cultural authenticity.

In contrast to the focus on women wearing veils, little notice has been taken of "women wearing gold." In two major anthropological introductory texts on the Middle East, for instance, the meaning of gold jewelry to the women concerned is virtually ignored. In *The Middle East: An Anthropological Approach*, Eickelman (1989), provides an extensive description of various types of marriage arrangements in the region, listing all sorts of gifts women receive as dower. Only in the briefest way possible, however, does he refer to the jewelry also received in these settings and then only to immediately downplay it by noting how the jewels are often rented (1989: 174). While jewelry may indeed, on some occasions, be rented, the widespread practice of women (even those from lower class households) obtaining at least some gold at marriage is completely overlooked. Bates and Rassam (1983) in their *Peoples and Cultures of the Middle East* only discuss gold when arguing that the daughters of the better off families receive the dower themselves "in the form of jewelry, furniture, property, and so on" (1983: 202). While their book includes an illustration of three women wearing what appear to be necklaces with a substantial number of gold coins, the reader is left in the dark as to the nature of the jewelry involved, with the caption only stating, "Three Yörük brides from one household" (1983: 205).

Discussions about jewelry in the Middle East are, by and large, limited to books on "material culture." Such books tend to focus on what has been defined as "customary jewelry," and then mainly to silver items. It is true that at least until the 1920s wearing silver jewelry was, indeed, a more widespread practice in Palestine than wearing gold, especially in the rural areas (Weir 1989: 194). Still, in more recent times as well, gold has largely been neglected, with publications focusing on the considerably larger and more spectacular silver items, such as Bedouin women's facial jewelry and head dresses. As a result, Palestinian jewelry is mainly represented as customary and exotic.[2]

The issue here is, however, not simply that women's veils rather than their gold has caught the eye of Western observers. The main point is that there are major differences in the ways in which the relation of women to these two material objects is defined and analyzed. While veils and women tend to be fused, with the veil almost taking on a life of its own and speaking for the women concerned, jewelry tends to be discussed as artifacts separated from their female owners. Whereas veiling is usually, at least in the more traditional Orientalist approaches, analyzed in terms of relations of male dominance and female subordination, in descriptions of "women wearing gold" the issue of power relations tends to be absent.[3] This absence then is a strong indication of very different economies of value attached to "wearing gold." Whereas Western observers choose to neglect women's gold, to many women in Jabal Nablus the gold jewelry they receive as part of their dower has been an important economic resource. If veils have by and large been discussed in terms of women's subordination and an essentialized Oriental difference, a focus on gold as a major economic asset may reveal the possibilities for women to act as an economic agent of sorts, and in doing so point to potential similarities with Western notions of personhood.

BALADÎ GOLD: A WOMAN'S AFFAIR

The Middle East is not only a large consumer of gold, but most of this gold, delivered in the form of kilo bars, is used locally to manufacture jewelry.[4] As many other cities in the Middle East, Nablus has a sizable gold market, which is regularly frequented by groups of women, with or without their male relatives, actively involved in the buying and selling of gold. For not only wearing, but also owning gold is, to a considerable extent, a woman's affair. While the size of their possessions may vary greatly, the large majority of married women in Jabal Nablus were and are owners of gold jewelry.

Jabal Nablus is part of an area in which wearing gold jewelry has a long history.[5] In rural Jabal Nablus, up till the 1960s most women acquired their gold largely in the form of Ottoman, and to a lesser extent, British gold coins (*lîrât dhahab*). These they wore, sewn together on a cloth ribbon, as necklaces inside their dresses (*qilâda dhahab*).

The value of such coins, which are facsimiles of official coins ("fake coins"), is determined by their gold content (usually 22-carat) and their weight. As such they can be seen as "bullion" coins, as a way of holding gold bullion in "small denominations."[6]

In Nablus city gold jewelry was also worn in other shapes and sizes. Rather then wearing a coin necklace, or in addition to wearing such and other necklaces, urban women wore their gold in the form of many different types of gold bracelets, such as the heavy "twisted wire" (*mabrûma*), "pear" (*injâsa*) or "snakes" (*hayâya*) bracelets, and the lighter *sahab*. Beginning in the late 1960s these gold bracelets also became more popular in the rural areas. Also the value of these bracelets, which were quite standardized, but with small variations in style, was determined largely by weight; the gold content was invariably 21-carat. At times combinations of bracelets and bullion were also popular. Some bracelets mainly consist of gold coins, while off and on bracelets with small gold bars between two gold chains were available in the gold market.

This type of gold, both the 21-carat bracelets and the 22-carat coins, is called *baladî*, a complex notion referring to the local, indigenous, and authentic. The main characteristic of such *baladî* gold is that the option of selling it is never far away. As jewelers pointed out, the main question women have when they come to buy gold is how much they will lose when selling it again. While what they will eventually receive is, of course, partly determined by the price of gold on the international market, losses due to labor and other additional costs are limited; labor costs are often less than 5 percent.

The economic value of gold depends on the relation between the local currency and internationally determined gold prices. In Palestine holding *baladî* gold was usually seen as a sound investment, and as a more secure way of keeping one's wealth than would be the case with cash money or bank accounts. Cash holdings were considered risky because of theft, inflation, and the possibility of currency depreciation, while international acceptability is less than with gold. A banking system has been largely absent in Jabal Nablus. Under the Israeli occupation, bank deposits with Israeli banks were unattractive because of fear of confiscation for political reasons, while bank deposits in Jordanian banks were relatively unaccessible (Harris 1988: 215–16). And gold has not only been a relatively secure, but also, at times, highly profitable way of investing money. Especially when the international gold standard collapsed and the link between currency and gold was broken, prices of gold have risen phenomenally.[7]

WOMEN ACQUIRING GOLD:
THE DOWER AS GENDERED PROPERTY

As I have already suggested, for Western authors, at least for those taking Muslim women's subordination as their point of departure, *women* owning gold is a difficult issue to deal with. This matter is further complicated because the main mechanism for women to acquire gold was and is through dower payments (the *mahr*, which is to be paid by the groom to the bride). Both in popular fiction and in academic work there is a tradition which equates dower payments with the sale of women, which is then commonly taken as yet another indication of women's alleged subordination. Hilma Granqvist, a Finnish anthropologist who, in the 1920s, did extensive fieldwork on marriage conditions in a village near Bethlehem, found it necessary to elaborate at length against these assumptions. As she points out, the village women themselves do not consider the *mahr* a form of sale and purchase:

> If one directly questions the fellahîn women about this and says: "Is it not the custom among you for a man to buy his wife?" or if one suggests that a father sells his daughter as a bride to a man—which is the same thing—they deny it with as much indignation as the educated Arabs in the town. The bride money does not appear to them to be payment for a purchase; it is only Westerns who unhesitatingly called the giving of a bride price in Palestine a purchase (. . .) (1931: 143).

Interestingly, educated urban men, well aware of such Western perceptions of the *mahr*, reformulated the issue of marriage payments in European terms and turned the tables when comparing the Arab *mahr* with the European dowry. Granqvist again:

> In Jerusalem I once discussed this matter with an educated Arab and he said: The Arabs again say that European women buy themselves husbands, and only if the Westerns agree to call the dowry a form of bridegroom purchase can the Arabs agree to see bride purchase in the giving of a bride price. (1931: 134).

Not only does the local population reject a conceptualization of the *mahr* as a form of "bride purchase," Islamic legal thought also firmly rejects such a point of view. According to both classical Islamic law and later legal reforms, the *mahr* is supposed to be the property of the bride herself over which neither her husband nor her father or other

kin would have any control. Social practice may, of course, diverge
from legal doctrine, but as Granqvist has argued, even if the bride
does not receive the full amount registered as her dower, she does obtain part of the *mahr* as property which she can deal with in whatever
way she likes (1931: 132, 145).

In my own work on women's access to property in Jabal Nablus I
also argue that the dower was and is a major mechanism for women
to acquire property (Moors 1994; 1995). Women commonly received
at least part of their *mahr* in the form of gold jewelry at marriage. The
ways in which women deploy their gold in economic transactions,
has, however, been affected by major shifts in the political-economic
structure of the region. From the 1960s on, male migration wage-
labor has rapidly gained the upper hand over agriculture as the major
source of livelihood in the rural areas. Up till then rural women had
commonly sold their gold and bought goats, cows, and occasionally a
piece of land. Such options became increasingly less attractive in the
context of the general marginalization of agriculture. Women subsequently began to invest their gold in their husband instead of in animals or land, for instance, in order to enable him to migrate or to
build a house, as well as in their children's education. In line with the
greater centrality of husbands as providers, not only women's ability
to act with their gold, but also the meaning and nature of the gold itself, has been affected.[8] One visible sign, for instance, has been the
appearance of 18-carat Italian gold in the Nablus markets and on
women's bodies. These shifts tie in with changes in dower registrations and marriage arrangements, some of which can be read from
the marriage contracts, while others are presented in women's narratives on the dower and gold.

ITALIAN GOLD AND THE TOKEN DOWER

Gold jewelry is not only an economic resource. For elite women,
wearing gold had always been more a statement of their status and
marital or kin relations than a means of gaining some sort of financial security or safeguarding against its absence. As one of them told
me, she never had any reason to sell her gold; her husband always
bought her more whenever there was a new model on the market,
and she liked to keep the older items as they reminded her of the
occasions when she had received them. In addition, amongst the
wealthy jewelry did not only consist of gold, but also diamond-set
items were included. With the diamond trade of a different nature

than that of gold, risks of losing money when selling such items were considerably greater.

Beginning in the 1960s a new trend in wearing jewelry developed. Those who could afford to do so began to wear smaller but more exclusive pieces of jewelry, commonly imported from Italy. They often referred to this gold as "small pieces," or *môdêlât* (that is, gold which, because of its greater hardness, could be made in a much wider variety of models and fashions). As this Italian gold was only 18-carat and a substantially larger part of the price was made up of labor costs and import duties, it was less valuable as an investment. Selling this gold, women would incur a considerable loss. Even so, wearing Italian gold rapidly became also more popular amongst the less well-off in the city and in the rural areas, even if for these women the 21-carat bracelets remained the central items in their dower gold. Younger brides liked the large variety of nicely made Italian necklaces, bracelets, pendants, rings, earrings and so on. Yet, at the same time, they (and their family) were also intent on acquiring *baladî* gold as a means of economic security.

Around the same time a major innovation in registering the dower also started to become a trend. Rather than registering a high amount of money as prompt dower, in some marriage contracts only a token amount was written down, such as one JD (Jordanian dinar) or one gold coin. Registering such a dower did, however, not result in brides' exclusion from gold and other items. Often they received gifts similar in value to what they would have obtained, had a set high dower been recorded in the marriage contract. The crucial difference, however, was that women no longer received these things as their legal right, but rather as a gift, voluntarily provided by the groom. As such, the token dower indicated above all that the bride and her family could afford to fully trust the groom and forego legal guarantees, while the jewelry she received displayed the groom's ability and willingness to give.

Registering the dower in this novel way was "invented" by the urban modernizing elite, and rapidly became the common practice in families where women themselves were well educated and at times professionally employed. Gradually also some families from the middle and lower classes, and from the rural areas started to participate in this trend. For them, however, this could be a risky thing to do, for if the groom's gifts did not live up to expectations no legal redress would subsequently be possible. Especially amongst the less well-off, ambivalences about registering a token dower can be read in the marriage contracts. In a considerable number of contracts with a token dower, the value, and sometimes the nature of the household goods to be provided by the groom were registered, and, less often, also gold of a specific carat content and weight. In this way the uncertainties of the token dower were somewhat hedged insofar as at least some financial guarantees were written into the contract.

Women's arguments in favor of registering a token dower are simi-. lar to their statements about why they only desire simple gold or "smaller pieces." Self-conciously "modern women" consider both registering a high dower and wearing a large number of heavy gold bracelets as old fashioned. Some of these women themselves compared registering such a dower with "the sale of women." One of them, for instance, told me how, when her brother had asked her whether she wanted a dower, she had indignantly responded with the query: "Am I a donkey that he has to pay for me?" These women would still receive gold jewelry at their weddings, but, especially amongst the better-off, this would consist of expensive, finely worked pieces of "Italian gold," and also may include diamond-set rings with a large solitaire, and so on. To them both registering a token dower and wearing Italian gold was a means of affirming their modernity, an announcement that they did not need financial guarantees upon marriage. Their husbands, or, if need be, their own families, could be fully trusted to provide them with anything they might need. And for those employed in the professions, it was a statement on their own earning capacities. They did not need the dower (or, for that matter, marriage) to gain access to property, as their own professional labor provided them with the means to do so. While women from the lower classes may register a token dower in order to claim higher status, and also liked to have some smaller, but less expensive items of Italian gold, they often did not want to take the risk of foregoing *baladî* gold altogether.

Wearing Italian gold and registering a token dower also coincide with another trend, that is women's increased say in their choice of a marriage partner. Actually, women sometimes attempted to downplay the economic side of marriage (a high dower and heavy gold bracelets) in order to facilitate arranging a marriage with someone they themselves preferred to marry. Within such a context Italian gold has become associated with love marriages in which women see their husbands as a partner and companion, rather than with strictly arranged marriages with stronger gender hierarchies. Still, whereas many younger women point out that the older system objectified women as it linked them to the dower, others, in particular those feeling excluded from this process of "modernization," argue that it is the very emphasis on the "person" of the bride which may lead to her objectification. As a peasant woman in her early thirties commented about a man who had demanded to see his future bride before the marriage contract was concluded: "Is she a cow that he needs to see her?"

THE "NEW" QILÂDA AND EMOTIONAL INVESTMENTS IN BALADÎ GOLD

The shift to Italian gold, as well as to registering a token dower, is far from complete.[9] In fact, there are indications that, by the later 1980s, Italian gold had already lost some of its popularity. Young rural women showed me with pride the *qilâda dhahab* they had received upon marriage, consisting of thirteen gold coins, with a larger one in the middle, contained within a heavy frame; these coins were not sewn on a ribbon, as had been common in their grandmother's day, but were attached to a heavy gold chain. And amongst the urban lower middle classes, the "Indian set" (*taqm hindî*) was becoming popular, a set of 21-carat gold, either brought from the Gulf region or locally made, consisting of at least a necklace and earrings, elaborately decorated with many small pendants and other attachments. Even if the labor costs involved in these were higher than for the traditional bracelets, they were less than in the case of Italian gold. While brides still liked fashionable jewelry, they seemed to be turning again to more secure types of gold. In a similar vein the rapid increase of token dower registrations has also halted. Guaranteeing some form of economic security apparently has become once again more important.

Yet, there is more to *baladî* gold than its monetary value. Women actually *wear* this "investment" gold on their bodies. Even if they do not necessarily do so all the time, at festive occasions they bring out their gold. And while they may wear their *qilâda* inside their dress, enough of it is visible for people "in the know," as it were, to know what is there. Wearing such gold coins and bracelets involves the public display of specific social relations, because in doing so, women make statements on their bodies about the various meanings of "being given" valuable gold. When a woman wears *baladî* gold it is evident that the groom's side has been willing to spend a considerable sum of money; it entails not only a claim about the groom's financial status, but also about his respect for and high evaluation of the bride's own family. Displaying *baladî* gold may, at the same time, also be read as a statement about the relation of a woman to her father. The *baladî* gold on the woman's body proves that her father did not pocket the dower himself, but instead has spent it generously on his daughter. As such, many read it as a sign of fatherly love and protection of her. *Baladî* gold is then more than "simply" an economic resource, it presents emotions to the world at large.

DISCUSSION

Gold is a fetish par excellence. As Pietz has pointed out, the term "guinea" came to designate the West African gold and slave coast as well as an important gold coin (1988: 105). Gold, which people themselves have created as "valuable," has gained tremendous power over people's lives. Gold discoveries have both led to concentrations of tremendous wealth and to ethnocide. Through the gold standard different parts of the world have become part of an international monetary system. Rather than representing value, as money does, gold is value. Still, the value of gold depends on trust. At the same time, gold is surrounded by much mystery. Major transactions of gold are conducted secretly, some countries do not disclose information about their gold reserves, and others have forbidden their citizens to hold bullion gold. Trading and smuggling gold have been highly lucrative, while gold has also been a convenient way of laundering money from dubious sources.

Discussing "women wearing gold," I have addressed fetishism in a more specific sense. In dealing with gold jewelry as a border fetish, my focus has been on the various ways in which women through their use of different types of gold jewelry mark off and negotiate such distinctions as locality, class, and gender. The strategies women themselves pursue in regard to gold jewelry indicate the ways in which wearing gold produces, transgresses, and undermines such crucial differences and hierarchies.

The great paradox of dower gold is that women acquire it by entering into marriage. Women generally are less able to act in respect to arranging their marriages than men, and have a more limited control over their own person after marriage. Yet, it is exactly through entering such a relation that they gain considerable access to property (in particular in the form of gold), a potential source of economic power, with which they can act in whatever way they wish. The very same dower that in some senses may be seen as objectifying women also turns them into owners of, at times considerable, movable property.

Dower gold does not only link person and property, it also connects gift and commodity. In legal terms the dower has been defined as a set amount of money, registered in a marriage contract, which the groom is obliged to pay the bride. In social practice, the dower is also a gift, as the bride's father, to whom the dower is usually paid, turns it over to his daughter in the form of "gifts" of gold jewelry, with some fathers keeping part of it for themselves, while others add to it. In the case of the token dower the gift element has become central, with the groom himself providing his wife with gifts of gold.

What women claim about their relations with their kin and husband ties in with the nature of the gold involved in sedimenting these social ties. *Baladî* gold is closely associated with a marriage system based on arranged marriages and high registered dowers. This gold points to the groom's respect for the family of the bride, and to her father's willingness and ability to transfer at least a considerable part of the dower to his daughter. As a result the daughter enters marriage endowed with considerable movable property. Italian gold and registering a token dower belong to a different, more "modern" life style, with marriage arrangements leaving some space for a more individualized choice of marital partner, and the groom providing the bride with gifts, rather than fulfilling dower obligations. Whereas *baladî* gold provided women with some economic autonomy, but within a marriage system in which women were less able to act independently in other ways, Italian gold works in somewhat the opposite fashion. Women claim more personalized marital arrangements and relations, yet they lose out in terms of the economic security they formerly enjoyed through their ownership of and rights over gold. Not only has the dower increasingly turned into a gift, also the gold given is of lesser value in economic exchange.

Through wearing different types of gold women make a statement both about their property holdings and about their kin and marital relations. Wearing *baladî* gold can be seen as negotiating gender and class borders by claiming economic autonomy and kin protection. Wearing Italian gold does so in a different way, as a token of a "modern" marriage and by concretizing status claims. But this distinction is not fixed, and ambiguities abound. Quite some marriage contracts with a token dower negate women's need for economic security, yet reaffirm it at the same time through the registrations of household goods and occasionally gold. In a similar vein, women may well employ multiple strategies with respect to their jewelry. Whereas the wealthy refrain from wearing *baladî* gold, but do obtain rings with a large solitaire, women from lower class households not only acquire *baladî* gold, but also some small pieces of fashionable Italian gold. Not only through wearing different types of gold, but also by combining these in various ways, women in different positions negotiate and revalue the differences and hierarchies of their gendered, class, and geographical subject positions.

Finally, a short note on the importance of the mechanisms through which women gain access to gold. In this paper dower gold has been central, which ties the ownership of gold directly to marriage. Such an emphasis fits well with local notions. When younger women wear lots of gold jewelry it often is assumed that they have recently married. There are, however, also other ways for women to acquire gold, such as through inheritance or through paid labor.

Acquiring gold through inheritance brings a very different relation to the fore. Whereas in Jabal Nablus women often forego claiming the share in the inheritance they are legally entitled to, it seems more difficult to disinherit women from gold than from any other type of property (Moors 1995; see also Mundy 1979; Pastner 1980). Yet, investigating the woman-inherited gold relation, it become evident that it is not so much the nature of the property that counts, but rather the fact that gold is mostly inherited from mothers. Inherited gold, then, can be seen as expressive of the strong emotional bond between a mother and her daughter (in fact, a woman may well give some of her gold pre-mortem to a daughter she feels particularly close to and responsible for, such as a daughter who herself has postponed marriage in order to support her mother in old age). In the case of such inherited gold, the emotional and "personalized" side of it is more central than was the case with dower gold. Even if mothers give their gold to their daughters as a guarantee of economic security, to the daughters the person of the mother is present in the gold concerned. Their gold speaks to them.

Buying gold from one's own income may in the first instance be seen as a mirror image of the inheritance story, as such gold clearly is a commodity and not a gift. Yet, also in this case wearing gold carries with it a highly specific message about kin relations. Being able to buy gold with income from one's own work indicates the freedom such girls are allowed by their families to spend their income. While legally women are under no obligation to support their families from their income, a notion which is also socially current, many girls go and work to assist their families when these are in financial need. Through wearing some gold, they undermine the idea that their fathers and brothers would not live up to their obligations as providers, and thereby show that their families are not stingy. Their gold speaks for itself.

NOTES

1. The discussion on gifts and commodities is informed by both Appadurai (1986) and Bloch and Parry (1989). In taking issue with the distinction between things that are commodities and those that are not, Appadurai (1986: 13) emphasizes that things may be one and/or the other at various moments during their life-cycle. Bloch and Parry (1989: 10–12) argue that differences in processes of fetishizing cannot simply be explained by the economic system involved and the use of money. The gendered nature of discussions on things and people, and on power and property is informed by Strathern (1984) and Whitehead (1984).

2. Whereas elsewhere in the Middle East wearing jewelry (and wearing the veil) could also be part of a discourse on the erotic—in which case women's undressed bodies were central in the display of such jewelry—the erotic has not been popular in Western discourse on Palestine, as Palestine has first and foremost been defined as the Holy Land.

3. Weir (1989: 174 ff) is an exception to this trend. While she also focuses on silver jewelry, her analysis does take into account the economic importance of such jewelry to its female owners.

4. At times 25 percent of all gold coming on the market was destined for the Middle East (Green 1980: 191).

5. The extent to which gold jewelry was in use before the twentieth century is not easy to judge. Various authors employing archival material in writing on property relations in Ottoman times mention gold jewelry (e.g. Tucker 1988 for Jabal Nablus).

6. Countries such as Syria, Kuwait, and Saudi Arabia produce large amounts of such coins. The great increase in gold coin production in Saudi Arabia in the late 1970s is explained in part by the fact that migrant laborers (and pilgrims) bought such coins as a secure way to take their savings back home (Weston 1983: 58).

7. After the gold price peaked during the 1930s and the 1970s considerable amounts of gold were sold by the private sector, also in the Middle East (Weston 1983: 70).

8. The shift in conceptualizing women from "productive daughters" to "consuming wives" has in itself stimulated women's investments in their husbands rather than their independent ownership of, and active dealing

with, productive property. And women are less able to buy productive property, as the value of the dower has declined relatively, especially in comparison to land and real estate prices.

9. Whereas during the 1970s the percentage of contracts with a token dower increased rapidly and, by the mid-1980s, a token dower was registered in almost half the urban contracts, thereafter there was no further increase.

REFERENCES

Ahmed, Leila (1992) *Women and Gender in Islam.* New Haven: Yale University Press.

Appadurai, Arjun (1986) "Introduction. Commodities and the Politics of Value," in Arjun Appadurai, ed. (1986) *The Social Life of Things: Commodities in Cultural Perspective.* Cambridge: Cambridge University Press. Pp. 3–64.

Bates, Daniel and Amal Rassam (1983) *Peoples and Cultures of the Middle East.* Englewood Cliffs, (N.J.): Prentice-Hall.

Eickelman, Dale (1989) *The Middle East: An anthropological approach.* Englewood Cliffs (N.J.): Prentice Hall.

Granqvist, Hilma (1931) *Marriage Conditions in a Palestinian Village I.* Helsingfors: Akademische Buchhandlung.

Green, Timothy (1980) "Changing Patterns in the Middle East Gold Market," *Journal of Social and Political Studies* 5, 4: 191–199.

Harris, Laurence (1988) "Money and Finance with Undeveloped Banking in the Occupied Territories," in George Abed, ed., *The Palestinian Economy: Studies in Development under Prolonged Occupation.* London and New York: Routledge. Pp. 191–223.

Moors, Annelies (1994) "Women and Dower Property in Twentieth-Century Palestine: The Case of Jabal Nablus," *Islamic Law and Society* 1, 3: 301–331.

Moors, Annelies (1995) *Women, Property, and Islam: Palestinian Experiences, 1920–1990.* Cambridge: Cambridge University Press.

Mundy, Martha (1979) "Women's Inheritance of Land in Highland Yemen," *Arabian Studies* 5: 161–187.

Parry, Jonathan and Maurice Bloch (1989) "Introduction: Money and the Morality of Exchange," in Jonathan Parry and Maurice Bloch, eds., *Money and the Morality of Exchange.* Cambridge: Cambridge University Press. Pp. 1–33.

Pastner, Caroll (1980) "Access to Property and the Status of Women in Islam," in J. Smith, (ed.), *Women in Contemporary Muslim Societies*. Lewisbury: Bucknell University Press. Pp. 146–186.

Pietz, William (1988) "The Problem of the Fetish, IIIa," *Res* 16: 105–123.

Strathern, Marilyn (1984) "Subject or Object? Women and the Circulation of Valuables in Highlands New Guinea," in Renée Hirshon, ed., *Women and Property, Women as Property*. London and Canberra: Croom Helm. Pp. 158–176.

Tucker, Judith (1988) "Marriage and Family in Nablus, 1720–1856: Towards a History of Arab marriage," *Journal of Family History* 13, 2: 165–179.

Weir, Shelagh (1989) *Palestinian Costume*. London: British Museum.

Weston, Ray (1983) *Gold: A World Survey*. London: Croom Helm.

Whitehead, Ann (1984) "Men and Women, Kinship and Property: Some General Issues," in Renée Hirshon, ed., *Women and Property, Women as Property*. London and Canberra: Croom Helm. Pp. 176–191.

9

Crossing the Face

Michael Taussig

Transgression incessantly crosses and recrosses a line which closes up
behind it in a wave of extremely short duration.

—Michel Foucault

The problem set forth by the editor of this book concerns fetish-effects
of crossings,[1] of culture-crossings, such that a word like *fetish* can
emerge as a pidgin word from its Portuguese mouthings dislocated
and punched up in a cross-cultural trading language along the West
African coast from the fifteenth century onwards, the trade eventually
being so many African slaves for so much European cloth and guns
and . . .[2] And if words are unstable "at the best of times," so full of
promise, at the best of times, how much more might this be the case
with pidgin words born of trading and misunderstandings concerning
matters spiritual where thought and matter by definition cohabit unfinished philosophies? Indeed it is to this sense of instability and more
emphatically unfinishedness and permanent incompleteness that the
word *fetish* has, I think, directed us at least since Enlightenment by
promising in the excitement it provokes no less than its disappointing
consequence more than it can deliver, an "always-beyond" bound to a

sense of of richness and mystery in elusive word-magic, the fetish of the fetish, we might say, testimony to etymolgies and histories cosmic and violent—no less than to the promises proffered by trade itself.

It is to this promise, to infinitude and its associated sense of frustration, that I want to raise the face—specifically the face as a fetish-crossing forever crossed, the ur-border zone, the mother of all borderlands. One does not look at the face, says Emanuel Levinas, but is granted access to it as an ethical act. Why this might be is surely beyond our knowledge, just as it is the basis of knowledge, beginning with sociology, but what we can do is constellate this not-looked-at site with the Infinite. At least this is what Levinas does where he recalls the Cartesian idea of the Infinite as an idea aimed at something "infinitely greater than the very act through which one thinks it. There is a disproportion between the act and that to which the act gives access."[3]

This is one way of thinking the fetish.

THE SECRET

In pursuing this disproportion in terms of crossing the border that is the face, I want to suggest—strange as it may seem—that what's crucial here is secrecy, and not just secrecy but more particuarly what I call the "public secret."

First let us note with what remarkable ease secrecy conjures fetish powers—as in Elias Canetti's remarkable chapter on secrecy in his book *Crowds and Power*, a book preeminently concerned with masking and transformation. "Secrecy lies at the very core of power," he begins, plunging us into an animal world despite the fact that the secrecy that concerns him is urgently human and social. "The act of lying in wait for prey is essentially secret," he writes. "Hiding or taking on the color of its surroundings and betraying itself by no movement, the lurking creature disappears entirely, covering itself with secrecy as with a second skin."[4] Total annihilation of the prey is the aim of this activity, yet patience, infinite patience, is an outstanding prerequisite for the hunter. There is something human in the restraint required here; not just human but superhuman. The animal and the superhuman seem to complement one another. They form a unity.

Then the aesthetic radically changes. Speed intervenes in the moment of seizure, flashing out "like lightning illuminating its own brief passage." Secrecy is abandoned for it is no longer necessary, at least for the moment. Annihilation takes its place. "The final seizing of the prey is open," says Canetti, "for terror is part of its intended effect, but from the moment of incorporation onwards, everything happens in the dark again."[5]

This second darkness is not hiding or waiting in order to kill, but secrecy in the image of a profound innnerness. Its scene is that of the moving yet lightless mucoid membranous interior of the gastrointesinal tract, rippling in peristaltic good health. "The mouth is dark and the stomach and bowels still darker. No one knows and no one thinks about what goes on inside him. Of this fundamental process of incorporation by far the larger part remains secret. It begins with the active and deliberate secrecy of lying in wait and ends as something unknown and involuntary in the secret recesses of the body."[6]

Fetishism is what also lies in wait for us in this stepwise revelation of the character of secrecy—from its lying at the core of power, to lying in wait, to killing, and to the incorporation via the mouth into the intestines—for now the secret acquires a life of its own. The term itself—*the* secret—provides terse testimony to the ease with which secrecy becomes fetishized as self-activating transcendance with a destiny of its own, in everyday life let alone with the paranoic whom, like the despot, says Canetti, has many secrets and "he organises these secrets so that they guard one another." We slip easily from the person keeping *a* secret to an understanding in which *the* secret keeps the person and organizes the social world of persons. What is more, like the fetish, *it* becomes godlike—"everything is subordinated" writes Canetti of the secret, "to its apotheosis." It is hard to resist the notion that this apotheosis is a consequence of an apocalyptic telos, the eventual self-destruction of the secret, shattering in its consequences. "Every secret is explosive," warns Canetti, "expanding with its own inner heat."[7]

THE PUBLIC SECRET

This is a frightened and frightening view of secrecy in which the secret as fetish, like paranoia, swarms across the emotional range, contaminating all in its swirling path, your fear frightening others.

But if secrecy is fascinating, still more interesting is "the public secret," by which I mean that which is generally known but cannot be acknowledged. Much social knowledge is of this sort and perhaps most of most important knowledge is too. Like families and universities, all institutions breed such secrecy and would die without it. Truer to life and more complex and mischievous than the old stalwarts of "discourse" and "ideology," public secrecy is a mobile, evanescent, power-laden knowing of unknowing, a perpetually renewed social contract as to knowing what not to know. This is equally true of the modern state, and the implications for democracy are profound.

So where does the face fit in? As both mask *and* window to the soul, the face can be considered the "bench-mark" of the public secret—that which is known but cannot be acknowledged—and now, like the public secret of sex in Michel Foucault's rendering, its turn has come to be turned inside out as the secret about which we cannot stop talking.[8] After all, the face and the genitalia are not only poles apart, but intimately connected, the one covered, the other exposed, such that inappropriate exposure of the one leads to a thoroughly appropriate surge of shame, the blush, across the other. (Indeed, might it not be a form of blushing in which I write here, about that form of inappropriate exposure known as defacement?)[9]

CROSSING THE BORDER

This coexistence in faciality of both mask and window to the soul is more than contradiction. Crossing back and forth across the face as mask *and* window to the soul is our necessary task and it is due to such "disproportion" that we discern the "always beyond" that spills out from the fetish. Such a formulation leads us away from cognition—as I think is implied in Levinas' notion that one does not "look" at the face—and directs us towards ethics, surely the beginning and end of all inquiry, just as it skips playfully past the rigid categories that are paraded as the mark of "rigorous thought," that harbinger of *rigor mortis*. Seismology, not semiology, obscene rather than upright, and above all proneness—a nervous proneness to the disturbing effects of its presence—is what faciality as both masking and windowing the soul entails. Either of these functions is a wonder; together, an orgy of disproportionateness.

If such disproportion is akin to an "always beyond" that is the face, how are we to resolve the difficulty that the face never exists alone; that it is fated in its very being to become only when faced by another face. Here is where the impossible but true coexistence of the mask and the window flares in recognition of a certain tenderness, a shyness, before the gaze of the other with a studied incapacity to "recognise" either the masking or the windowing capacity and certainly not their coexistence. All this happens "under the table," secretly, as it were, as necessary to social life as it is forever bound to the unsayable. Thus to the need to deny the mask when looking through the window, and to the need to deny the window when espying the mask, try computing the added complexity when it is (and has to be) not one but at least two faces facing these reciprocating denials. Truly, an orgy of disproportionateness and one of the seven wonders of the world; all the more so on account of us pulling this off unthinkingly most every moment of the day, the bench-mark, the bottom line, of being a social being. Of language itself and signifying, says Levinas.[10]

THE ANIMAL WITHIN

Canetti's fear of the secret has already alerted us to the always-beyond of "withinness," to what is more than a fact of space or of anatomy, but a fact of metaphysics, religion, and ontology. What is revelatory—if one can trade in language like this—is the connection of "innerness" to both the fetish power of the secret and animality.

Why animality? Why is it second nature for Canetti, with his obsessive interest in the mask and transformation, to dovetail secrecy with the animal and thence with the intestines, with the insides of the intestines, these insides that we never seem to get inside of, rippling in peristaltic good health, each inside harbinger to another, still further and deeper innerness (the secret of the secret, we might say)? It is trite to say that a profound addiction to innerness is here at work. We are talking of a whole situation of being in the world, an all-consuming practice dedicated to behindedness in a world replete with screens.

Physiognomy, that ancient science of reading the face, of reading insides from outsides, often connected the human face to the animal so as to perform its reading. In fact the connection seems absolute. Used as a mechanism for defining the human form, zoomorphism appears to be indispensable to physiognomists, notes a student of such arcane yet everyday concerns.[11] And this despite the fact that such reading indulges in astonishing disproportionateness, astonishing paradoxicality in which mirror is held to mirror—the animality discerned by the physiognomist in the face of a particular human being an animality which only means something because it is endowed with a human quality . . . the hook nose of a vulture as the sign of cruelty, the cunning of the fox, the sharp-toothed muzzle of the rat.

Yet disproportionateness works! And how! Perversity recruited for the ever keener study of reality, beginning—as always—with faciality. Sergei Eisenstein pointed out—confessed might be more appropriate—that far from dying out as Lavater's and Aristotle's defunct science, physiognomy was boosted by modernity thanks to the invention of the camera and the moving pictures, as in the famous "soliloquy of the silent language of the face" discovered by the close-up.[12] Eisenstein's point was that a defunct science was not necessarily a bad art, and in any event physiognomy was the natural practice of the filmmaker. I would say further that the everyday arts of physiognomy—honed to ever greater skills by the arts of cinema making and viewing—are precisely the everyday arts of reading the disproportion that is the face, of defining the human, the inner being, not to mention the insalubrious arts of making through such reading racial and gendered types and sub-types, in short the great cast of characters stalking the human stage in modern times.[13]

As if by magic in Eisenstein's first film, *The Strike* (1924), the human faces of the police spies are transformed one by one in front of our eyes into animal faces and back again into human ones. It is the power and magic of film that is proudly and lovingly displayed here, no less than the power of the state and the spies. (Which is greater? you ask.) Most of these spies have animal nicknames and this is how they are introduced as the first line of attack against the strikers when the police chief pulls out from his right hand desk drawer his spy-file consisting of photographs of the faces of his agents. As their animals names are revealed, the photographic portraits become animated, leaping ecstatically out of the frames of the portraits in the police file, ready for action. Animalization and transformation is essential to their secretive being and to their heightened capacity to observe as through a one-way mirror.

Central to the action here in startling opposition to the offices of the police precinct and the bureaucratic spaces of the state is a species of pet-shop, a mysterious alchemical laboratory of zoomorphosis in whose shadowy debris of animal figures and junk predominates a live monkey encircled by a hoop suspended from the ceiling. The monkey plays in the hoop. The hoop rotates slowly, back and forth. Whenever there is a human facial transformation into an animal, thanks to the montaging capacity of film, the hoop and the monkey swim briefly into focus as if to tell us something.

This hoop is the magical circle of transformation, of secrecy and fetish powers as released by the physiognomics of film.

This hoop is the human face.

It is the face of transformation—not of men into animals but of Double-Men, transforming men whose metamorphosing capacities are established through face-animal physiognomics.

The "Organization of Mimesis"

Why Double-Men? What is the significance of this? Double-Men are figures who can change back and forth from animals into men, and from men into animals. This is the mark of the ancestors no less than of spies working for the modern state—as if the state is the select social organ for appropriating those ancient powers, and cinema is the select instrument for revelation of this mighty appropriation that Horkheimer and Adorno termed "the organiziation of mimesis."[14]

Let us return to Canetti, for he loves human-animal transformation. He is in thrall to it. This is more than an intellectual thing, but we shall concentrate on it as intellection for the moment. He sees what few of us see. He writes:

> The talent for transformation which has given man so much power over all other creatures has as yet scarcely been considered or begun to be understood. Though everyone possesses it, uses it, and takes it for granted, yet it is one of the great mysteries and few are aware that to it they owe what is best in themselves.[15]

". . . that to it they owe what is best in themselves."

What is more important here, the being into which one is transformed, or the sheer fact of transformation itself? It is hard to tell. And probably unimportant except too often we focus on the end-result and not the magical capacity itself, the capacity to "which we owe what is best in ourselves," a certain quality of "mimetic excess" lack of which may lead to profound melancholia as when one cannot escape; one cannot find fresh metamorphoses . . . .[16]

Deterritorializing the Face

Writing in exile in Hollywood in the wake of the Holocaust, Max Horkheimer and T. W. Adorno built (together with Gretel Adorno) an argument to the effect that this sort of mimetic prowess was not so much sundered by Enlightenment as reconfigured. The massive deterritorializing power of nineteenth- and twentieth-century Euroamerican capitalism had dislodged, so to speak, the mimetic faculty from its magical and primitivist moorings in myth and ritual, only to relocate and reterritorialise those powers, perhaps more metaphorical than literal, in the state itself.[17]

"A very special mechanism" is how Giles Deleuze and Felix Guattari denote the face—or not so much the face, as "faciality"—the mechanism of the intersection of the two great axes, the wall of the broad plane of the face as screen, and the black holes of the eyes; the axis of signifiance and the axis of subjectification, respectively. Already here, as with Levinas, we can discern not merely the fundamental role of signification being granted the face alongside the interiority of the autonomous subject, but the public secret of the coexistence of the face as mask and the face as window to the soul, harbinger to the "always beyond," to the ineffability and fetish quality of the face.

But like Horkheimer and Adorno, Deleuze and Guattari have a decisive historicist bent and, furthermore, in keeping with the "always beyond," a utopic one as well, as when they write that "if human beings have a destiny, it is rather to escape the face, to dismantle the face and facializations, to become imperceptible, to become clandestine, not by returning to animality, nor even returning to the head, but by quite spiritual and special becomings-animal . . ."[18]

Once again, this unexpected confluence of animality and the face in the shaping of the world's signifiance.

To escape the face! Impossible! you say. Terrifying! they say. And not by returning to the animal but to the "becomings-intense, becomings-animal" in the volatility of modernity—as with Kafka's tic moving across the face of the actor acting the state official in the Yiddish theater in Prague, spasms contracting across the face with merciful quickness. "I mean the haste but also the regularity, of a second hand," he wrote in his diary. "When it reaches the left eye it almost obliterates it. For this contraction new, small, fresh muscles have developed in the otherwise quite wasted face."[19]

DEFACEMENT

Can the fetish "pass"? Can it lurk undetected in the everyday? Am I that fetish? asks the face. Can this sensate and mobile tissue evoking an obscure innerness be truly the zone of the fetish? And all along we thought that it was just our familiar friend, old face, far from the traders on the West coast of Africa and Christian fantasies concerning pagan ritual objects.

But then the fetish—as we use the term, and as the term uses us—does have this remarkable twofold property of being either in-your-face exotic *or* hidden in the everyday. Just think of those familiar icons of fetishism, black raincoats, sex-bespattered leather and shoes, on the one hand, and Marx's capital, on the other; goose-bumped spectacularity to one side, the everyday mundane self-nourishing life-and-death force, on the other. And if the whole point of leather's goose-bumps is—as we read Freud especially his essay on the uncanny—to arouse-through-concealment by means of elaborate games of castrating peek-a-boo, now you see it, now you don't, then the fetish power of capital—as we read Marx—lies in its quiet invisibility as a Deus Ex Machina, the ghost in the machine, its virtual camoflage passing into the genetic structure of normality, we might say, in a quite other dialectic of revelation and concealment. Adam Smith's Invisible Hand, no less. And it is precisely in this invisibility rendered by ordinariness—as we read Marx—that there lies the source of fetish power.

Here is where the negative strikes with unparalleled force and consequence, as with *defacement*, drawing on the invisible account and rendering it holy in an act of sacrilege. Strange powers erupt as meaning hemorrages in active, abject, force, as in the defacement of flags and statues whereby the baseness within the sacred billows forth.

DEMASKING

In some and perhaps many rituals of initiation it is the reality of demasking and not the illusions of masking that is crucial—as when, at the culminating point, the men masked as spirits are stripped of their disguise. It is precisely at this point of revelation of artifice and make-believe that the reality of the spirit world, far from being destroyed, is deepened and achieves full force. This apparent paradox serves many useful functions, not least for unmasking our own masking of the question as to what we might mean by the power of the mask, let alone masking of the difficulties we have had selecting certain words such as "disguise," "acting," and "demystification" . . . words that seem so powerful and no less dramatic than the drama they point to, yet so provisional and empty as well.

It is a curious thing, this, that far from demystifying, demasking can heighten the masking power of the mask. This is more than curious; it is the begining of philosophy, of knowing, and of being, for demasking is a peculiar form of defacement, a sort of double or meta-defacement returning the face to its home in faciality—only to discover, but not accept, that once left, home changes.

Martin Gusinde, an ethnograper of the Yamana as they lived in the early 1920s in Tierra del Fuego, has a good deal to tell us about one particular unmasking. It is an account of the initiation of young people, especially young men, into what are called the secrets. He tells us about the unmasking of Yetaita, the underground spirit, and his encounter with an initiate.

The young man who shall personify Yetaita has taken off his clothing and smeared his whole body with white paint, on which he evenly arranges short vertical lines five centimeters long and as wide as a finger.

His face is covered with thick red paint, and many delicate white lines, like rays, extending in all directions from the corners of his mouth.

Feathers hang from shoulder to shoulder. His hair stands on end. Imi powder has been rubbed into it.

When the initiate has been shoved into his place, the men in the Great Hut motion to the man who represents Yetaita.

The moment a leather blindfold is removed from the initiate, Yetaita leaps in front of him. Because the fire has been stirred up, it looks as though he has emerged from the flames. He keeps his face averted so as not to be identified and attacks the initiate cruelly for some ten minutes to the accompaniment of drumming and stamping on the ground by the other men. The initiate is greatly distressed, sweating, and has become limp like a dummy.

Suddenly everything stops, and Yetaita crouches motionless in front of the initiate who is forced, now, to look his tormenter full in the face and recognize him. A counsellor says, "Look closely, that is your kinsman, not Yetaita! (He specifically says "That is your uncle, that is your father . . .") The true Yetaita looks like your kinsman here who is painted like Yetaita. Watch out for Yetaita! . . . Keep strict silence among other people about what you will experience here. Now you know that Yetaita is much rougher than your kinsman. This man is not Yetaita himself, but you should know now to watch out for him."[20]

It's the revelation as to the hoax that perfects the illusion; the divulgation of the deception that makes for supernatural power . . . "But beware of Watauineiwa, that is the real Yetaita," advises an older man who warns the initiate to keep absolutely silent about the impersonation. "This means," says Gusinde, "that Watauineiwa threatens and punishes as a truly living spirit, in the way that this is maintained of Yetaita who, however, is only an invention."[21]

No sooner is one figure's reality dissolved as mere invention, than a more powerful figure appears behind it as real . . . and here amid the swirling currents we have to choose or at least acknowledge the fork in the epistemic path; one way to the flickering reality behind the illusion, or, the Other way wherein the reality is that there is none, other than brilliant attempts at its staging.

Analyzing Gusinde's copious Tierra del Fuego ethnography some fifty years after its publication, and having spent almost five years between 1966 and 1976 with the handful of Selk'nam survivors in Tierra del Fuego, Anne Chapman is perturbed by what she sees as his tendency to define the Selk'nam men's elaborate initiation ritual as an elaborate hoax aimed at striking fear among the women and uninitiated in order to control them. She notes for instance that his own work reveals that the masks used by Selk'nam men were treated by them with a degree of veneration that would not be accorded an actor's prop or disguise. Great care was taken that they were carefully stored and did not fall. If a mask was damaged, it was thought that its user would fall and injure or even kill himself in the next performance. Gusinde had difficulty obtaining masks for museums.[22] The older men refused to give or sell any.

Thus she cannot bring herself to agree with the concept of a hoax and tries to resolve the issue by calling the participants not actors but "actors," noting that they "are somehow imbued with the supernatural personality of their prototypes" (the term prototype being a significant choice of words here).

Yet there is something deeply unsatisfying in proposing this either-or dilemma between hoax and sincerity, deception, and heartfelt religious expression, theater and ritual, and the attempt to then force a resolution through the use of the ambivalence achieved by quotation marks around the word "actors" seems more like an elegant evasion of the disturbing possibility that the sacred at stake here, if not most elsewhere, is in some profound sense precisely a massive hoax in which truth is teased and the arts of representation deployed so as to represent representation itself. Here, we might say, quotation marks are equivalent to both masking and demasking—ie. to crossing the face and escaping faciality.

Summarizing Gusinde's account of the climactic moment in the initiation of young men among the Selk'nam (who had a more rigid division between male and female than the neighboring Yamana who feature in my first account of unmasking), Chapman describes how the Selk'nam initiate is ushered into the hut to find a circle of men standing in a tight circle against the inner wall staring at the fire. His clothes are stripped off and the spirit Shoort squats hidden behind the men, pounding the floor. The very earth seems to tremble. The initiate's head is held so he is forced to look upwards as

Shoort springs into the center of the hut as if emerging from the fire to pace around the initiate, sexually excited, body swaying, breathing hard. Suddenly he grasps the initiate's genitals, pressing them hard, panting with agitation. The initiate suffers acute pain without resistance, being told he has to keep his hands folded on his head and being held by a supervisor. Shoort pulls the initiate's genitals violently with both hands, giving out a shrill yell before releasing them, and the initiate is then ordered to fight the spirit.

They circle one another. Shoort threatens to bite his penis. The initiate lunges at Shoort but is strictly forbidden to touch his mask. He has been warned that Shoort would ram him with his head of rock if he so much as brushes against it. If Shoort loses control he may burn the initiate with a firebrand or actually bite his genitals. The initiate has little chance of dominating his opponent because he is held back by the supervisor. When he is in a state of frantic despair the contest is suddenly stopped and and the supervisor, pointing to Shoort's head, gives the starling command (to quote the dialog directly from Chapman's account).

"Grasp it!"

Another man shouts, "Is he rock or is he flesh?"

Encouraged, the initiate passes his fingers over Shoort's head and neck. With further urging he he finally grasps the head, feels the mask, and starts to pull it off as Shoort covers his face with his hands.

A counseller orders the initiate to pull Shoort's hands away from his face.

He stares with amazement at the unmasked face.

"Who is he? Could he be an ancestor?" shouts an elder.

"Who could he be? Maybe an Airu? Or a Woo?" (These are the names of neighboring people.) "Perhaps a Joshe?" (This is the name of a killer spirit.)

Others break in with their questions.

"Don't you know him?"

"Name him!"

"Don't you recognize the face?"

Minutes usually pass before the young man identifies the face—in part because it is is blackened and the muscles are contracted and the eyes tightly closed.

He calls out the man's name.

"Push him!," someone yells, and the spirit tumbles to the ground. The men roar with laughter.[23]

At which point, Gusinde notes, the initiate relaxes, but in E. Lucas Bridges' account of the ceremony to which he was invited at the turn of the century, something different occured. "He attacked him with such fury," said Bridges of the initiate, "that he had to be dragged off, to the accompaniment of roars of laughter in which Shoort joined heartily."[24]

IS SACRILEGE THE INVERSE OF SACRIFICE?

Claude Lévi-Strauss has suggested that sacrilege can be thought of as the inverse of sacrifice, as when extremes are brought too close together—as in incest and bestiality—compared with sacrifice in which an item of mediation ambiguously attached to both extremes is selected, destroyed, and in its thus manufactured absence is made a space for a "compensatory continuity" and hence communication with the divine.[25]

I want to reconsider this strange space achieved though killing or destroying the object ambiguously attached to extremes—and the first thing to notice is that sacrilege is itself a type of sacred act and that this is both obvious and surprising.[26] Thus problematized, we are encouraged to further scrutinze the type of "space" created by destruction of the victim, as in sacrifice, or—and this is the decisive issue—by too close an abutment of extremes, as in sacrilege. For this abutment, too, can be thought of as a space, albeit an explosive space—perhaps a "space in time" might be a way to grasp it, the space of imploding time—an outstanding result of which is not the satisfying clasp of the harmoniously frozen universe envisaged in Lévi-Strauss's vision but, to the contrary, a bounteous spilling over and proliferation of inconstant meanings and identities released by the way that defacement acts upon the fetish of interiority bound to the public secret of faciality.

SUBCOMANDANTE MARCOS UNMASKED   *1. THE UNMASKING*

On Saturday, February 11th of this year, 1995, the *New York Times* reported on page one "Mexico's New Offensive: Erasing Rebel's Mystique."

The continuation on page six was headlined "Offensive To Erase a Rebel's Mystique," and the window inserted into article read

> *UNMASKED HE'S A FURNITURE SALESMAN'S SON*

"Yuck!" exclaimed a young acquaintance of Alma Guillermoprieto's in Mexico City on seeing the unmasked face. Before that she'd swoon at mere mention of his name.[27] "Stripped of the myth that went with his ever-present mask . . . government officials said today that they hoped the disclosure of his identity would by itself help to break a rebel movement that has never been militarily strong," began the *New York Times*. "The moment that Marcos was identified and his photo shown and everyone saw who he was, much of his importance as a symbol vanished," one official said. "Whether he is captured or not is incidental."[28]

"It was like a game of peekaboo," wrote Alma Guillermoprieto, who as a journalist was invited to the demasking and hence was able to describe how an official took an oversized slide of a ski mask with a pair of large dark eyes, in one hand, and a black and white photo of a "milk toast" looking young man with a beard and large dark eyes, in the other. He then then slipped the slide of the mask and eyes over the photo of the unmasked face.

"*Voila*! Subcomandante Marcos! The idol is a Clark Kent!" noted Guillermoprieto.

He kept superimposing and separating the two images, now you see it, now you don't, until the storm of camera flashes subsided. . . .

Other things are going on here alongside demasking, more "abstract" things, perhaps, more fundamental and philosophical things, perhaps, of which this new form of guerrilla warfare is part—as amid the flashing cameras the state attempts to restore *faciality* to its proper function—as Deleuze and Giattari see it; namely the

almightiness of the signifier as well as the autonomy of the subject. You will be pinned to the white wall and stuffed in the black hole. This machine is called the faciality machine because it is the social production of face, because it performs the facialization of the entire body and all its surroundings and objects, and the landscapification of all words and milieus.[29]

Faciality: the white wall/black hole system of signification and subjectification, semiosis and interiority.
But then
Others break in with their questions.
"Don't you know him?"
"Name him!"
"Don't you recognize the face?"

Minutes usually pass before the young man identifies the face—in part because it is is blackened and the muscles are contracted and the eyes tightly closed.

He calls out the man's name.

"Push him!," someone yells, and the spirit tumbles to the ground. The men roar with laughter.

SUBCOMANDANTE MARCOS UNMASKED   *2. THE RE-MASKING*

That was Wednesday. By Sunday demonstrations had occurred with thousands of people wearing the same masks as Subcomandante Marcos, and the Mexican press had received and published the first comunique from Marcos since the unmasking. It bore three of his trademarks; the postcripts he attaches to his letters to the press.

P.S. that rapidly applauds this new "success" of the government police:

I've heard they've found another "Marcos," and that he's from Tampico. That doesn't sound bad, the port is nice. I remember when I used to work as a bouncer in a brothel in Ciudad Madero [near Tampico], in the days when [a corrupt oilworkers'-union leader] used to do the same thing to the regional economy that Salinas [the recently retired President of Mexico] did with the stock market; inject money into it to hide poverty. . . .

P.S. that despite the circumstances does not abandon its narcissism:

So . . . Is this this new Subcomandante Marcos good-looking? Because lately they've been assigning me really ugly ones and my feminine correspondence gets ruined.

P.S. that counts time and ammunition:

I have 300 bullets, so try to bring 299 soldiers and police to get me. Legend has it that I don"t miss a shot; would you like to find out if it's true?) Why 299, if there's 300 bullets? Well, because the last one is for yours truly. It turns out that one gets fond of things like this, and a bullet seems the only consolation for this solitary heart.

Vale again, and *Salud,* and can it be that there will be a little spot for me in her heart?

Signed, the Sup [Subcomandante], rearranging his ski mask with macabre flirtatiousness.

"In five short paragraphs," concludes Alma Guillermoprieto, "the Sup reestablished his credentials as an outlaw hero, brought sex into the issue, and, yanking back the mask his pursuers had torn off, donned it once more."[30]

But we must ask here whether remasking the unmasked face returns us to the status quo ante, or whether, as seems more likely, some quite other force, a proliferating magical force amounting to a sort of hypermasking, consequent to and created by unmasking, takes over? For in Marcos's case, unmasking by the state through the deployment of the photo on a driver's license or similar document to dramatically reveal the real Marcos to the flashing lights of the photographic equipment of the media seems to have totally backfired—a result anticipated by no one—which is to say that a certain deterritorializing potential in masking was thus brought to full flower because the state itself is seen as the most masked entity of all possible masked beings to have ever crossed the threshold of the human imagination.

It was common knowledge that around the conference table up there in San Cristóbal in Chiapas that the representatives of the state were distinctly uncomfortable having to negotiate with masked beings. "It's impossible!" they said.

"But the state is always masked," was the Zapatista response.

So the negotiations proceeded between the masked rebels—whom Alma G. sees as faceless—and the faceless bureaucrats of the state—whom the Zapatistas see as masked.

And what seems to me crucial to the backfiring-effect of unmasking was the role played by *refacement* as a result of the the state attempting to exercise its prohibition on transformation.

UNMASKING AND PROLIFERATION

Prohibitions on transformation are a social and religious phenomenon which have never properly been understood.
                                          —*Elias Canetti*, Crowds and Power

Alma G. has characterised the postscript as "the Subcomandante's contribution to epistolary art. Now swaggering, now full of righteous fury, now impudent and hip, the Marcos of the postscripts is at all times both elusive and intimate, and this seductive knack has allowed him to become a faceless stand-in for all the oppressed. . . ."[31]

What is so wonderful here is that being "faceless" in this way is not so much being without a face as it is a reorganization of faciality creating a new type of face—a deterritorializing face that both Brecht, with his demand to show the actor acting, and Nietzsche, with his search for a Dionysian triumph over the mask of of power, would, each in their own way, have recognized as part of their own carnivalesque efforts at entering into the masquerade that is history. This type of face reconfigures the public secret—that which is known but cannot be stated, of the face as both mask and window to the soul— such that there is a type of "release" of the fetish powers of the face in a wild proliferation of identities no less than of the very notion of identity itself, a discharge of the powers of representation. Now you see it. Now you don't.

A reporter asked if Marcos is gay.

"Marcos is gay in San Francisco, black in South Africa, an Asian in Europe, a Chicano in San Ysidro, an anarchist in Spain, a Palestinian in Israel, a Mayan Indian in the Streets of San Cristóbal, a gang member in Neza, a rocker in the National University, a Jew in Germany, an Ombundsman in the Defense Ministry, a Communist in the post–Cold War era, an artist without gallery or portfolio, a pacifist in Bosnia, a housewife alone on a Saturday night in any neighbourhood in any city in Mexico, a reporter filing stories for the back pages, a single woman on the subway at 10 P.M., a peasant without land, an unemployed worker, a dissident amid free-market economics, a writer without books or readers, and, of course, a Zapatista in the moutains of southern Mexico." [32]

POSTSCRIPT

And we . . . mere writers performing, at best, without masks and nothing but (faceless) words, cannot we take heart here and rework the figure of the double, the figure of the totem, in a new understanding of the art of criticism as an art of defacement—so long and only so long as we feel confident in our ability to direct the surge of fetish power issuing forth when that skin we call "face" stretched across the "always beyond" is thus crossed? Here enters writing as a permanent suplement, the postscript as unmasking splattering meaning no less than identity in a perpetually penultimate movement called forth not only by the conflicts and instabilities the text conceals, but most decisively by the masks it uses to disguise its masking.

NOTES

1. Epigraph is from M. Foucault, "A Preface to Transgression," in *Language, Counter-Memory, Practice*. (Cornell University Press: Ithaca) 1977, 34.

2. William Pietz, "The Problem of the Fetish, 1." *RES* 9 Spring, 1985: 5–17.

3. Emanuel Levinas, *Totality and Infinity: An Essay on Exteriority* translated by Alphonso Lingis (Martinus Nijhoff: The Hague), 1990, and *Face to Face With Levinas* edited by Richard A. Cohen (State Unversity of New York Press: Albany), 1986.

4. Elias Canetti, *Crowds and Power* (Farrar, Strauss, Giroux: New York), p. 290.

5. Canetti, p. 290.

6. Canetti, p. 290.

7. Canetti, p. 296.

8. "What is peculiar to modern societies, in fact, is not that they consigned sex to a shadow existence, but that they dedicated themselves to speaking of it *ad infinitum*, while exploiting it as *the* secret. " Michel Foucault *The History of Sexuality, Volume I: An Introduction* (Vintage, New York), p. 35.

9. I am tempted to think of the blush as an exemplary "crossing" the face and "revelation" of fetish-power. More than a covering, as a substitute for covering the exposed genitalia, the blush serves as a signal of the impossibility of innerness, of the "always-beyond" that access to the face initiates. (A blush, physiologicallly, in the first instance, is a rapid expansion of facial vasculature.) Dark hued faces escape this.

10. In *Totality and Infinity* Levinas says, "Meaning is the face of the Other, and all recourse to words takes place already within the primordial face to face of language. . . . And the epiphany that is produced as a face is not constituted as as are all other beings, precisely because it 'reveals' infinity" (pp. 206–207). "The face is the evidence that makes evidence possible," he says, "like the divine veracity that sustains Cartesian rationality" (p. 204).

11. See Patrizia Magli, "The Face and the Soul," pp. 87–127 in *Fragments for a History of the Human Body, Part 2* (Zone Books: New York) 1989, p. 100.

12. See for instance Chapter 7, "The Close-Up," and Chapter 8 "The Face of Man," in Bela Balazs, *Theory of the Film* (Arno Press and The New York Times: New York) 1972, pp. 52–89.

13. "Exploring the inner man through the outer man [in Euroamerica from the late 18th century on] sets the foundations for a sort of physiology, whose parameters do not significantly differ from those once adopted by ancient people. Animality emerges again in an unsettling way in those beings which are at once man and beast: lunatics, women, primates, children." Magli, p. 124.

14. Max Horkhermer and T.W. Adorno, *Dialectic of Enlightenment* (Continuum: New York), 1987. In following this line of thought I am also of course indebted to the aspirations of the members of the College of Sociology (Bataille, Caillois, et al.) with the attempt to re-cycle into the study of modern politics the anthropology of so-called primitive societies, notably the lessons to be learnt therefrom regarding mimesis and sympathetic magic.

15. Canetti, p. 337.

16. Canetti, p. 347.

17. Cf. Nietzsche's sense of mimesis and the Dionysian impulse in *Twilight of the Idols* and Max Horkheimer and T.W. Adorno's *Dialectic of Enlightenment* with its argument about magic as the first step of Enlightenment.

18. Giles Deleuze and Felix Guattari, *A Thousand Plateaus: Capitalism and Schizophrenia* (University of Minnesota Press: Minneapolis), 1987, p. 171.

19. Franz Kafka, *The Diaries of Franz Kafka: 1910–1913*, edited by Max Brod, (Schocken: New York), 1965, p. 81.

20. Martin Gusinde, *The Yamana: The Life and Thought of the Water Nomads of Cape Horn*, translated from the German by Frieda Schutze (Human Relations Area Files: New Haven), 1961, vol 3, pp. 699–700.

21. Gusinde, p. 746.

22. Anne Chapman, *Drama and Power in a Hunting Society: The Selk'nam of Tierra del Fuego* (Cambridge University Press: Cambridge), 1982, pp. 86–87. I move between Gusinde's ethnography of the Yamana and the Selk'nam, both of which contain fascinating and extraordinarily lengthy descriptions of the masking and un-masking rites of the public secret of male initiation. Like Chapman, Irving Goldman is also perturbed by the notion of a hoax and spends much time anxiously disclaiming his own analysis of Kwakiutal Winter ceremonial and shamanic ritual which with absolute unambiguity is directed by the notion that such ritual is guided by simulation or mimesis. What is crucial is his (curious and to me totally unwarranted) assumption that if one imitates one is therefore inauthentic and has abandoned all claim on the sacred. See Irving Goldman, *The Mouth of Heaven*, (John Wiley: New York), 1975, pp. 102–104.

23. Chapman, pp. 106–06. Note that some crucial parts of this un-masking material comes directly from Chapman's ethnographic diary compiled between 1966–76 and is not only a digest of Gusinde. It should also be

noted—and this is a major point—that Chapman understands Gusinde to be claiming that the Selk'nam men do not believe in the spirits they are impersonating, which would throw my argument about the power on un-masking off course. But (1) un-masking certainly increases the power of the secret, and (2) "belief" (in the spirits) is too elusive a thing to be easily or decisively settled on the evidence to hand.

24. E. Lucas Bridges, *Uttermost Part of the Earth* (Hodder and Stoughton: London), p. 421.

25. Claude Lévi-Strauss, *The Savage Mind* (University of Chicago Press: Chicago) 1966, pp. 225–26. This reference was brought to my attention by Deleuze and Guattari, op. cit., in their chapter "Becoming-Animal, Becoming-Intense. . .".

26. A field explored earlier and in considerable depth by Georges Bataille coming out of Surrealism, Hegel, Marx, Nietzsche, medieval texts, and early twentieth century ethnography.

27. Alma Guillermoprieto, "Letter From Mexico: The Unmasking," pp. 40–48, *The New Yorker*, March 13, 1995, p. 44.

28. *The New York Times*, Ibid.

29. Deleuze and Guattari, op. cit., pp. 181.

30. Guillermo Prieto, op. cit., p. 44.

31. Guillermoprieto, op. cit., p. 42.

32. This was taken off the Internet and forwarded to me in Sydney, Australia, April 1995, by my urban anthropologist friend, Kostas Gounis, Department of Anthropology, Teachers' College, New York City.

BIBLIOGRAPHY

Balazs, B. (1972) *Theory of the Film* (Arno Press and The New York Times: New York).

Bridges, E.L. (1951) *Uttermost Part of the Earth* (Hodder and Stoughton: London).

Canetti, E. (1984) *Crowds and Power* (Farrar, Strauss, Giroux: New York).

Chapman, A. (1982) *Drama and Power in a Hunting Society: The Selk'nam of Tierra del Fuego* (Cambridge University Press: Cambridge).

Deleuze, G. and F. Guattari (1987) *A Thousand Plateaus: Capitalism and Schizophrenia* (University of Minnesota Press: Minneapolis).

Foucault, M. (1977) "A Preface to Transgression," in *Language, Counter-Memory, Practice* (Cornell University Press: Ithaca).

Foucault, M. (1980) *The History of Sexuality, Volume I: An Introduction* (Vintage, New York).

Gusinde, M. (1961) *The Yamana: The Life and Thought of the Water Nomads of Cape Horn,,* vol 3., translated from the German by Frieda Schutze (Human Relations Area Files: New Haven).

Goldman, I. (1975) *The Mouth of Heaven* (John Wiley: New York).

Guillermoprieto, A. (1995) "Letter From Mexico: The Unmasking," pp. 40–48, *The New Yorker*, March 13.

Horkhermer, M. and T. W. Adorno (1987) *Dialectic of Enlightenment* (Continuum: New York).

Kafka, F. (1965) *The Diaries of Franz Kafka: 1910–1913*, edited by Max Brod (Schocken: New York).

Levinas, E. (1979) *Totality and Infinity: An Essay on Exteriority*, translated by Alphonso Lingis (Martinus Nijhoff: The Hague).

Levinas, E. (1986) *Face to Face With Levinas*, edited by Richard A. Cohen (State University of New York Press: Albany).

Lévi-Strauss, C. (1966) *The Savage Mind* (University of Chicago Press: Chicago).

Magli, P. (1989) "The Face and the Soul," pp. 86–127 in *Fragments for a History of the Human Body, Part 2* (Zone Books: New York).

Pietz, W. (1985) "The Problem of the Fetish, 1." *RES* 9 Spring, pp. 5–17.

Afterword

How to Grow Oranges in Norway

William Pietz

Unlike introductions, afterwords to books are in the pleasant position of addressing those who have already read the text and who, presumably, have found the material interesting enough to finish. But to find something interesting does not necessarily mean one finds it serious or useful, something that might productively alter one's own way of thinking. Perhaps the value offered is merely that of entertainment: The book might have been worth reading as a pleasant but trifling diversion, as a sort of postmodern Wunderkammer, a cabinet of curiosities taken from exotic but unimportant places like Sumba and Surinam that has been assembled during the decade of post–Cold War globalization for the amusement of intellectuals who have a taste for such things. Or is there something of real substance to be gained by reading the nine essays of this collection and thinking one's way into the notion of "border fetishisms" that they develop? This is the question I would like to consider in this afterword.

Since I wish to argue that there is something of real value to be gotten from this book, let me speak in what counts as the most serious of contemporary languages, the discourse of international economics. This is not to say that I think it likely an international economist would ever read this book. Indeed, I assume that, were such an improbable thing to happen, the economist would likely regard the authors' arguments in the manner that the naturalist's wife, Anna Forbes, in the anecdote cited by Spyer, regarded a group of Aruese villagers who attempted to communicate the murder of their local political authority to the passing representatives of the global economy. To read about the outlandish uses to which commodities and currencies have been put, as in Foster's discussion of the noncommercial uses of 20 kina banknotes in Papua New Guinea, might be as amusing to an international economist as, for Anna Forbes, was the look of Aruese costumes, whose crosscultural appropriation of Western fashions appeared to be nothing more than a travesty. The villagers' attempt to communicate the serious news of a murder was rendered impossible by the most trivial of things: The truth of their words was erased by their taste in clothes. As Stallybrass discussed, Karl Marx, for one, knew all too well that a respectable look is required for admission into the space of truth: He needed a gentlemen's overcoat to get into the British Museum Reading Room, and he needed the overcoat's literary equivalent, the philosophical form of critique, to demonstrate in an authoritative fashion that societies structured by the categories and logic of political economics are not merely unjust but inherently unsustainable. So while I assume I am not addressing real international economists in this afterword, it is their authoritative discourse that functions as the mantle of respectability required for thought to be taken seriously beyond the confines of particular academic disciplines such as anthropology and art history. There is at least one perfectly good reason for this: Whoever actually reads this text will have done so only after purchasing it (or by having access to a library that decided to buy it). While one wishes to think that the value of a scholarly book exceeds its mere commodity value, its value as an economic object is a necessary modality of its existence. For this reason, the question I wish to raise about this book concerns what economists call the "gains of trade." What may be gained by trading one's (or someone's) hard-earned money for this book? And what has this to do with price of oranges in Norway?

The problem of growing oranges in Norway is a favorite illustration used by international economists wishing to bring home the point that in global free trade everybody gains, even those who are exploited in the Marxian sense that the goods they receive "contain" less labor time than the goods they sell (Krugman and Obstfeld 1994: 3–4). Norway (standing for the technologically advanced North) could conceivably grow its own oranges in expensive hot houses, but

Norwegians can get more oranges for the same amount of labor by making some other commodity (refrigerators, say) in which their natural resources and technology give them a comparative advantage, and then trading these for foreign oranges grown in some underdeveloped nation in the tropical South (Indonesia, say) whose natural climate and cheaper labor gives it a comparative advantage in orange production. The latter will also gain since it will get more refrigerators through trading oranges than it could by diverting its own cheap labor and poor technology from orange growing to the domestic manufacture of refrigerators. And this is so despite the truth of the Marxist complaint that the labor value of the Indonesian oranges exchanged for Norwegian refrigerators is unequal. Because exploitation (for lack of a better word) is good for everyone. Properly understood, international exchange is simply another way of producing the goods demanded by nations that happen to have different "tastes and technology" (Krugman 1990: 100). This is the happy lesson of the parable: The best way to produce oranges in Norway is to build refrigerators and trade them for fruit from the tropics. International trade itself is what provides the gains, the surplus value, and it does this for both Norway and Indonesia, for the advanced North and the underdeveloped South alike.

Here, then, is the Disneyfied world picture of simple commodities circulating across cleanly drawn national borders as it is rendered by the secular clerics of the latterday House of Orange. As Taussig might put it, to introduce the notion of border fetishisms into this happiest of global images is one way of defacing it, of reminding us that it is nothing more than a lie made plausible not by the methodology of a scientific discipline but by the desire of political powers who wish to remain concealed, revealing themselves only in rare moments that can be dismissed as singular and non-normative: Soeharto's "stabilization" of Indonesia in 1965–66 and its counterparts in Mexico City in 1968, Chile in 1972, Kwangju in 1979—one could go on assembling the list, but however many nation-stabilizing massacres one might add up, for economists there will never be enough to aggregate them into any sort of norm. What have they to do with the problem of where "added value" comes from? Or even with the economic demand for exotic luxury goods like hats made from beaver fur or bird-of-paradise feathers? Surely the demand for such passing fashions follows a logic of sheer caprice and has nothing to do with exterminations that, surely, are merely an unintended consequence . . .

Let me suggest that it was to mark this embarrassing point of scientific unthinkability—of a factual relation that must at all costs imply nothing—that the discourse about fetishism first entered European intellectual culture. It did so in the literary figure of a mutilated, fetish-worshipping slave who had escaped from a plantation in Surinam. In a scene belatedly added by Voltaire to his popular novel *Candide*, the fetish-worshipper, displaying to Candide his own concrete condition of misery, destroys that innocent's faith in the Enlightenment by informing him, "It is at this price that you eat sugar in Europe" (Voltaire 1981: 60). Fifty years later a neologism would be invented to name the idea being expressed in this scene: "exploitation." A couple of decades after this, Marx in *Capital* would try to explain what exploitation looked like and how it was conceived within the perverse social logic of political economics. But to show that the categories of Ricardian economics work out rationally only by calculating the surplus exchange value realized in capitalized commodities as uncompensated labor time is only to show how things must appear from the perspective of capital. As Stallybrass argues in his essay for this collection, for Marx the point was not to advance the science of economics by correcting its errors, but to render implausible its false pretensions as a social science. Capitalism, the generalized principles of international trade, has never been able to organize a healthy or even viable society. This is the point of characterizing capitalism as a form of fetishism, in the sense of a historical mode for endowing material objects and people with the objective values necessary to build a sustainable social world. To repeat Stallybrass's point, for Marx the problem was not that capital was a fetish, it is that capital is such a poor fetish. Of course, such a statement could no more be taken seriously by international economists than Calvinist missionaries in Sumba can take seriously the claim of the *marupu* followers discussed by Keane that a bit of sacrificial meat or a gold ornament can be a material form of "the ancestral body." The sort of social materiality that realizes the transgenerational solidarity of a people is something as much outside the conceptual horizon of social science as it is outside that of Christian ontotheology. And as long as the transcendentalist premises of such worldviews hold sway—as long as the leading American ideologue of the coming "Information Age" can begin his book of scientific prophecy with the statement, "The central event of the twentieth century is the overthrow of matter" (Gilder 1989: 17)—then the materialist discourse about fetishism will retain its viability.

To appreciate why this is so it might be useful to return to problem of the orange as fetish, that is, to the "use values" at stake in international commerce and to the logic of destruction this seems to entail despite itself. A classicist could, of course, genealogize the problem of the destruction entailed in the demand for luxury goods, for spices and relishes, for oranges and sugar, within the Western tradition itself, perhaps tracing it back to Plato's Republic. It was Socrates' young admirers, after all, who insisted that he include luxuries in his verbal construction of the ideal city; this requirement to build "the feverish city" rather than "the healthy city" assured that all possible forms of the state would be temporally unstable and impermanent (Plato 1968: 49 [372 c–e]). For Plato, the problem was simply a given of what might be termed political consumer demand. A world historian like William McNeill might even attempt to relate the thematization of this problem to the ascetic premises of the discourse of ontotheology that emerged, rather suddenly, a bit before Plato's day across the band of civilized countries stretching from the Mediterranean Sea to the Ganges River—the intellectual movement that achieved its institutional actualization in the great cosmopolitan religions. However, the peculiar discourse about "fetishes" is not really a part of "the Western tradition," nor even of the broader intellectual tradition of the so-called great religions. It developed in an early modern border zone of crosscultural trade between Africans and Europeans, an interstitial "world" where the presumptions of ontotheological religion and mercantile economics alike broke down; and it entered high European intellectual culture (by way of published "travelogues") during the period of the Seven Years War, the first war waged between European states primarily for control of overseas possessions. The methodological force of the theory of fetishism formulated at this time by the Burgundian aristocrat Charles de Brosses is found in his insistence that philosophy and social theory could no longer be based upon the unexamined presuppositions of the intellectual tradition of Western Christendom, but must more radically derive its authority from what might be called a method of "ethnographic materialism," of cultural interpretation based on the "direct observation" of contemporary peoples, including those outside Europe and its traditions. De Brosses was framing this novel project on the basis of his own direct experience. His own world had been changed in its substance by the new global economy: the monetary value of the landed estates that were his ancestral inheritance, and that he rented out (among others, to Voltaire) to support himself, had plummeted as the overseas war went badly for France. He invested his remaining cash in a Paris-based overseas company, where he lost most of it. For de Brosses there could be no doubt that the non-European world was part of his world. No more than there could be any doubt for Voltaire, who, at the same time he was writing his heart-wringing scene of the fetish-worshipping slave, was penning desperate letters about the fate of a Spanish fleet of slave traders in whom he had invested much of his money. The appearance of the discourse about fetishism in learned European culture was less an expression of "the Enlightenment mentality" than it was a symptom of the effects of the Seven Years War. Indeed, while Voltaire's literary vignette, along with the argument of Helvetius (from whom Voltaire stole the conceit) that the sweetness of sugar was mixed with the blood of slaves, was an early expression of a moral sensibility that would crystallize in the call for universal human rights and the abolition of the slave trade, the irony that Voltaire's own capital was so heavily invested in the very business he condemned testifies to the role the displaced discourse about fetishism played in suturing a fracture point in the ideology of scientific enlightenment.

It is inside this fracture, in the "heterospaces" where capitalism and noncapitalism coexist (Gibson-Graham 1996: 5), that the idea of border fetishism operates. In this volume, Moors's study of the gold jewelry worn by Palestinian women in Jabal Nablus perhaps best exemplifies the usefulness of the idea of border fetishisms. We do not see a local or "indigenous" people merely adapting their cultural forms to a "hegemonic" global economy or "resisting" it. They have their own good reasons for sometimes preferring the more fashionable Italian jewelry, despite its inferiority to the old 21-carat jewelry as an effective popular form of offshore banking. (One can imagine what laughter would be evoked if some banker-evangelist tried to show them a Palestinian version of *The Luluai's Dream!*) Where international economists may see only local fetishes that must be turned into global commodities, in these essays we see that the process also runs in the other direction, a direction that might be termed the social appropriation of capitalism.

But the notion of border fetishisms proposed in this collection can provide a useful framework for thought, it seems to me, only if one comes to terms with another issue raised in these essays: the value of shoplifting. Pinch's essay on "Stealing Happiness" might be read in the light of one of the more common claims in the air today: the claim that Marxism failed—or, in any event, the Soviet empire collapsed—because people wanted to shop. Socialist societies have proved as unsuccessful at producing satisfactory consumer goods as socialist theories have always been at finding any sort of positive value in luxury goods. The ascetic morality of socialist ethics could find no legitimate necessity in the desire for sumptuary excess. The outcome of the Cold War indicates otherwise, and the question Pinch's essay raises is whether consumer desire is simply a utilitarian desire for more things or whether there is a deeper truth about the gratifications enjoyed in shopping that is revealed in the compulsion to shoplift. Is some secular version of the sacred in play within the complusive pleasures of shoplifting? While not overtly destructive of objects in the way one finds in sacrifice, a transgressive violence is being enacted in some way analogous to the antisocial performances found at the center of sacramental practices that, by some seemingly perverse logic, function to renew the social. If there is an important truth here, it is one I cannot yet articulate. But I do hear whispering in my ear the ghost of a surgically altered man I once met in Nicaragua during its brief attempt to hold back the capitalist tide. He is telling me that if I want to understand the real "surplus values" represented in the gains of trade now being reaped in the real Norway (whose national income derives primarily from its legal control over rapidly depleting North Sea oil reserves) and in the real Indonesia (where multinational mining firms like Freeport McMoRan and Barrick Gold are chewing up "resources" to the local benefit of no one outside Indonesia's corrupt national government), then I should end this afterword with an unconscionable recommendation.

STEAL THIS BOOK!

References

Gibson-Graham, J.K. (1996) *The End of Capitalism (as we knew it)*. Cambridge, Mass.: Blackwell.

Gilder, George. (1989) *Microcosm: The Quantum Revolution in Economics and Technology*. New York: Simon and Schuster.

Krugman, Paul R. (1990) "Trade, Accumulation, and Uneven Development." In *Rethinking International Trade*. Cambridge, Mass.: MIT Press. Pp. 93–105.

Krugman, Paul R., and Maurice Obstfeld. (1994) *International Economics: Theory and Policy*. Third edition. New York: HarperCollins College Publishers.

Plato. *The Republic of Plato*, trans. Allan Bloom (1968). New York: Basic Books.

Voltaire. (1981) *Candide*, in *Candide, Zadig, and Selected Stories*, trans. Donald M. Frame. New York: New American Library. Pp. 15–101.

Contributors

Robert J. Foster teaches anthropology at the University of Rochester, Rochester, N.Y. He is the author of *Social Reproduction and History in Melanesia* (Cambridge 1995) and editor of *Nation Making: Emergent Identities in Postcolonial Melanesia* (Michigan 1995). His current research interests include globalization, mass consumption, and comparative modernities.

Webb Keane is Associate Professor in the Department of Anthropology at the University of Michigan (Ann Arbor) and the author of *Signs and Recognition: Powers and Hazards of Representation in an Indonesian Society* (1997). His current project is about language, material objects, money, and modernity in Indonesia.

Susan Legêne is a historian, since 1985 publisher at the Royal Tropical Institute (KIT), and as of 1997 Head Curator at the Tropenmuseum. She is completing a dissertation on representations of non-Western culture in early nineteenth-century Holland.

Annelies Moors, teaches anthropology at the University of Amsterdam and Leiden University. She is the author of *Women, Property, and Islam: Palestinian Experiences 1920–1990* (Cambridge University Press, 1995), coeditor of *Discourse and Palestine: Power, Text, and Context* (Het Spinhuis, 1995), and has published articles on the biographical method, on women and Islamic law, and on Orientalism. She is presently writing on photographs of women in Palestine, and involved in a research project on women wearing gold.

Peter Pels is Lecturer at the Research Centre Religion and Society, University of Amsterdam, and research fellow of the Netherlands Foundation for the Advancement of Tropical Research. He is author of *The Microphysics of Colonial Contact, Interactions between Missionaries and*

Waluguru in Late Colonial Tanganyika (Harwood Academic Publishers, in press) and edited, with Lorraine Nencel, *Constructing Knowledge: Authority and Critique in Social Science* (Sage, 1991) and with Oscar Salemink, *Colonial Ethnographies* (special issue of *History and Anthropology)*.

William Pietz is Director of the Asymmetrical Research Foundation in Los Angeles. He coedited with Emily Apter *Fetishism as Cultural Discourse* (Cornell University Press) and has written essays on the history of the idea of fetishism. He lives in Los Angeles.

Adela Pinch is Associate Professor of English at the University of Michigan (Ann Arbor). She is the author of *Strange Fits of Passion: Epistemologies of Emotion, Hume to Austen* (Stanford, 1996), and articles on eighteenth- and nineteenth-century British literature and culture. The essay in this volume is part of a book in progress called *Fetishes at Home: How English Literature Construed Its Objects, 1750–1850.*

Patricia Spyer is Lecturer at the Research Centre Religion and Society, University of Amsterdam. She is presently completing a book entitled *The Memory of Trade* (forthcoming, Duke University Press), and has published articles on ritual, conversion, and trade.

Peter Stallybrass is Professor of English and of Comparative Literature and Literary Theory at the University of Pennsylvania. He is the coauthor with Allon White of the *Politics and Poetics of Transgressions* and he has just completed a book with Ann Rosalind Jones entitled *Worn Worlds: Clothes and Identity in Early Modern England and Europe.*

Michael Taussig is a precocious fetishist, having virtually begun his writerly life expounding upon the (marxist) fetish, as in *The Devil and Commodity Fetishism* (1980), the fetish of the Other, as in *Shamanism, Colonialism and the Wild Man: A Study in Terror and Healing.* (1987), and the fetish of the system as in *The Nervous System* (1992), and of course the fetish of the fetish as in his article in the present volume. He teaches fetish anthropology in New York.

Index